ALIEN BODIES

HOW DID DANCERS ON EACH SIDE OF THE ATLANTIC CHOREOGRAPH THE DISTURBING NEW RHYTHMS AND SPACES OF MODERNITY?

Blurring the conventional distinction between modern dance and ballet, African American dance, gymnastics and dancing as popular entertainment, *Alien Bodies* looks at the way the dance of the 1920s and 1930s mediated the experience of modernity. It focuses in particular on ways in which dance became a form in which ideologies of national and 'racial' identity were expressed and contested.

Through an examination of work by key dancers and choreographers including Josephine Baker, Jean Börlin, George Balanchine, Katherine Dunham, Martha Graham, and Doris Humphrey, *Alien Bodies* argues for a revision of the way dance history is written. Burt shows how during the 1920s and 1930s – the jazz age – dance became a privileged site for defining the lived experiences of modernity. The disturbing experience of living in the ever changing modern city through successive waves of industrial restructuring created new desires and new types of embodied identities.

Alien Bodies places European and white American uses of ritual alongside the work of African American dancers and their struggle to define their own relation to modernity and to their African roots in relation to dominant cultural trends. Dance, it argues, can help us see that what individuals fear about the difference between themselves and others is actually inscribed within themselves, and it is this strangeness that, during the 1920s and 1930s, was expressed on both sides of the Atlantic by the alien dancing bodies of modern dance artists.

Ramsay Burt is the author of the highly acclaimed *The Male Dancer* (Routledge 1995). He is currently Senior Research Fellow in Dance at De Montfort University, Leicester.

ALIEN BODIES

Representations of modernity, 'race' and
nation in early modern dance

Ramsay Burt

London and New York

First published 1998
by Routledge
11 New Fetter Lane, London EC4P 4EE

Simultaneously published in the USA and Canada
by Routledge
29 West 35th Street, New York, NY 10001

©1998 Ramsay Burt

Typeset in Garamond by Routledge
Printed and bound in Great Britain by
Biddles Ltd, Guildford and King's Lynn

British Library Cataloguing in Publication Data
A catalogue record for this book is available from the British Library

Library of Congress Cataloguing in Publication Data
Burt, Ramsay, 1953–
Alien bodies: representations of modernity, "race," and nation in
early modern dance / Ramsay Burt.
p. cm.
Includes bibliographical references (p.) and index
1. Modern dance–Social aspects–United States–History. 2. Modern
dance–Social aspects–Europe–History. I. Title.
GV1783.B87 1998
792.8–dc21   97–23360
                                                     CIP

ISBN 0–415–14594–5 (hbk)
ISBN 0–415–14595–3 (pbk)

CONTENTS

CONTENTS

FIGURES

ACKNOWLEDGEMENTS

Many friends and colleagues have contributed to this book, listening to me and brainstorming ideas, sharing their own research or reading drafts of chapters and giving me feedback. These include Christy Adair, Thea Barnes, Valerie Briginshaw, Deena Burton, Angela Deluca, Millicent Hodson, Michael Huxley, Ursula Pellaton, Stacey Prickett, and Linda Tomko – I am grateful to all of them, but any shortcomings in the book are, of course, my own.

I also wish to thank the staff of the Dance Collection at the New York Public Library and of the Scraptoft Library at De Montfort University. Some parts of this study go back to papers which I presented at recent conferences. Parts of Chapter 2 were presented at the City Limits Conference, Staffordshire University in September 1996; Chapter 8 grew out of a paper I gave at the conference 'Fallen Angels', Twentieth Century Represention of Women's Spirituality, at LSU College, Southampton in June 1996; some of the ideas in the Conclusion were presented at a Symposium at the Kanonhallen, Copenhagen, in March 1997 at the invitation of Toni Cotts. The discussion in Chapter 7 of Doris Humphrey's *New Dance* and *With My Red Fires* developed out of an article which Ann Nugent asked me to write for an issue of *Dance Theatre Journal* celebrating the centenary of Humphrey's birth (Burt 1995b). Irmgard Thorne kindly translated for me material about Valeska Gert from the original German. I am very grateful to Millicent Hodson and Kenneth Archer for inviting me to Zürich to observe the final stages of their work reconstructing *Skating Rink* with Zürich Ballet and generously sharing their research with me, and to Zürich Ballet for giving me access backstage to watch rehearsals. I am also grateful to Katherine Dunham and Jeanelle Stovall for their time and patience. In addition, I wish to thank Julia Hall, Talia Rodgers, Sophie Powell, Jason Arthur, and Shankari Sanmuganathan.

The author and publisher wish to thank the copyright holders for their kind permission to reproduce visual images in this book. Detailed acknowledgements are made with the captions.

The research for this book was made possible by the generous support of De Montfort University, Leicester, who awarded me a fellowship to write it and have funded my research trips to New York and Zürich.

1

INTRODUCTION

While doing her field research in Haiti in 1936, Katherine Dunham found herself giving a complicated explanation to a surprisingly well informed and intellectually curious Haitian Bush Priest about why she was doing research into Haitian ritual practices. Her concern was with the function of cultural forms in creating social identity. In explaining this, she drew a comparison between the need for identity among de-racinated American Negroes and the lack of national identity felt by the German people that had led them to accept a leader like Hitler.

> I explained my theory that people de-racinated, denied full partici-pation in a society in which they are obliged to live, inevitably turn backwards to ancestral beliefs or follow any leader who can propose a solution to their immediate distress, who can offer a future if not a present. I mentioned the disorientation of the German people after World War I and their subsequent need for a leader such as Hitler, nonbeneficent as he was.
>
> (Dunham 1994b: 198)

She then told him about the Black Muslim group in Chicago[1] about whom she had written a research paper:

> American Negroes seeking social and economic stability, first banded together, my study showed, by a Japanese in Detroit but soon transferr[ed] their headquarters to Chicago and call[ed] the new establishment Temple Number Two. According to press reports Temple Number One was disbanded under pressure; rumour had it that some of the Detroit members had been intercepted in a basement in the act of dismembering a white policeman in prepara-tion for ritual feasting. My thesis was . . . that people would not fall

victim to such accusations were they not deprived of full benefits in the social structure, their own or imposed, in which they lived.

(ibid.: 198–9)

In essence Dunham explains here her underlying motive in going to the Caribbean and looking for dances that retain elements of African traditions from before the Diaspora: her overall aim could be broadly stated as the recovery of dance material that could be used to help re-establish a positive sense of American Negro identity. When approaching people in the Caribbean to find out about their ritual practices she usually exploited the fact that, as an African American, local villagers recognised her as someone who, like them, was a descendent of Africa, but from a group who had forgotten their religious practices and therefore needed help in rediscovering them. The reason why she took a different line with this priest is because of the reputation of the cult to which he belonged. This was the Moundong cult who, some said, practised human sacrifices and cannibalism, and kept Zombies. Zombies and the darker side of Caribbean magical and religious practices were to feature in her 1939 ballet *L'Ag Ya*. Presumably Dunham told the priest sensational rumours about Temple Number One to try to draw him on these subjects.

What fascinates me about this story, however, is the way it reveals Dunham in 1936 as someone who brought together Europe and America, black and white, anthropology and the urban sociology of modernity, and the ideas of the recently exiled German psychologist Erich Fromm. Furthermore Dunham was, at the time, someone who had experience of both ballet and modern dance and would draw on these in developing an African American style of dance. Dunham's early dance training was in ballet with Mark Turbyfill and Ludmilla Speranzeva in Chicago (Barzel and Turbyfill 1983). Her first significant professional appearance had been in a ballet with Ruth Page. Speranzeva herself had initially trained at the Kamerny Theatre in Moscow but she had also studied in Germany with Mary Wigman. Dunham had taken lessons from, among others, the German dancer Harald Kreutzberg (who was also a pupil of Wigman's) when he had been in Chicago working with Ruth Page. In an early statement that is undated but was presumably written some time in the 1930s, Dunham expresses an interest in studying with both Mary Wigman and Martha Graham 'so that I would be capable, in every sense of the word, to train a group of dancers with which to interpret the [African and Caribbean] materials collected in research, and produce ballets which I am confident such research would inspire' (Dunham 1978a: 199).

It should not be surprising that Dunham felt confident about linking together European and American modern dance, ballet, African American (including popular vernacular) traditions and African and Caribbean dance, given the brilliant, highly educated, and self-confident woman she undoubtedly was at the time. The point is, however, that such cross-overs do not easily fit into the way the history of modern dance has until recently been told. The books that established the canonical history of modern dance have until recently done so by excluding European modern dance altogether. Similarly, books on modern dance have dealt with the work of white dance artists, while books on black dance discuss the work of black dance artists. My aim in this book is unashamedly revisionist, and I have therefore purposely chosen to discuss a range of material that encompasses both Europe and America, black and white, modern ballet, modern dance, and African American dance, and leads me to consider examples both from theatre dance as elite culture and from dancing as popular entertainment.

There is now ongoing research that is beginning to reconsider the work of the pioneers of modern dance in the United States and to re-situate their contribution in relation to European developments. There is also, of course, a growing body of German research into early European modern dance, and there is beginning to be research into the relationship between the two. A review of literature about the period reveals a number of coincidences and connections between, on the one hand, ballet and modern dance and, on the other hand, dance in musicals and revues.

The inter-relationships between dance as popular entertainment and dance as a serious art form during the period was a complex one, as is demonstrated in the following collection of juxtaposed examples. During the war years, the avant-garde dance artist Valeska Gert started her career as a dancer in a cinema, performing on stage between films. Massine started his choreographic career with Diaghilev, Picasso and Satie, but in New York in the late 1920s produced ballets that were also performed in the intermissions between screenings of films. Meanwhile in Paris during the ballet *Relâche* (*Postponed*) (1924) a now famous film *Entracte* (*Intermission*) by René Clair was screened in the 'entracte' between two acts of the ballet. Ninette de Valois (b. 1898) is best known as the founder of the Royal Ballet (initially Vic–Wells Ballet) but she gained her initial stage experience dancing for three years in music halls and West End revues before joining Diaghilev's Ballets Russes. In her book *Come Dance with Me* (1957), she recalls the tradition that second house audiences on Monday nights in the provinces (i.e. outside London) always gave the acts, regardless of quality, a hard time (1957: 56). One of the revues in which De Valois appeared was *You'd be Surprised* (1923) choreographed by Massine (1895–1979). Also in the cast was the ballerina Lydia Sokolova (1896–1974) who had danced the role of the Chosen One three years earlier in Massine's 1920 revival of the *Rite of Spring*. *You'd be Surprised* was designed by Duncan Grant (1885–1978),[2] a painter associated with the Bloomsbury group. The Ballets Russes themselves appeared for a few seasons as part of music hall shows in London. It was there that members of the Bloomsbury group 'discovered' ballet modernism. It is interesting to observe that Nijinsky, Pavlova, Karsavina and other ballet dancers who had trained in St Petersburg all appeared at some time on a London music hall bill. Roger Fry observed in 1920:

> Now that . . . Picasso and Derain have delighted the miscellaneous audience of the London Music Halls with their designs for the Russian Ballet, it will be difficult for people to imagine the vehemence of the indignation which greeted the first sight of their works in England.
>
> (Fry 1928: 292)

Across the Atlantic, similar inter-relationships between dance as popular entertainment and dance as a serious art form existed. It is well known that the Denishawn Company toured vaudeville circuits and appeared on Broadway in spectacular Ziegfield productions. Martha Graham (1892–1991), leaving Denishawn to do something more 'serious', nevertheless initially danced in the (commercial) *Greenwich Village Follies* in 'artistic' dances choreographed by Ichio Ito (1892–1961), another 'serious' modern dance artist. In 1932 Graham and her company danced her *Choric Dance for an Antique Greek Tragedy* as one of the acts on the opening night of the Radio City Music Hall, New York. Doris Humphrey (1895–1958) and Charles Weidman (1901–75) broke with Denishawn for reasons similar to Graham's. But Humphrey's *Water Study* (1928) and *Shakers* (1931) and Weidman's *Ringside* (1928)[3] were performed by their own dancers in J. J. Schubert's Broadway revue *Americana* (1932) (see Cohen 1972: 111; Siegel 1993: 127–8). While Humphrey tried to distance herself from the commercial stage, Weidman continued choreographing shows throughout the 1930s and 1940s. According to Marcia Siegel, he increasingly got himself into a mess and Humphrey would have to come along at the last minute and pull it all together for him.[4] In Paris, George Balanchine (1904–83) not only worked for the Ballets Russes but also gave Josephine Baker ballet classes and then choreographed a few numbers for her appearance in the 1930–1 revue *Paris Qui Remue* at the Casino de Paris. When she briefly returned to New York in 1935 he again choreographed some of her numbers in the *Ziegfield Follies*. In the 1940s, it was with money he had earned on Broadway that Balanchine commissioned a suite of music from Paul Hindemith (1895–1963) which he then used when creating his ballet *The Four Temperaments* (1946).

Recent research on African American concert dancers has also shown up connections that have until now been hidden. For example, among the fascinating details that John Perpener has brought to light is the fact that Katherine Dunham's first New York concert – the 'Negro Dance Evening' in March 1937 – was organised by two black modern dancers, Edna Guy and Alison Burroughs (Perpener 1992: 114). Guy had trained with Denishawn and maintained a long but emotionally tortuous relationship with Ruth St

Denis, while Burroughs had studied Dalcroze eurythmics at the Hellerau-Laxenburg School near Vienna in 1931. Also sharing the programme with Burroughs, Dunham and Guy was the African-born, European-educated dancer Asdata Dafora Horton. With Graham on the bill for the opening night of the Radio City Music Hall in New York were Kreutzberg and Georgi (who Dunham had seen in Chicago and who inspired both José Limón and Erick Hawkins to study dance), and the tap dancer Ray Bolger. Bolger is probably best known for his role as the Scarecrow in the film *The Wizard of Oz* (1939), but that same year he also performed in Balanchine's ballet *Slaughter on Tenth Avenue* and in the Broadway musical *On Your Toes* (see Mason 1991: 153–8). Dunham and her company would also work with Balanchine on the Broadway musical *Cabin in the Sky* (1942) and star in a Hollywood feature film – *Stormy Weather* (1943).

There is ample evidence therefore that points to the coexistence and interdependence of the many different forms of theatre dance during the interwar years, and of connections and cross-overs between them. In recounting these here, I do not wish to suggest that distinctions between 'high' and 'low' culture and between ballet and modern dance did not exist during the first four decades of the twentieth century. Such distinctions, however, were more fluid and dynamic during that period than they subsequently became in the period following the Second World War. Rather than presenting a detailed historical chronicle of the period that fits together the many overlaps and correspondences between different dance forms, this book develops a series of arguments about modernity, 'race', and ideologies of national identity and internationalism as these were represented in theatre dance and contested in critical writings about dance during the period. In doing so it traces the development during this period of a series of critical positions that articulated the differences between the work of black and white dancers, between ballet and modern dance, and between dance as art and dance as part of modern mass entertainment.

The process of researching and writing about this series of critical positions has often therefore reminded me of a detective story. The assembling of clues and following up of leads in order to establish what happened is of course detective work, but underlying this is the attempt to understand the motivation – why certain events happened. In some of the best crime novels (or at least the ones I like reading) the detective is not really concerned with finding out who actually committed the crime but with trying to work out who's calling the shots and what power structures are at play in the situation she or he is investigating. These power structures are generally masked and dark secrets inevitably lie beneath a seemingly innocent normality. Most of the best crime novels are also visceral. Julia Kristeva, who has herself written a *roman policier*, recently quipped that Lacan was wrong when he suggested the unconscious is structured like a language: rather, she suggests, it is structured like a carnage.[5] At its best, too, modern dance has a visceral quality and powerfully moves the spectator in ways she or he doesn't always understand but nevertheless responds to.

This visceral quality is an aspect of the affective power of the body and poses a problem for ways of thinking that are conditioned by the Judaeo-Christian value system. Within such dualistic ways of thinking, the body is generally marginalised and ignored although it may occasionally be wildly overdetermined. I have advanced the argument elsewhere that social prejudices about the male dancer during approximately the last 150 years have served the function of policing dominant white norms of heterosexual masculinity (1995a: 10–30). Similarly, notions of physical hygiene and of the body's capabilities that are mediated through dance are gendered and are socially and historically specific. The subjective experience of embodiment is also conditioned by ideologies of national identity. As Mary Douglas (1966) has observed, the body is an image of society, and it therefore follows that nations can be spoken of in embodied terms: they have boundaries, life blood, vitality, their health can be a cause for concern, and wounds may be sustained to national honour. Since the body is the primary means of expression in dance, romantic discourses about the national character of national dances have been in circulation since the Enlightenment. I am not especially interested here with the fact that nationally identifiable dancing bodies conveyed political meanings during the 1920s and 1930s. My aim is to examine the relationship between notions of national boundaries and with the differing ways in which these were mediated by dancing bodies. Thus, for example, ideologies of national community were defined in an exclusive manner in some German mass performances while notions of the French 'spirit' of French modern ballets produced by 'Russian' and 'Swedish' companies in the 1920s were interpreted in an inclusive way.

Any attempt to define collective identities necessitates the exclusion of strangers and their alien bodies. These and other alien bodies, I argue, were a central subject of modernist dance. A significant aim of this book is to elucidate points of view that have tended to be marginalised in the unreconstructed, modernist account of (American)[6] modern dance. Hence, as I have already indicated, the breadth of the range of material I have chosen to discuss. The project of reinstating marginalised voices and points of view is not, however, a straightforward one. What it often reveals are perspectives that differ radically from hegemonic ones. In some cases the contrast between a dominant and alternative points of view is a useful and informative one, leading to adjustment and accommodation. However, some of the instances I have come across while doing the research for this book are ones in which dance performance and the dancing body have become a locus for contestation between different groups and formations. In writing about this I have found that in certain circumstances no single account can be made that gives an adequate idea of the knowable dance community. To put this another way, what is at issue here is the validity of the old claim that modern dance constituted a single, universal language. For example, in my chapter about Josephine Baker, different narratives are presented which all focus on the same dance event but account for its significance in widely divergent ways. Here, as elsewhere in the book, it is not enough just to recognise that certain voices and points of view (particularly black ones) have been marginalised; to try to pull these divergent voices together and infer from them an all-embracing, hegemonic conclusion would be to repeat the actions which marginalised these voices in the first place. Trying to understand them changes the way one assesses dominant points of view, in some cases revealing silences or inconsistencies that have not until now been noticed or had not previously been considered significant. Underlying these silences and inconsistencies is discontent with modernity and unease at the sense of strangeness that it arouses. The notion that modern dance constituted a universal language served the function of hiding these silences, disavowing these inconsistencies and reinforcing the power relations which underlay dominant points of view.

A basic premise of this book is that a conceptual structure based upon a particular, socially and historically constructed definition of modern dance has determined the way the canonical history of (American) modern dance has been told. Such structures enable certain kinds of discourse while closing off others. It is obvious that to ask questions that don't easily fit into such histories may reveal a different and fuller picture. To ask such questions also constitutes a challenge to the methodologies that underpinned this history of modern dance. It is to the question of methodology that I now turn.

The novelist E. M. Forster begins his theoretical essay *Aspects of the Novel* (1927) by admitting 'The novel tells a story, oh dear me yes'. Dance history tells stories too, and this book is itself structured through narratives on many levels. But, oh dear me yes, there are many different ways in which stories can be told. I look with awe, admiration but also with disbelief at the work of past historians like the Victorian scholars who pieced together detailed, authoritative accounts of English and European history with such quiet, confident certainty about what happened. Many historians of the 1990s are far more sanguine about the extent of their competencies. Simon Schama has observed that, since historians are unable to travel back in time, they:

> are left forever chasing shadows, painfully aware of their inability ever to reconstruct a dead world in its completeness, however thorough or revealing their documentation. Of course, they make do with other work: the business of formulating problems, of supplying explanations about cause and effect. But the certainty of such answers always remains contingent on their unavoidable remoteness from

their subjects. We are doomed to be forever hailing someone who has just gone around the corner and out of earshot.

(Schama 1991: 320)

Given the ephemeral nature of the performing arts, the situation for the dance historian is even less certain.

All the source material I have evaluated, reviewed and marshalled while writing this book must be seen as partial and provisional. June Layson's invaluable distinction between primary and secondary sources is pertinent here:

> Primary sources are those that came into existence during the period being studied: thus they are first-hand and contemporary, and provide the raw materials for dance study. . . . Secondary sources, as the term suggests, are second-hand, processed, after the event accounts, often using hindsight to trace developments in the dance over a span of time.
>
> (Layson 1983: 15)

While interrogating primary and secondary source materials, I too bring the benefit of hindsight to my evaluation of dance in the 1920s and 1930s. It is possible to make judgements now about past events on grounds that could not have been known at the time. While it is sometimes problematic to judge fairly instances of individual human behaviour on the basis of knowledge to which individuals at the time did not have access, hindsight affords valid and useful insights into the way social structures impact upon cultural forms and vice versa. Hindsight is an inevitable factor in the way histories are used to make sense of the present. But histories are sometimes also used to escape the present: my choice to write about the 1920s and 1930s may on one level be an avoidance of the rat race of trying to keep up with the latest in high postmodernist theory and apply it to the newest discoveries of postmodern dance and physical theatre. The reader may, however, recognise in some of this book's concerns recent additions to the academic agenda. Recent theoretical approaches to the city, the body, colonialism and decolonisation, and current work on psychoanalytic accounts of cultural forms all in my view offer valid and useful insights about the dance history of the 1920s and 1930s.

I have no illusions about my role as a writer about dance now, and am equally sceptical when approaching the dance of the past. Schama refers to the widespread recognition that impartiality is unattainable. Feminist scholarship has recently led the way in challenging the notion that it is possible to adopt an impartially objective and transparent view point from which to make value-free judgements: hence the many scholars who adopt pragmatic approaches towards epistemology. I bring to bear on the dance history of the inter-war years both a point of view and a manner of putting it into words that are partial – are socially, psychologically and historically specific. But, as Peggy Phelan has pointed out, any writing about dance performance has the effect of altering not just memories of the original but in effect the performance itself.

> To attempt to write about the undocumentable event of performance is to invoke the rules of the written document and thereby alter the event itself. Just as quantum physics discovered that macro-instruments cannot measure microscopic particles without transforming those particles, so too must performance critics realise that the labor to write about performance (and thus to 'preserve' it) is also a labor that fundamentally alters the event.
>
> (Phelan 1993: 148)

A criticism that has been levelled at some recent dance historical writing is that, in drawing on new theoretical approaches, the writers tend to neglect and marginalise the movement material that is its raison d'être. I have tried in this book to ground my theoretical excursions on analyses of particular dance examples and where relevant to give descriptions of these. The performances to which I refer took place between fifty and eighty years ago; hardly any have survived in repertory, few were filmed at the time or notated, and in most cases all that survives of them are photographs, reviews, interviews and reminiscences. I take Phelan's point that writing inevitably alters the performance event as an incentive to 'own up' to the writerliness of my descriptions. I try to bring the pieces I am interested in 'alive' by bringing out the qualities I find significant. As Simon Schama observes: 'Even in the most austere scholarly report from the archive, the inventive faculty – selecting, pruning, editing, commenting, interpreting, delivering judgements – is in full play' (1991: 322). I am arguing here not for a stylish postmodern relativism but for a pragmatism without which, it seems to me, dance history cannot reach back beyond living memory. In writing about dance events beyond this barrier the dance historian delivers an interpretation informed by his or her overall knowledge of the period and of its economies of choreographic, iconographic, corporeal, visual, musical, literary and other images.

When dance historians look backwards to try to comment, interpret and deliver judgements, the question of progress arises, particularly in the context of dance modernism. Walter Benjamin's observations about looking back at the past, in his ninth thesis on the philosophy of history, are often cited in this context:

> A Klee painting named 'Angelus Novus' shows an angel looking as though he is about to move away from something he is fixedly contemplating. His eyes are staring, his mouth is open, his wings

are spreading. This is how one pictures the angel of history. His face is turned towards the past. Where we perceive a chain of events, he sees one single catastrophe which keeps piling wreckage upon wreckage and hurls it in front of his feet. The angel would like to stay, awaken the dead, and make whole what has been smashed. But a storm is blowing from paradise; it has got caught in his wings with such violence that the angel can no longer close them. This storm irresistibly propels him into the future to which his back is turned, while the pile of debris before him grows skywards. This storm is what we call progress.

(Benjamin 1970: 259–60)

Writing in 1940, just before his suicide, Benjamin is at his most pessimistic about modernity. It is Benjamin's insight into the hollowness of most ideologies of progress and their underlying symptoms of the failure of modernity that informs most of the analyses of modernist theatre dance that I present in this book. Hence my recurring preoccupation with ways in which what is strange and disturbing in modernity is mediated by the alien bodies of modern dance artists.

Although it is easily done, modernism should not be conflated with modernity. Janet Wolff has pointed out that modernism in art is not necessarily or straightforwardly the representation of modernity. To illustrate this she points out that, although Baudelaire is 'undoubtedly the poet of modernity since he writes of the experience of the modern age and the modern city, [he] is not by any definition a "modernist" writer in aesthetic terms. Yet there is a relationship between the two' (1990: 57). It is with the relationship between the modernism of theatre dance during the 1920s and 1930s and the experience of modernity that this book is concerned. By focusing on modernity, my intention is to shift discussions about the modernism of early modern dance away from the type of formalist, modernist aesthetic theory derived from the writings of Clement Greenberg on the visual arts. Instead my concern is with the ways in which the modernisms of early modern theatre dance in Europe and North America constituted particular responses to the experience of modernity, and specifically with the experience of metropolitan living. The majority of the dance artists whose work I discuss in this book lived and worked in Paris or New York. All showed their work in either one of these metropolises but significantly few did so in both.[7] Clearly European and American experiences of modernity were different from one another. Underlying these differences are the harsh economic realities of the period and their impact upon individual national sovereignties. During the 1920s and 1930s, Europeans looked to the United States as an example of a more highly developed industrial culture. It has been argued that, for Europeans, one consequence of industrial modernisation at this time was the progressive blurring and dismantlement of the residual nineteenth-century social distinction and cultural hierarchies upon which ideologies of national identity depended (de Grazia 1989). European artistic modernisms were in some cases highly nationalistic. Modernism in the United States during the same period also tended towards a celebration of the national rather than the international. From an American point of view one of the factors that helped American art to free itself from its previous status as a peripheral and provincial outpost of European civilisation was American recognition of its status as a leading industrial country. In both Europe and North America during the 1920s and 1930s one response to modernity was therefore to focus attention on questions of national identity. The nationalism inherent in Jean Börlin and Rolf de Maré's folkloristic ballets for the Ballets Suédois, and of Nijinska and Stravinsky's ballet *Les Noces*, the nationalism inherent in statements by Mary Wigman about the German-ness of modern dance, and Martha Graham's statements about its American-ness and her comments on American pieces such as *Frontier* and *American Document* – all these need to be seen in the context of the impact of modernity on national sovereignty during the period.

Given therefore that modernity was strange and disturbing, the individuals who, during the period covered in this book, articulated a theory that is closest to accounting for this aspect of modernity, were Walter Benjamin and Siegfried Kracauer. The different but related views of modernity which they developed, writing first in Frankfurt and Berlin and then in exile in Paris after Hitler's rise to power, blend an avant-garde sensibility and Marxist historical materialism with a developing critique of the Enlightenment. Shorn of their avant-gardism, these can be seen historically as a precursor of the views of the so-called Frankfurt School – Adorno, Horkheimer and Marcuse. On a philosophical basis, the theory of aesthetic modernism developed by Greenberg shares one important aspect with this German view of modernity: both look back to the modernist project of the Enlightenment and in particular to the work of Emmanuel Kant. According to Greenberg, modernism is the use of theoretical procedures which derive from Kant. Greenberg proposes that Kant was the first modernist because he: 'used logic to establish the limits of logic, and while he withdrew much from its old jurisdiction, logic was left in all the more secure possession of what remained to it' (Greenberg 1983: 5). Thus the arts under modernism have been encouraged to undergo a process of Kantian self-criticism – using art to establish the limits of art – leading to the conclusion that: 'Realistic, illusionist art had dissembled the medium, using art to conceal art. Modernism used art to draw attention to art' (ibid.).

Adorno and Horkheimer's most pessimistic book *The Dialectics of the Enlightenment* (1947) was of course a critique of the effectiveness of the kind of Kantian self-criticism Greenberg advocated. As Zygmunt Bauman has proposed:

[the Enlightenment] has spectacularly failed in its drive to 'extinguish any trace of its own self-consciousness' (Adorno and Horkheimer's own work is, to be sure, one of the many proofs of that failure), and that myth-shattering thinking (which the Enlightenment could not but reinforce instead of marginalizing) proved to be not so much self-destructive, as destructive of the modern project's blind arrogance, high-handedness and legislative dreams.

(Bauman 1991: 17)

Underlying Adorno and Horkheimer's pessimism was horror at the Holocaust: as Adorno famously proposed, there can be no lyric poetry after Auschwitz. The history of modern dance in the 1920s and 1930s has been overshadowed by the events of the Second World War and the Holocaust – both in relation to ideologies of nationalism and of modernism.

As a result of the Second World War the United States changed its foreign policy from isolationism to an internationalist stance that was informed both by the commercial logic of opening up international markets and the political objective of combating international communism. American definitions of modernism developed by Clement Greenberg leant support to the export of American visual art and modern dance as the most advanced art of the most advanced country of the free world (see Orton and Pollock 1985). While modernism thus became associated with internationalism, nationalism became associated in many people's minds with extremist brands of populist politics, and in particular with the racist basis of German nationalism under the National Socialist regime. As a result of the writings of Horst Koegler, Hedwig Müller, Valerie Preston-Dunlop, Susan Manning, Marion Kant, Lilian Karina and others, it is now well known that many leading German modern dance artists during the early years of the Nazi regime became involved in the work of the Reich Chamber of Culture under Joseph Goebbels. This process reached its apogee when most of the leading German dancers and choreographers participated in the dance performances celebrating the 1936 Berlin Olympic Games. Statements about the Germanness of German modern dance that are made both before and after Hitler's rise to power are sometimes, therefore, over-simplistically read as proto-fascist.

One of the problems with this way of thinking about modern dance in Germany is that it is rarely accompanied by an attempt to place nationalistic statements by German dancers in the broader context of ideologies of national identity and internationalism in other countries at the time. There are three other obvious examples of the way these ideologies were mediated in theatre dance during the period. First, there is the French nationalism inherent in the rappel à l'ordre – the call for a return to the French classical spirit in the arts in the immediate aftermath of the First World War. As

John Willett has pointed out, this return to classicism was not particularly restrictive and actually supported the development of modernist architecture and avant-garde painting (Willett 1978: 63–4). The ballets in whose creation Jean Cocteau was involved – from *Parade* in 1917 to *Le Train Bleu* in 1924 – could all be said to associate progressive modernism with a putative French classical spirit. Second, there is the isolationist, American nationalism of Martha Graham's modern dance on American themes during the 1930s and 1940s – exemplified by pieces like *Frontier*, *American Document* and *Appalachian Spring* and evident within some of her published statements during the 1930s. Third, there is the internationalism of the ballets Kurt Jooss created in the 1930s: these were both international in their themes and in their assimilation of traditional academic ballet technique with movement vocabularies and ideologies developed by Laban, and with methods of staging and lighting developed in German expressionist theatre and cinema.

Susan Manning has developed a revisionist reassessment of the nationalism and internationalism of early modern dance. Ballet, she suggests, has historically tended to be more international than modern dance:

> As modern dance institutionalised after World War I, it fragmented into two self-consciously national movements, the German and the American. The domestication of Russian ballet in America, England, and elsewhere in Europe veered away from Soviet derivations from the same heritage. Modern dance became an arena for the forging of national identity, while 20th-century ballet became an arena for international competition.
>
> (Manning 1988: 36)

Manning's primary concern has been with German dance, and it is certainly true that Mary Wigman as a modern dancer was primarily concerned with ideologies of German nationalism and that, as Kurt Jooss moved away from *ausdrucktanz* towards ballet he choreographed pieces which were informed by internationalist ideologies. Manning's proposition also illuminates the relationship between Graham's work and notions of the specificity of modern American experience. It is my contention, however, that where the modernism of early modern dance and ballet is concerned, some works were informed by international modernist aesthetic concerns while others developed a specifically national aesthetic. Historically there is a shift during the period from national to international that is a response to the impact on dancers of changing political circumstances.

Manning's discussion about nationalism and internationalism came in the context of a response to the re-publication of Sally Banes' seminal study of American postmodern dance *Terpsichore in Sneakers* (1980, 1987). Manning was taking issue with Banes' assertion that 'It has been precisely in the area of postmodern dance that issues of modernism in the other arts have arisen' (1987: xiv). Manning had argued that Wigman and Graham's works in the 1920s were modernist in their formalism, abstraction and self-referential acknowledgement of dance's specificity as an art form. This drew from Banes the response that Graham's dances of the late 1920s and early 1930s are not relevant to a discussion of modernism as it emerged in the dance world under the Greenbergian gallery aesthetic (1989: 14) – i.e. the view of modernism in the visual arts largely proposed by Clement Greenberg.

Many other dance historians and theorists have, like Banes, drawn on the Greenbergian account of modernism in the visual arts to theorise the modernism of modern and postmodern dance: these include Marshall Cohen, Roger Copeland, David Michael Levin and Stephanie Jordan. It is sometimes assumed that Wigman and Graham were not engaged in the particular process of purist abstraction that typifies the high modernist painting of the 1950s and 1960s with which Greenberg and his followers are principally concerned. Greenberg's proposition that the arts under modernism have been encouraged to undergo a process of Kantian self-criticism – using art to establish the limits of art – is an account of modernism as a progression from one generation of modernist practitioners to another, each reacting against the aesthetic paradigms of their predecessors and progressing towards a goal of pure abstraction. Although it is not always stated in these terms, the view that the work of expressionist dance artists like Wigman and Graham is not modernist is based on the idea that, in their use of primitivist material, they are ideologically opposed to modernity and progress. This, however, is to oversimplify the relationship between modernism and modernity. As Zygmunt Bauman has observed:

> History of modernity is a history of tension between social existence and its culture. Modern existence forces its culture into opposition to itself. The disharmony is precisely the harmony modernity needs. The history of modernity draws its uncanny and unprecedented dynamism from the speed with which it discards successive versions of harmony having first discredited them as but pale and flawed reflections of its foci imaginarii.
>
> (Bauman 1991: 10)

Bauman draws the concept of foci imaginarii from Richard Rorty (1989) and defines these focuses as 'absolute truth, pure art, humanity as such, order, certainty, harmony, the end of history' (ibid.). Wigman and Graham, in different ways and for differently stated reasons, were both involved in a quest for 'absolute truth, pure art, humanity as such'. This led them to strip down the expressive means of theatre dance and this stripping away of inessentials is typical of modern consciousness as Bauman defines it:

a suspicion or awareness of the inconclusiveness of extant order; a consciousness prompted and moved by the premonition of inadequacy, nay non-viability, of the order-designing, ambivalence-eliminating project; of the randomness of the world in as far as it reveals ever new layers of chaos underneath the lid of power-assisted order.

(ibid.: 9)

My assumption in this book is that Wigman, Graham and many other modern dance artists of their time should properly be considered modernists.

The reading of the modern dance of the 1920s and 1930s that is proposed in this book is informed by this view of the relationship between modernism and modernity: that modernism is not a direct aesthetic expression of positivist ideologies of progress but a progressive deconstruction of outmoded aesthetic conventions and traditions. Through most of the twentieth century, artists have produced work that purposely avoids utilising certain artistic conventions which up to that time had been considered essential to the creation of art. It is this practice of abandoning traditional conventions that is generally recognised as making such art 'modern' and it can also be recognised as an instance of the kind of critical modern consciousness described by Bauman.

This critical modern consciousness can also be seen at work in the ways in which ideologies of national identity and internationalism are represented and expressed through the modern dancing body. In the 1920s and 1930s older ideologies of national identity were being undermined both by the actuality and the social effects of industrial and financial modernisation. Benedict Anderson (1991) has suggested that nations are imagined communities.[8] The sort of national communities that individuals imagined themselves to belong to were substantially different in the 1920s to the communities that had existed in the last decade of the previous century. It is not just that so many geographical boundaries and political affiliations were changed as a consequence of the First World War. From the beginning of the century, national and regional distinctions were increasingly being eroded by modernity. Mass production and the accompanying new methods of marketing were increasingly creating a more homogeneous society, while the new mass media cinema, radio and mass-circulation illustrated magazines were altering individuals' awareness of their place in the world. Anderson points out that, in addition to political factors, technology and the mass media play an important role in the construction of the individual's sense of national membership. He also allows that the arts mediate ideologies of national identity. However, because he sees nations as constructions, the question he admits to finding most difficult to answer is: why are individuals prepared to die for an imagined, constructed community that they think of as their nation? To answer this, it is necessary to consider the relationship between the concept of national identity as an historical variable and the historically specific, psychological construction of subjectivity. This is what Julia Kristeva addresses in her famous 1979 essay 'Women's time'. This opens with an overview of the period covered in this book:

> The nation – dream and reality of the nineteenth century – seems to have reached both its apogee and its limit when the 1929 crash and the National-Socialist apocalypse demolished the pillars that, according to Marx, were its essence: economic homogeneity, histor-ical tradition and linguistic unity. It could indeed be demonstrated that the Second World War, though fought in the name of national values (in the above sense of the term), brought an end to the nation as a reality: it was turned into a mere illusion which, from that point forward, would be preserved only for ideological or strictly political purposes, its social and philosophical coherence having collapsed.
>
> (Kristeva 1986: 188)

While the social and philosophical coherence of the nation may have been collapsing during the period under consideration in this book, the psychic importance for the individual of being a part of a nation – and through this, as Kristeva puts it, of accessing 'the cultural and religious memory forged by the interweaving of history and geography' (ibid.) – must not be underesti-mated. Kristeva's suggestion that national identity is about origins – about where the individual comes from and how the individual subject relates to the collectivity – provides a useful way of understanding how dance (and dancing bodies) articulated notions of national and racial identity during the period.

It has also to be remembered that many people during the inter-war years conflated 'race' and nation, and thus understood national differences in the biological terms that were developed during the nineteenth century. The word 'race' is often now placed within inverted commas to mark the fact that the concept still exists on an ideological basis although the scientific evidence on which the notion of 'racial' difference was initially posited has long since been discredited. In the inter-war years, difference was often expressed through bodily metaphors, 'pure race' being understood in terms of 'pure blood', while anxiety over national boundaries (cultural, geograph-ical) was equated with concern over bodily boundaries, pollution and degen-eration. Dance, whose primary means of communication is of course the body, therefore became a locus of anxieties over loss of national and racial identity as a consequence of the impact of modernity.

This focus on nationalism was, as Hannah Arendt (1958) has pointed out, one of the consequences of the Enlightenment. She identifies as a key failure of the French Revolution the inability to extend universal human rights to all human beings. This is due, she argues, to a slippage in the Declaration of Human Rights between the rights of all human beings and the rights of citizens: individuals, within the Declaration, gain access to universal rights through the democratic constitution of the enlightened modern state. As the ideas of the French Revolution spread throughout Europe they triggered a demand for the national rights of peoples rather than universal rights for all. As Kristeva (1991: 149) points out, strangers – those who were stateless or from diasporic groups, and those from outside the enlightened West – were excluded from an otherwise universal, liberally democratic polity. It is only through becoming a citizen that an individual's obligations and enjoyments are protected or that she or he faces punishment for any infringment of these. Katherine Dunham undoubtedly appreciated this connection between political rights and the freedom to express cultural identities when she referred to 'people de-racinated, denied full participation in a society in which they are obliged to live' (1994b: 198). Kristeva has argued that what disturbs individuals in their encounters with foreigners or strangers is an uncanny recognition (or refusal to recognise) that the alterity that the stranger represents is a projection of an alterity inscribed already within the most intimate interiority of the self. By calling modern dancing bodies 'alien bodies' I am drawing attention to the fact that, where modernity undermined ideologies of national identity, it created needs for new definitions of origins that, during the 1920s and 1930s, were partially satisfied through the appreciation of primitivism in the arts. The alien bodies after whom this book is named are those modernist dancing bodies that articulated the disturbing new spaces and rhythms of modernity in pieces like Graham's *Lamentations*, and Wigman's *Witch Dance*, as well as in the choreography and performance of artists like Josephine Baker and Katherine Dunham. My argument is that what seemed alien about modern dancing (in the theatre as well as at the dance hall and nightclub) was nevertheless uncannily familiar because of the extent to which individuals were themselves alienated by modernity.

The three categories – modernity, 'race' and nation – which I have included in the subtitle for this book, were therefore closely interconnected, particularly where representations in dance were concerned during the 1920s and 1930s. My aim in writing this book and offering a revised history of dance during the inter-war years is to look at the ways in which modernity, 'race' and national identity determined the development of modern dance, and how dance too often reinforced but occasionally undermined individuals' understandings of these concepts. The first half of this book therefore examines European responses to the fragmentation and alienation that resulted from the metropolitan experience of modernity: in doing so it focuses on critical writing about the impact of American modernity and jazz music in popular theatrical dance of the period. Then, turning to American modern dance, the second part examines the way notions of American-ness and primitivism, that are examined in the first part in a European context, were important in creating an aesthetic response to the experience of modernity in the United States.

The book proceeds as follows. Chapter 2 examines European ballets and dance pieces which take the city and metropolitan life as subjects through which to explore an underlying unease at the disturbing new spaces and rhythms of modernity. It also identifies an historical shift: from a nationally focused avant-garde optimism about the potential of the 'shock of the new' to bring about the demise of capitalism and a consequent, utopian (re)integration of art and life; to an internationally focused modernism that constituted a site of resistance against right-wing nationalism. It is this historical shift which establishes the social and artistic contexts for the critical positions on jazz dance that are discussed in Chapters 3 and 4.

Chapter 3 examines three mutually exclusive and largely contradictory views of Josephine Baker's dancing in Paris in the 1920s and early 1930s. It points out that Baker was originally presented under the auspices of the Parisian avant-garde, her primitivist dancing being valued as a utopian alternative and a much needed injection of 'natural' vitality into a supposedly dying European civilisation. Baker herself was fully aware of the contradictions and inconsistencies in this imaginary white fantasy which bore little relation to her own sense of her African heritage. Another view of Baker valued her dancing body as an ideal image of the socially and psychologically constructed slender modern female body which, it is argued, represented a positive escape for women from domesticity and restrictive nineteenth-century ideologies of femininity. Chapters 4 and 5 are also concerned with the modernity of the slender modern, female dancing body as perceived by Siegfried Kracauer in his 1927 essay 'The mass ornament'. Following the historical shift identified in Chapter 2, Chapter 4 discusses Kracauer's initial optimism about the potential of the mass ornament while Chapter 5 shows how this changed in the light of National Socialist uses of the mass ornament. Thus Kracauer's avant-garde influenced hope that such mass cultural phenomena as the dancing of the Tiller Girls might portend the disintegration of capitalism is seen to have turned sour in a general condemnation of German body culture as inherently and generically fascist. This is an understandable conclusion in the light of the Holocaust and yet one which I shall argue is nevertheless flawed.

The rest of the book takes these European concerns about the alien dancing bodies of modernity and finds parallels with contemporary developments in the United States, while accounting for some of the differences in the way modern dance developed across the Atlantic. Chapter 6 presents an overview of the overlaps and connections between modern dance in Europe and the United States. It thus challenges the view that each developed in isolation from the other, locating this in ideological and critical positions taken up by artists and commentators as a consequence of the Second World

War, the Holocaust and the cold war. Chapter 7 looks at positivist but isolationist American views of American modernity during the 1930s and their expression in American modern dance and ballet that implicitly or explicitly deals with the experience of modern life. While on some levels this work is radically different from the European work considered in Chapter 2, an underlying unease with the social consequences of modernity is again identified. Chapter 8 revisits the issues of primitivism introduced in Chapter 3, presenting an analysis of three pieces which each use 'primitive' ritual to develop modernist theatrical dance vocabularies. It situates an underlying modernist fascination with otherness within ideologies of acculturation and assimilation, and discusses the ethical issues implicit within dominant Western appropriations of the cultural forms of subordinate 'primitive' peoples.

In so far as this book (oh dear me yes) tells a story, it is one that starts in Paris during the 1920s and progresses from France and Germany to the United States and Haiti during the 1930s and 1940s. On the way it identifies within choreography, performance and critical writings about performance, a number of differing views about modernity, 'race' and national identity and internationalism. Underlying these are different attitudes towards the rigidity or fluidity of the imaginary boundaries set up between self and other that are mediated by the dancing body – boundaries which are socially and psychologically constructed and politically and historically situated. While this book is written from the point of view that modernity has failed, it does not take up this position in order to propose that modern dance has also failed, or that modern dance is therefore no longer relevant to postmodern times. Instead, its aim is to inspire a revisionist approach to the study of the work of early modern dance artists and, with it, a re-evaluation of what their work can tell us about the embodiment of ethics in our own responses to the spectacle of those alien dancing bodies which we need to own as a product of our own fears, desires and fascinations.

2

CHOREOGRAPHING THE DISTURBING NEW SPACES OF MODERNITY

'Brother, if you can't be an artist in Paris, you might as well go on home and marry the boss' daughter.' Even as Gene Kelly was recording these words for the voice-over at the start of the MGM musical *American in Paris* (1952), New York was taking over from Paris as the centre of advanced artistic activity (or, as Suzi Gablik has put it, was stealing the idea of modern art). Be it Paris, New York, Berlin, London, or whichever metropolitan centre, the metropolis exudes a special allure. Cultural life is richer and more diverse there than anywhere else. Munich, in some accounts, was the birth place of theatrical modernism, though Moscow and St Petersburg were undoubtedly also important. Berlin and the idea of Berlin impinged on the German consciousness as representative of all that was good and all that wasn't about modernity, and became a symbol of this in the work of many German artists and writers of the first few decades of the twentieth century. Cities, and capital cities in particular, have been crucial in the development of the modern arts. The reasons that draw artists to capital cities are fairly obvious. By and large it is there that they can see work in galleries and theatres, meet like-minded individuals, or lose themselves in the crowd. It is also something like good business sense or good career planning that draws artists there. Nowhere else can they have the same chances of coming to the attention of the 'right' people: for visual artists the patrons and dealers; for performers the directors, impresarios and theatre managers; for writers the editors and publishers; and of course all artists at some time need to be noticed by the opinion formers, writers and critics.

In the early 1900s the modernist writers Guillaume Appolinaire (1880–1918), James Joyce (1882–1941) and Gertrude Stein (1876–1946), and the modernist visual artists Pablo Picasso (1881–1973) and Constantin Brancusi (1876–1957) all moved to Paris. All of them were foreign immigrants. It was in *Le Figaro* in Paris that the Italian poet Filippo Marninetti (1876–1944) published his first Futurist Manifesto in 1909: only there would it have been noticed. Paris similarly, in 1909, made the Ballets Russes' reputation and in 1932 did the same for Kurt Jooss (1901–79) when his ballet *The Green Table* (*Der Grüne Tisch*) won an international choreographic competition.[1] Rudolf Laban (1879–1958) and Mary Wigman (1886–1973) may have worked their theories and artistic ideas out during the 1914–18 war in the peaceful, pastoral tranquillity of Ascona in southern Switzerland, but they had previously taught, created work and attended advanced theatrical performances in Munich before the war and did the same in Zürich during it. Isadora Duncan (1877–1927) and Ruth St Denis (1879–1968) both received their first big critical successes in Munich in 1902 and 1906 respectively. Duncan subsequently settled in Paris, as did Josephine Baker (1906–75). These artists in the early years of the twentieth century would have experienced the social effects of modernity more intensely in these cities than they might have done had they lived in smaller towns or in the country.

If everything was up to date at the turn of the century in Kansas City for the cowboys of Oklahoma in the Rogers and Hammerstein musical of 1943, things were even more advanced in Berlin, London, New York and Paris. Not only was the metropolis the epitome of modernity but for nearly all these artists it was also foreign. This generally alienating social experience was crucial to the development of the new formal and expressive artistic vocabularies of modernism. Raymond Williams has suggested that the experience of exile, and of being an immigrant in a foreign metropolis, was central to the creation of the formal innovations made by the early modernists. Discussing early modernist writers, Williams argues that the experience of being an immigrant:

> underlies in an obvious way the elements of strangeness and distance, indeed of alienation, which so regularly form part of the repertory. But the decisive aesthetic effect is at a deeper level. Liberated or breaking from their national or provincial cultures, placed in quite new relations to those other native languages or visual traditions, encountering meanwhile a novel and dynamic common environment from which many of the older forms were obviously distant, the artists and writers and thinkers of this phase found the only community available to them: a community of the medium; of their own practices.
>
> (Williams 1989: 45)

This concentration on the medium itself (which is recognisably a hallmark of modernist work in all the arts including theatre dance) took the form of a progressive deconstruction of outmoded aesthetic conventions and traditions. Modernist dance artists embodied the deconstructive modern consciousness (discussed in Chapter 1) by purposely avoiding the utilisation of conventions and traditions which up to that time had been considered essential to the creation of theatre dance. The resulting 'modern' dance and ballet was by implication independent of the past and indeed a transitory tracing of an ever-disappearing present. The city, both as subject matter and as example, played a catalytic role in this process: it too, with the building sites and road works of its ever-changing streets, its newly opening shops and businesses, and the built-in redundancy of its trend setting fashions in clothes and popular entertainment – all this embodied the transitory nature of the experience of modernity. Dance, by embracing the transitory nature of the modern city, was of course breaking away from the values of nineteenth-century bourgeois society and its stagnating cultural conservatism. This rejection was clearest in the new, reflexive relationship between modernist ballets and dance as popular entertainment. The cowboy in *Oklahoma* who had just returned from Kansas City sang not only about its artefacts – skyscrapers seven storeys high, elevators, 'Bell' telephones, indoor water closets. He also sang about urban mass entertainment – ragtime and burlesque. The metropolis is the natural home of the entertainment industry. If in the early years of the twentieth century dance and ballet were emerging as serious art forms, they were doing so by distancing dance as art from dance as entertainment. But to complicate matters, dance as entertainment in dance halls, on stage or in rehearsals had been a favoured subject through which painters and writers, from the mid-nineteenth century through to the mid-twentieth century, represented modern life. Significantly, this was generally female dancers being described or depicted by male artists.

While in the first two decades of the twentieth century, dance was only beginning to be recognised as a serious art form in its own right (in many cases primarily because of the 'serious' composers, writers and visual artists who collaborated with choreographers on ballet productions), dancing and prostitution had for some time been established as characteristic forms of metropolitan entertainment. These latter were key subjects which painters and writers, from Baudelaire (1821–67) and the Impressionists on, had used to depict modern life. Metropolitan life was perceived as feminine – indulgent, luxurious, corrupting – and having an enervating and feminising effect on men. By the middle of the nineteenth century, dance was primarily associated with femininity. While (or because) dance was not itself considered a serious art form, it was therefore available for use by artists as an exemplary modern subject.

From 1917, when the Ballets Russes premiered *Parade*, to 1932, when Jooss' company the Folkwang Tanzbühnen first performed *The Big City* (*Die Grosstadt von Heute* – literally *The Big City of Today*), some European choreographers (both male and female) followed the lead of visual artists in using popular dance and mass entertainment as a key subject through which to explore the social experience of modern life in the big city. While Chapters 6 and 7 consider the relationship between modernity and modern dance in New York, it is with this group of European works that I am concerned in this chapter. The group comprises some ballets premiered in Paris by de

Maré's Les Ballets Suédois and by choreographers associated with Diaghilev's Ballets Russes, a few modern dance works and dance plays produced in Germany by Laban and Jooss and a few small-scale recital pieces by the German dancer Valeska Gert (1892–1978). My intention is not, however, to document these works and to place them in a stylistic slot within a supposed evolution of modern dance. In many ways these works defy any such collective categorisation: what they have in common is their subject and the social, cultural and political meanings which that subject had at that time. Here again I am not primarily concerned with developing an interpretation of these works that is informed by a fuller understanding of their context, although one of my intentions is to show how these works illuminate this context more fully for us. Through revealing the complex inter-relationships that existed between 'popular' mass entertainment and 'serious' modernist and avant-garde theatre dance during this period, my intention is to open up the theoretical issues that I use to underpin the discussion of dancing on the commercial stage by Josephine Baker and the Tiller Girls in the next two chapters. What is at issue in these modernist and avant-garde works is the extent to which it was believed that dance could actively bring about positive social change.

In the first few decades of the twentieth century a tradition of radical thinking about the role of the arts had its roots not in marxist political thinking but in a utopian, anarchic socialism. As Andreas Huyssen points out, links between the avant-garde and political radicalism were particularly evident in 'substantial segments of the bohemian subcultures of the turn of the century' (1986: 5). For some radical dance artists and their audiences in France and Germany during the 1920s, the hope still existed that dance could develop into an emancipatory mass culture through the elimination of the artificial barriers between work and leisure, production and culture. It was the political events of the 1930s and 1940s that finally killed off this hope. The erosion of this hope is outlined later in the chapter, through comparing the ideological premises of ballets from the period which used modernist visual, theatrical and choreographic vocabularies and explored themes from popular mass entertainment to evoke the alienating anonymity of metropolitan experience. What emerges from this discussion are differing ideologies of national identity and of internationalism. Susan Manning has proposed that during the twentieth century 'modern dance became an arena for the forging of national identity, while 20th-century ballet became an arena for international competition' (Manning 1988: 36). Some of the ballets that take as their starting point modern life in the big city were informed by international modernist aesthetic concerns while others developed a specifically modernist national aesthetic.

By pointing out the connections between modernist theatre dance and popular entertainment, I am not suggesting that distinctions between 'high' and 'low' culture and between ballet and modern dance did not exist during the first four decades of the twentieth century. These distinctions, however, were understood differently at that time from the way they were understood during the period between the end of the Second World War and the advent of ideas about postmodernism. As Huyssen observes, the theoretical arguments that defined the distinction between high modernism and kitsch were developing during the 1930s and 1940s in the writings of Clement Greenberg and Theodor Adorno (1986: 56). Huyssen proposes that, prior to this and particularly during the 1920s, the distinction between modernism and mass entertainment was understood in gendered terms. Although in his discussion of this he doesn't consider dance, this insight is particularly pertinent. Because dance at the time was considered a feminine realm (and still is to a certain extent at the end of the century), it is a useful area within which to examine the particular forms which concerns and anxieties about changing gender roles took in the 1920s.

Many middle-class men in the early 1920s felt demoralised by the experience of war and by the social and economic changes that followed. Modernity represented a threat through its erosion of the distinctions that determined class and national identities. It is now argued that, despite the success of the women's suffrage movement, by the 1920s women did not in fact enjoy significantly greater political influence than they had before winning the vote. Nevertheless, women's new found independence and their greater visibility within the job market constituted an erosion of the nineteenth-century phenomenon that has been called the culture of separate spheres (Wolff and Seed 1987). From a male point of view, the 'new women' of the jazz age became on some levels a symptom of an increasing sense of masculine insecurity. These masculine concerns were mediated through the roles and stories in some ballets of the period. From a female point of view, modernity offered an escape from the restrictions of nineteenth-century definitions of femininity. The predominance in the dance profession of women dancers and choreographers largely from middle-class backgrounds meant that during this period theatre dance (both popular and artistic) was an area in which the differences between male and female responses to modernity were particularly clearly articulated.

This chapter therefore proceeds as follows. First, it considers ways in which modernist artistic practice drew on characteristic, gendered aspects of metropolitan experience; it thus surveys ballets that explore the (masculine) flâneur's view of the city, and ballets and dance pieces by female choreographers that explored 'modern' activities which at the time promised to allow an escape from gender stereotyping. It then considers the ideological shifts in notions of national identity and internationalism that can be identified in three ballets: *Parade* (1917), *Skating Rink* (1922) and *The Big City* (1932). It is shown that *Skating Rink* was informed by utopian socialist ideas while Jooss was interested in left-wing, anti-fascist ideas around the time he made *The Big City* and *The Green Table*. What is argued, however, is that despite the political radicalism of these ballets, some (though not all) of the ways in which women are represented in them are conservative and sentimental, and do not refer to women's actual historical experience of modernity but are determined by increasing masculine insecurities. These are also exemplified in the way the idea of prostitution, particularly in Weimar Germany, came to stand for the alienating social experience of individuals under capitalism. The chapter therefore concludes by comparing and contrasting differing ways of representing prostitution in *The Green Table* and in Valeska Gert's *Canaille*.

The social experience of metropolitan modernity

The social experience of time and space has recently become an object of research. Andreas Huyssen has given a useful overview of the way social history, history of technology, urban history and philosophy of time have converged:

> We only need to think of the well-documented changes in the perception and articulation of time and space brought about by rail-road travelling, the expansion of the visual field by news photography, the restructuring of city space with the Hausmannization of Paris, and last but not least the increasing imposition of industrial time and space on the human body in schools, factories, and the family. We may take the periodical spectacles of the World Expositions, those major mass-cultural phenomena of the times, as well as the elaborate stagings of commodity in the first giant department stores as salient symptoms of a changing relationship between the human body and the object world that surrounds it and of which it is itself a major part.
>
> (Huyssen 1986: 18–19)

If modernity created new spaces and new experiences of time, then modernism in theatre dance explored these dimensions in choreographic terms. Modern subjects for ballet and modern dance demanded modern treatment. Blaise Cendrars, for example, in a eulogy for the choreographer Jean Börlin, wrote:

> Billboards and loudspeakers have made you [Börlin] forget the pedagogy of the Académie de Danse, with its bouts of sciatica and measure, bars [of music] and good taste, affectation and virtuosity. When you've forgotten all this you've discovered rhythm, the beautiful rhythm of today, which opens five continents to us: discipline, balance, health, strength, speed.
>
> (quoted in Håger 1990: 291)

25

Cendrars, by asserting that the rhythms of today are beautiful, is taking an affirmative, celebratory stance towards modernity and progress. His hope was that modernity would bring about a breakdown in the residual bourgeois capitalist world order and lead to a liberation of everyday life. Yet it is clear from contemporary sources that the city and its transitory new spaces could sometimes appear disturbing. Modernist art that celebrated modernity couldn't avoid evoking these potentially disturbing qualities. The early German sociologist George Simmel identified agoraphobia, neurasthenia and an over-exaggeratedly blasé attitude as psychological responses to, and effects of city life (Simmel 1971). It is within discussions of the figure of the flâneur that this ambiguously affirmative yet simultaneously critical and predominantly masculine response to the city is most clearly identified. It is the moment when dancing makes its transition from being the object of the flâneur's gaze, as he wanders through the city, to being the subject of inspiration of what might be called the choreography of modern life, that dance finally became a modernist art form.

In Paris during the second half of the nineteenth century artists, writers and gentlemen of leisure enjoyed a freedom, derived from their class position and gender, to wander through the vast, modernised metropolis created by Baron Haussmann (1809–91), and, in a detached and disdainful way, to seek the object of their (generally heterosexual) desires. Eunice Lipton has linked the daily haunts of this social group in a discussion of some paintings and drawings by Degas (1834–1917):

> [Degas'] daily haunts were also the haunts of dandies: opera and theatre foyers, cafés, brothels, racetracks, the boulevards. Dandies were attracted to lower-class, sexually accessible women; that they were also repulsed by these women seemed to make the encounters all the more exciting. Dancers were an obvious choice for such men, laundresses were another. Chroniclers of 'la vie élegante', the dandy life – artists like Eugène Lami, Constantin Guys and Gavarini – in fact depicted laundresses and ballet dancers as well as milliners and café singers.
>
> (Lipton 1982: 279–80)

And so, of course, did Degas. In this context then it is not surprising that dance, whose primary means of expression is the body in space and time, should become such a frequent subject for the depiction of the disturbing new spaces and rhythms of modernity. Degas' drawings and paintings of ballet dancers, together with scenes of dance halls in Montmartre by French painters including Henri Toulouse-Lautrec (1864–1901) and Auguste Renoir (1841–1919) are the forerunners of similar subjects in early twentieth-century paintings by Pablo Picasso (1881–1973), Ludwig Kirchner (1880–1938) and Otto Dix (1891–1969)[2] in which the threatening

Otherness (for the male spectator) of female dancers and prostitutes comes to stand for an increasingly paranoid, middle-class, masculine vision of metropolitan life. The act of representing such subjects was an act of attempted mastery as the male modernist artist strove to provide, as Andreas Huyssen has suggested, an active and productive alternative to the (feminine) pleasures of mass cultural entertainment (1986: 47–53).

The prototype for the flâneur cruising the city was the poet Baudelaire. Probably the best description of this Baudelairian concept comes in the 1939 essay 'Some motifs in Baudelaire' by Walter Benjamin (1892–1940):

> There was the pedestrian who would let himself be jostled by the crowd but there was also the flâneur who demanded elbow room and was unwilling to forgo the life of gentleman of leisure. Let the many attend to their daily affairs, the man of leisure can indulge in the perambulations of the flâneur only if as such he is already out of place. He is as much out of place in the atmosphere of complete leisure as in the feverish turmoil of the city.
>
> (Benjamin 1970: 174)

Strictly speaking, the flâneur should be seen as an historically specific phenomenon who existed in the particular social and economic circumstances of Baudelaire's day. Benjamin and Kracauer, and even to some extent Simmel, were all interested in the idea of the flâneur and flânerie although their class positions were quite different from that of Baudelaire. Nevertheless, the flâneur has been widely adopted by social theorists as a useful figure through which to identify and articulate aspects of social experience of the modern city, and it is in this partly ahistoricised sense that I use it in this chapter.

As Benjamin observes, the flâneur is out of place and this is because he wants to be so; what he seeks in the city is an Other who will confirm for him his sense of identity – a privileged identity that the scale of the modern metropolis and the social changes brought about by modernisation threatened to erode. The city becomes associated with this desire for the Other, a desire that becomes projected onto its fabric. Even its public spaces are perceived not as rational architectural constructions but as sexualised, uncanny and threatening.

> As I was walking, one hot summer afternoon, through the deserted streets of a provincial town in Italy which was unknown to me, I found myself in a quarter of whose character I could not remain long in doubt. Nothing but painted women were to be seen at the windows of the small houses, and I hastened to leave the narrow street at the next turning. But after having wandered about for a time without enquiring my way, I suddenly found myself back in

27

the small street, where my presence was beginning to excite attention. I hurried away once more, only to arrive by another detour at
the same place yet a third time. Now, however, a feeling overcame
me which I can only describe as uncanny, and I was glad to find
myself back at the piazza I left a short while before, without any
further voyages of discovery.

(Freud 1951, vol. 17: 237)

Freud's seemingly aimless wanderings were subconsciously motivated by
desires too shameful to admit consciously. His anecdote illustrates his
insight that those desires that are repressed are bound to return. Here the
return of the repressed and what he calls the compulsion to repeat, take on a
literally spatial dimension as he connects his impression of uncanniness with
the unknown urban landscape.

This was an experience that finds a parallel in Rudolf Laban's reminiscences in his 1936 autobiography *A Life for Dance* (*Ein Leben für Tanz*).
Recalling a going away party he had given as a young man on the eve of his
departure to study architecture in Paris, Laban wrote:

For a moment, in this happy-nostalgic farewell atmosphere, I felt a
shadow of foreboding as if beneath the brilliant, glittering cloak of
the lighted streets and buildings there was an enormous monster
that could crush all high hopes and expectations with one blow of
his paw. Was the city just another 'Queen of the Night'?

(Laban 1975: 32–3)

The 'Queen of the Night' was a society lady to whom Laban had been introduced.[3] Quite why he felt so repulsed by her attempts to involve him in
theatrical work is none too clear from his account. What is evident is that
yet again the big, nocturnal city is menacing and this menace is connected
with femininity. This response to the city was explored by Laban in his
dance play *The Night* (*Die Nacht*, 1927).

Another wanderer is perhaps more honest with himself than Freud
appears to have been about his search on the boulevards for sexualised
Others:

All young men do silly things. In the streets of Paris I went in search
of cocottes. I looked for a long time because I wanted the girl to be
healthy and beautiful – sometimes I looked all day long and found
nobody because I was inexperienced. I loved several cocottes every
day. I went for walks along the boulevards and often met cocottes
who did not understand me. I used to make use of all sorts of tricks in
order to draw their attention, as they paid very little attention to me
because I was simply dressed. I was dressed quietly in order not to be

recognised. One day I was following a cocotte when I noticed a young man staring at me. He was in a carriage with his wife and his two children. He recognised me and I felt terribly humiliated, so I turned blushing. But I continued my chase.

(Nijinsky 1937: 31)

The sense of shame that Nijinsky (1889–1950) expresses so infectiously in his journals, from which this extract comes, has tended to be read by dance historians in terms of the fragility of Nijinsky's mental health. Kenneth Archer and Millicent Hodson have uncovered further evidence of Nijinsky's flânerie in the form of quotations in his choreography to popular dances that Nijinsky would have come across in working-class dance halls. There is a reference to Apache dancing in *Le Sacre du printemps* (Hodson 1996: 59), to the tango in *L'Après midi d'un faune* and to the Turkey Trot and Texas Rag in *Jeux*.[4]

If Nijinsky slummed in the role of flâneur, he must be seen as someone situated in an extremely awkward social position in relation to flânerie. He himself, as a dancer, had more than once been on the other end, as it were, of the metropolitan dandy's quest for the desired Other. His sister, Bronislava Nijinska (1891–1972) recalls in her memoirs an elegantly dressed young man who was always hovering around her brother while the latter was rehearsing backstage at the Théâtre du Châtelet in Paris before the Ballets Russes' celebrated first performance there in 1909.

I found a moment to ask Vaslav who he was.
'He is a very talented young French poet.'
'But why does he wear makeup?'
'This is Paris . . . he advises me to do the same . . . to put some makeup on my cheeks and lips . . . ', laughed Vaslav. 'This is the poet Jean Cocteau.'

(Nijinska 1981: 265–6)

It is clear from her tone that, from this first encounter with Cocteau (1889–1963), Nijinska didn't warm to him (or perhaps that is the impression she retrospectively wished to convey). From a broader perspective, the elegantly dressed Cocteau in 1909, going backstage in search of the object of his desire, was cruising the same types of haunts as the dandies of Degas' time.

By Cocteau's time, or soon thereafter, new sites were being added to the list of haunts, including the cinema, and night clubs with jazz bands. It must of course have been in that perennial 'popular' venue, the music hall, that, prior to the arrival of dancers from the Imperial Russian Ballet, Cocteau would have first encountered ballet. While, for the Impressionists, flânerie had been a source of inspiration in developing the painting of modern life, so in the period 1917–32 it aided in the development of modernism in dance and ballet. Cocteau made appropriations from new mass cultural forms like jazz and the cinema, and from traditional popular culture such as the circus and applied them to ballet and avant-garde music theatre in works like *Parade* (1917), *Le Boeuf sur le toit* (*Ox on the Roof*) (1920), *Les Mariés de la tour Eiffel* (*Marriage at the Eiffel Tower*) (1921) and the two ballets with Nijinska: *Les Biches* (literally: *The Female Deers* but also slang for sweeties or dears), and *Le Train bleu* (*The Blue Train*) both from 1924.[5]

Cocteau's contribution to the development of modern ballet is, in my opinion, often unfairly dismissed. The problem seems to be that he doesn't fit into any of the current, competing views of the putative development of modern ballet. There is no room for Cocteau in the view that Balanchine was the rightful successor to Petipa, carrying forward the latter's academic classicism and stripping it of outmoded narrative conventions. Nor is there any room in a revised version of this which acknowledges the extent to which Balanchine introduced to the West the results of the choreographic innovations developed by Soviet choreographers during the early 1920s. Then there are those who rightly point out that, before Balanchine joined the Ballets Russes, Nijinska had already initiated the return by the Ballets Russes to the use of the classical, academic vocabulary. Fokine's legacy to the dancers of the Ballets Russes were roles that made greater demands in terms of personal understanding and interpretation than in terms of technical difficulties. Nijinska in ballets like *Les Biches* created roles that were much more demanding both in terms of interpretative understanding and of technical ability. The uses to which she put the classical academic ballet vocabulary were, however, as Sokolova recalled, strange and untraditional (Sokolova 1960: 215–16). These untraditional uses were the solution that Nijinska found to the problem of how to deal with a modern subject matter. It was Cocteau who first set her this problem.

In the 1920s Nijinska's choreographed oeuvre included a number of pieces on a range of 'modern' subjects which other choreographers and artists in other media were also exploring. For convenience, these can loosely be grouped in three categories: circus, sport, and jazz. Cocteau's *Parade* and Valeska Gert's *Circus* both take circus as their starting point. Cocteau and Nijinska's *Le Train bleu*, Nijinska's *The Sports and Touring Ballet Revue* (1925), and Gert's *Boxers* all present sport. Jean Börlin of the Ballets Suédois, together with the poet Blaise Cendrars, apparently planned a huge outdoor ballet spectacle on the theme of sports (Håger 1990: 279). Several of Cocteau's ballets and theatre pieces pioneered the use of jazz. *Le Boeuf sur le toit* was set in what he supposed to be the natural home of jazz: an American bar. Nijinska created a black-face duet *Jazz* (1925) with costumes by Alexandra Exter and set to Stravinsky's piece *Ragtime* (1919), while Gert created her own caustically parodic versions of the Charleston and of a variety chorus girl troupe performing kick dancing like an American chorus

Figure 1 Cocteau (centre) and Nijinska (right): *Le Train bleu*
Source: © Hulton Getty Picture Collection Limited

line in her piece *Variety-Show*. These references to modern America are part of a wider interest in American modernity by artists, writers and composers during the 1920s. Andreas Huyssen observes: 'In retrospect, it seems quite significant that major artists of the 1920s used precisely the then wide-spread "Americanism" (associated with jazz, sport, cars, technology, movies, and photography) in order to overcome bourgeois aestheticism and its separateness from life' (Huyssen 1986: 60). Manuel Peters summed up Gert's evocation of modern city life:

> She danced the *Traffic* of a Berlin crossroads with pedestrians rushing to and fro, with cars and a policeman. She danced Cinema with newsreel excerpts, a military *Parade*, dramatic actresses etc. She danced *Variety-Show*, *Circus*, and she danced *Sport* with all its different forms, *Boxing* in particular.
>
> (Peters 1987: 44)

For each of these choreographers in different ways, these modern subjects allowed them to distance themselves from nineteenth-century bourgeois aestheticism. It also allowed them a relative if circumscribed freedom from dominant definitions of gendered behaviour.

There is much more information available about Cocteau's ballets than there is about *Circus*, *Jazz*, *Variety-Show* or *The Sports and Touring Ballet Revue* (Baer 1978: 50–1). The only ballets on modern themes by Nijinska that much is known about are those based on Cocteau's librettos. Up until then Nijinska had not worked on modern themes, although there are certainly similarities between Nijinsky's *Jeux* (1913) and Nijinska's *Le Train bleu*. Frank Ries says that it was Cocteau who showed Nijinska news reels of the tennis champion Suzanne Langlen which she used to develop her own role in *Le Train bleu* (Hellman 1990b: 44). It was shortly after working on *Le Train bleu* that Nijinska created *Jazz*, and *The Sports and Touring Ballet Revue* for her own company Théâtre Chorégraphique Nijinska. For this company she also created *Guignol* based on popular puppet theatre, and then in 1926 for the Paris Opéra ballet company she created *Impressions de Music-hall*. Her modern ballets therefore owed something to her association with Cocteau. Nijinska more or less implicated Cocteau in her reasons for leaving the Ballets Russes by saying she felt too constrained by the narrative librettos which Diaghilev expected her to take as the starting point for her choreography. It was of course Cocteau who wrote the libretto that caused her most grief – that of *Le Train bleu*. Cocteau forced her in the final rehearsal period of this ballet to change her choreography so that it followed his libretto more closely. Thus Irina Nijinska called the recent revival of *Le Train bleu* (which she and Frank Ries are jointly credited with reconstructing) as 'after Nijinska' because the aim of the restoration was to show the ballet as it was performed and thus not as Nijinska had actually choreographed it (Hellman 1990a: 38). Nijinska and Cocteau's clash during the making of *Le Train bleu* clearly had something to do with their personalities. Nijinska spoke little French, was half deafened from living through the bombardment of Kiev during the Russian civil war, and had her own clearly defined choreographic agenda. Cocteau was not perhaps at ease with strong-willed women and was at the time still shattered by the sudden death of his young lover Raymond

Radiguet. But the clash between the two should also be interpreted in terms of their different gender positions. Cocteau's own position as a homosexual in relation to dominant (masculine) modernism and Nijinska's feminine modernist sensibility deriving from a different and less paranoid experience of modernity must also be taken into account.

Cocteau's flâneuristic response to modern subjects has to be seen in relation to his sexual orientation. What seems to have most attracted him to the world of performance was sexual ambiguity and illusion. When he engaged the Frattelli Brothers, clowns from the Circus Medrano, to appear in his piece *Le Boeuf sur le toit* it was to dance in 'Tango des femmes' as La Dame Décolettée and La Dame Rousse. Just as he had haunted the wings of the Théâtre Châtellet to watch Nijinsky, so in the mid-1920s he haunted the wings of the Circus Medrano to watch Barbette, the American female impersonator aerialist (Steegmuller 1970; Franko 1995: 95–100). The Little American Girl in *Parade* was inspired by the heroine of the Hollywood silent movie series *The Perils of Pauline*. Pauline became involved in hair raising stunts and adventures. Cocteau was surely attracted to the idea of a woman who blurred the boundaries between masculine activity and feminine vulnerability. In his discussion of *Les Biches*, it is the androgynous figure of the page boy (or girl) performed by Vera Nemtchinova (1899–1984) that clearly fascinated him (Cocteau 1926: 68–9). Neither Cocteau nor Nijinska approached the night life of the metropolis as threatened heterosexual men needing to reassert their sense of loss through mastering feminine mass culture. But clearly neither of them had much chance of understanding how the other felt about modernity.

For Gert and Nijinska the freedom from dominant definitions of gendered behaviour covered their roles both as performers and as dance creators. Sports and popular up-to-date jazz dancing were activities that reflected women's new freedoms to take part in daily life, and their release from nineteenth-century middle-class restrictions on women's involvement in the public sphere. Sport in particular was an area within which women in the 1920s were enjoying new freedoms from both physical and social restrictions about what was and was not considered appropriate feminine behaviour. There is another area in which Nijinska had to confront notions of appropriate feminine behaviour: the role of choreographer in a big, international ballet company was, of course, conventionally masculine. I have discussed elsewhere the ways in which Nijinska was perceived to be unfeminine (Burt 1995a: 93–5). This included dancing the male role of the dancing master in her ballet *Les Fâcheux*, when the male dancer for whom she had created this role had refused to perform it. As the choreographer it seemed not inappropriate for Nijinska to step in and dance this role. At roughly the same time, however, Diaghilev complained in a letter to Boris Kochno that the material Nijinska was choreographing for *Les Biches* appeared 'too feminine' (Buckle 1979: 418). Dealing with 'feminine' themes,

Nijinska risked being discounted as merely feminine, while as a fierce task master she might be considered too masculine.

In the mid-1920s Nijinska wanted to develop increasingly abstract, non-narrative ballets. One of the factors that precipitated Nijinska's resignation from the Ballets Russes in 1924 was Diaghilev's rejection of her ideas for abstract ballets (Baer 1978: 44). For Nijinska, modern subjects allowed her to explore an increasingly abstracted movement language and within that abstraction create a dancing body that was less gendered. Gert in comparison was totally against abstraction in dance, criticising Wigman and other 'pseudo-abstractionists'. Thus Gert asserted: 'I don't want to dance these vague movements, that have nothing to do with me nor with my time' (quoted in de Keersmaeker 1981: 58). Nijinska spoke of the need for modern dancers who could perform with 'the living movement of the automobile or aeroplane, those perfected machines representing the latest achievements of industry' (Baer 1978: 87). There is undoubtedly an echo here of the pre-war Italian Futurists' adulation of cars and aeroplanes that was taken up by Russian Cubo-Futurists like Nijinska's friend Alexandra Exter who designed all Nijinska's ballets for the short-lived Théâtre Choréographique Nijinska. Nijinska nevertheless turns this futurist idea into specifically choreographic terms when she writes of the 'dynamic rhythm of these machines, their breath = speed, deceleration, and the unexpected, nervous braking' (ibid.). Gert however saw the dance of modern life in very different terms: 'I want to dance the people and the variegated mixture of gestures and movements of their daily life' (quoted in de Keersmaeker 1981: 58). And for accompaniment she wanted:

> a town march made up of the roar of aeroplanes, cycling, people walking, women screeching and machines thundering. Such music can only come to us in sound films or on the radio; they shouldn't be sounds made artificially, but should be sounds that are taken from real life. All the artist does is make a montage of them. Such music will move us as much as Bach and Beethoven moved others.
>
> (Gert 1990: 44)

It was the avant-garde (for Gert the Berlin Dadaists, for Nijinska the Russian Cubo-Futurists) who had put the speed and violence of modernity as exemplified by cars and aeroplanes onto the artistic agenda. The obvious difference between Nijinska and Gert's approach to these are that Nijinska abstracts them into an impersonal, dynamic expression, while Gert sees modern life as the sounds and movements of people and machines montaged together. Despite these differences, both were concerned with modernity and clearly saw modern life in a different way from heterosexual male artists. What therefore unites them is the fact that they both presented the female dancing body in a way that corresponded to feminine experience and managed to escape the kinds of projective symbolisation female dancers generally assume in work that addresses a male point of view.

Three ballets of modern life: *Parade*, *Skating Rink* and *The Big City*

Joan Acocella succinctly sums up a widespread opinion of Cocteau among dance historians when she asks what was Cocteau's influence, if any, on the history of choreography? She points out that a dramatic revolution in dance had been set in process by Nijinsky, Nijinska and Balanchine: 'If Cocteau substantially aided this process,' she says, 'I would like to know about it' (1987: 44–5). When Cocteau had any direct influence upon the way movement material was created in his ballets, he tried to dictate a literal, pantomimic approach which in itself contributed nothing to the revolutionary process to which Acocella refers. However, Cocteau surely did contribute to the development of modernism in ballet by way of the challenge he provided through the themes he set the choreographers he worked with. These themes derived from his flâneur's view of modern life and of modern Paris in particular.

Discussing the ballets which, starting with *Parade*, Cocteau produced for Diaghilev, de Maré and others, Lynn Garafola has coined the phrase 'lifestyle modernism'. She points out that Cocteau primarily addressed an elite audience (which was of course true for ballet as a whole at the time and was largely also the case with the work of many avant-garde and modernist artists). She also states that the popular materials on which Cocteau drew in these ballets – variety, circus, cinema, jazz – were the pastimes and consumer styles of France's upper class: 'Where le tout Paris slummed, Cocteau, its self-appointed vanguardist, found material for its rarefied entertainment' (1989: 101). This is also true, but it should nevertheless be acknowledged that across Europe around this time visual artists, writers, composers, film makers and, as I have shown, dance artists, were all exploring these subjects. This popular material addressed a much wider audience than Garafola suggests. Cocteau must surely first have recognised that circus would be appropriate to an avant-garde aesthetic while in the company of Appolinaire and Blaise Cendrars, both of whom subscribed to utopian socialist views.

Garafola argues that: 'Cocteau's true genius lay not in the originality of his ideas, but in the ability to appropriate the ideas of the avant-garde for essentially conservative ends. Purged of radicalism, his sanitised art became the stuff of élite entertainment' (1989: 100). It is the case that Cocteau took up a conservative and patriotic position after the outbreak of the First World War, but this political move has to be understood in relation to its historical context. It is certainly true that, by the end of the nineteenth century, a populist politics was already emerging that presaged the later genocidal catastrophes of the twentieth century that were carried out in the name of nationalism. One should not, however, assume that nationalism necessarily implies right-wing politics in the first quarter of the twentieth century. Individuals thought in national terms because the notion of internationalism was at the time largely undeveloped. It was only in the 1930s that various left-wing alliances and coalitions developed with an international outlook, in an attempt to oppose the right-wing nationalism of totalitarian regimes in Italy, Germany and Spain. During the war Cocteau was not the only artist at that time living in France to discover patriotic feelings for France while that country was being attacked and occupied by the German army – Isadora Duncan, for example, in her dance 'The Marseillaise'. Cocteau's artistic activities during the war were largely concerned with aligning progressive artistic practices with ideologies of the French national character. Cocteau's work on the ballet *Parade* illustrates this.

Parade

While it now seems that the opening performance of *Parade* did not provoke the sort of outcry which some writers have described,[6] evidence indicates that there were a few muffled shouts from the audience of 'Salles Boches!' – 'dirty Germans' (Buckle 1979: 331). For some Parisians, avant-garde and modernist work in general and Picasso's paintings in particular were associated with Germany. When war broke out in 1914 Picasso's dealer Kahnweiler, who was a German, had to escape quickly from France. His entire stock of paintings was therefore impounded and sold off at very low prices. As a result, the market for Cubist painting collapsed and only subsequently recovered as a result of Picasso's association with the Ballets Russes, which itself came about through Cocteau and *Parade*. Picasso was Spanish, not French, and the cries of 'Salles Boches!' were inspired by Picasso's foreignness and his association with Kahnweiler. But, as Kenneth Silver has shown, an important visual source for Picasso's designs for *Parade* were the nineteenth-century French popular prints known as Images d'Epinal, after the town where some of them had been printed (Silver 1984). It was Cocteau who showed them to Picasso.

The *Parade* of the title is a pre-show put on outside a fairground or boulevard theatre in order to attract an audience and this would have recalled for many Parisians the nostalgic appeal for such Parisian boulevard and fairground theatres of the eighteenth and early nineteenth century. (The film *Les Enfants du Paradis* which was being filmed in Paris during the closing stages of the occupation of Paris during the Second World War, opens with an extravagant, nostalgic recreation of a boulevard theatre with rope walkers, freak shows and parades where managers entice onlookers into their theatres.) In the ballet *Parade* there are two managers, one French and the other American. Photographs of the complex Cubist constructions that

Picasso designed as costumes for these two characters are probably the best known element of the ballet. The American Manager carries on his back a Cubist skyscraper: Cubism is thus associated with modernity and with the United States as its exemplar. Crucially Cubism is not associated with Germany. Silver has shown that the French Manager, with his pipe, moustache and cap is partly inspired by figures in a popular nineteenth-century coloured prints of 'Alphabet Grotesque des Cris de Paris' printed in Epinal (1984: 101). In 1917, when *Parade* opened, Epinal was in the area of France occupied by the German army. The use of these popular prints and of circus imagery would have been recognised by audience members as specifically French. The United States had in 1917 just entered the war as a French ally. The jazz-inspired music by Eric Satie and the Little American Girl (based on Hollywood silent films) both referred to the United States. The films and music of this new ally were clearly aligned with the French and in opposition to the Germans. Within the cultural politics of the day, Cocteau was therefore disassociating avant-garde art from any connection with Germany and aligning it with ideologies of French-ness.

Skating Rink

In the early 1920s Cocteau took up Jacques Rivière's slogan 'Le Rappel à l'Ordre', the call for a return to the French classical spirit in the arts. But, as John Willett has pointed out, this return to classicism was not particularly restrictive and actually supported the development of modernist architecture and avant-garde painting (Willett 1978: 63–4). Diaghilev responded to the increasingly nationalistic spirit in France by producing ballets with strongly French sources; hence his wonderful but disastrous attempt to bring to Paris a production of a masterwork by Petipa, *The Sleeping Princess*, followed by new ballets based on much older French ones, like for example *Les Fâcheux* (1924).[7] While Diaghilev was going heavily into debt making *The Sleeping Princess* and trying with Nijinska to resolve the problem of performing its now hopelessly outmoded classical mime sequences, Rolf de Maré's Ballets Suédois was making *Skating Rink*, a ballet that took as its starting point the very different mimetic style of Charlie Chaplin's 1916 film *The Rink*. What contributed to Diaghilev's bankruptcy were Leon Bakst's sumptuous, historicising designs for *The Sleeping Princess*. *Skating Rink* was designed by the French painter Fernand Léger in a colourful Cubist style that was in accord with 'Le Rappel à l'Ordre'. Despite their national foci, what made *Skating Rink* and *Parade* modern were their American references: both looked to Hollywood – *Skating Rink* to Charlie Chaplin, *Parade* to *The Perils of Pauline*; both made references to jazz, and both referred albeit in indirect ways to American mechanical modernity. The motivation behind their evident admiration for the United States was the desire that France and other European countries might emulate American modernity and, through attaining its promised financial rewards, use them to create a better life.

Skating Rink, choreographed by Jean Börlin during 1921 and first performed at the Théatre des Champs Elysées in Paris on 20 January 1922, evoked the anonymous scale and monotony of city life through references to popular mass culture – skating, the dances of working-class dance halls, the silent cinema. Set in a city, it has a cast of generalised characters which spans a wide cross section of class and occupation. The ballet was based on a poem 'Skating-Rink à Tabarin' (1918) by Riciotto Canudo (which was itself inspired by Chaplin's *The Rink*). The set and costumes were designed by Fernand Léger (who was actively involved throughout the production) and the musical score was by the Swiss composer Arthur Honegger. It was choreographed by Jean Börlin who also danced the leading role. The original ballet is 'lost', none of it having been performed since 1929, but it has been painstakingly reconstructed by Archer and Hodson for the Zürich Opernhaus.[8]

What makes *Skating Rink* a modernist ballet is its evocation of the anonymous scale and monotony of city life. Set at a roller skating rink, it shows factory workers and market girls, prostitutes, immigrants, and young aristocratic dandies all skating together. In 1922 it was unusual for a ballet to deal with such a subject and treat it in such a way as to emphasise the characteristic isolation of the individual amidst the swirling indifference of the crowd. This is a modernist work, which responded to the artists' experience of metropolitan modernity. In his article 'Popular Music Halls' published in 1925, Léger argues that the sources for a new French choreography should be sought in the dance halls (Léger 1973: 77). As I have already pointed out, Léger's close friend Blaise Cendrars argued that the modernity of Börlin's choreography was gained by looking at billboards and loudspeakers and discovering 'the beautiful rhythm of today' (quoted in Häger 1990: 291). The rhythm of the 1920s that Börlin discovered and injected into *Skating Rink* was not unproblematically beautiful but, despite what Cendrars suggests, alienating and disturbing. The new spaces of modernity were gendered and sexualised. They are represented in the ballet as they were experienced from a male flâneur's point of view which reflects the more or less conscious demoralisation born of the war and its aftermath, and the alienating experience of metropolitan life. In *Skating Rink* what Börlin choreographed were the disturbing new spaces of modernity.

In 1921, while working on *Skating Rink*, Börlin, de Maré, Honegger and Léger together visited Parisian skating rinks and working-class dance halls. There they observed members of rough Parisian street gangs or 'Apaches' who are featured in the ballet. Photographs and surviving designs for the ballet *Skating Rink* show that the costumes which some of the men wear in the latter are abstracted versions of the clothes worn by the dangerous Apache gangs. Archer and Hodson discovered that some of the movement material for the ballet derived from Apache dancing which the choreographer would have seen in these dance halls (1994: 108). There is also a fox-trot and a shimmy. As well as the Apaches and working-class characters, the ballet also shows rich, ultra-fashionable young men 'slumming it' at the rink, dancing with working-class women. Like the Baudelairian flâneur, these dandies disdainfully explore (with a mixture of detached fascination and repulsion) urban spaces that are gendered and sexualised. The central character in the ballet is called the Poet, or the Madman. He is wealthy but an outsider whose brilliant skating disturbs the atmosphere at the rink. He steals the Young Woman, who is the girlfriend of the Man, an Apache, and the resulting struggle between the Poet and the Apache Man leads inadvertently to her collapse and possibly death.[9] The other skaters momentarily seem to register what has happened but then, callously, resume their dancing – such is the blasé indifference of the big city dweller. As the final curtain descends, the Poet is leaving the stage with the limp body of the Young Woman slung over his shoulder while behind them the crowd skate and dance in wild abandon. The Apache Man, alone in the crowd, looks on in despair.

My overall impression from watching the reconstruction of *Skating Rink* is of the busy crowd of circling skaters. Like the first act of the ballet *Petrushka* (1911) there is almost too much going on with disconnected incidents happening in unexpected parts of the stage. Like the crowd in *Petrushka*, the gliding skaters are not anonymous but each have their different roles and characters, and, just as the three main roles in *Petrushka* are puppets, there is something puppet-like about the skaters. Their abstracted circles and arcs blend with mimetic gestures as they react to the events that take place. The style of the dancers' reactions, as Archer and Hodson's research revealed, should be that of silent film actors. At times it is as if they are in a Chaplin comedy. Early on, when The Lady's Maid comes on stage, she is clearly not a confident skater and repeatedly appears about to fall over until The Sailor gallantly leaves the circling crowd to catch her and offer her his arm to lean on. Throughout the ballet there are spectacular collisions between skaters, one bringing down the whole corps de ballet in a large heap that spreads right across the stage. Everything is overdone for effect just as in a silent comedy. There are other more serious moments when the dancers look like a crowd in a German expressionist film – *Metropolis* or *The Cabinet of Doctor Caligari*. In packed groups, like 'loose' rugby scrums, dancers take up the angular arm gestures that are indicated in Léger's designs and in photographs of the original production. Millicent Hodson calls these 'cubist gestures' as Léger was a Cubist painter, but the effect is highly Expressionist. The groups resemble photographs of Dalcroze and Laban movement choirs. Bengt Håger writes in his book on the Ballets Suédois that Börlin worked with Dalcroze in 1912 in Stockholm and then again in Geneva in 1919 (1990: 10). That year Börlin is supposed to have

Figure 2 Jean Börlin as 'The Madman' in *Skating Rink*. Léger's design included a
dark rectangle of make-up on Börlin's face.

Source: Dansmuseet, Stockholm

visited Zürich and studied with Mary Wigman. There he and de Maré might also have met Laban and attended one of the final Dada soirées. Attractive though the idea of such meetings might be, there is at the moment no evidence to support it.

Whether Cubist or Expressionist, the modernist look of this gestural movement material is largely determined by Léger's set and costumes. Archer and Hodson believe that Léger's backdrop was slightly curved like a cyclorama, thus creating a curved space upstage for the circling motion of the skaters. The backcloth includes discs, segmented circles, pennants and railway signal shapes strung out rainbow-like across the stage. These presumably refer to the steel structure of the rink's roof. The cloth's visual language relates to that which Léger used in his paintings *Les Disques et la ville* (1919) and *Le Remorqueur* (1920) which de Maré had bought from Léger. A large arrow indicates the direction in which the skaters circle round the rink. The disruptive characters in the ballet make their entrances skating in the opposite direction. This arrow, as Peter de Francia has written 'propels the eye from left to right, high up and doubling the parabola of shapes below it, which in themselves form a fabulous horizon of colour' (De Francia 1983: 174). The dancers stand out clearly against this strongly coloured backdrop because the lower half of this is taken up with broad, simple areas of colour while the more complex, abstracted disc and girder shapes occur in the upper half. The costumes are largely made of plain, brightly coloured material with strong patterned areas on skirts or jackets. When the dancers form a tight group, the costumes cause them to merge visually into one another. Nevertheless the different characters and in particular their social status are indicated through costume – workers have a brick pattern on their clothes, the gambler has domino dots on his. Thus, when I saw a run-through of the ballet in practice clothes rather than costumes I found it hard to follow the action. The costumes are constructed in such a way as to affect the movements the dancers wearing them can make. As Archer and Hodson write in the Zürich programme:

> The men's jackets are cut and padded so that the torso, oversized and often asymmetrical, remains stable as the legs skate nimbly underneath, in the manner of marionettes. Conversely, the women's skirts are large, stiff geometrical shapes that hold their line as the torso moves freely above.
>
> (Archer and Hodson 1995: 15)[10]

The movements thus take on a frieze-like appearance occasionally reminiscent of *L'Après Midi d'un Faune*, and have the puppet-like quality already mentioned. The costumes in *Skating Rink* are exactly contemporary with those Oscar Schlemmer designed for his *Triadic Ballet* which also determined puppet-like movements. The dancers in *Skating Rink* were thus generalised and abstracted through the nature of the set and costumes and through the abstracted dance movement itself.

A central theme of the ballet is the (masculine) flâneur's view of metropolitan modernity – of modern city life. During the planning stage, when the collaborators cruised places of metropolitan mass entertainment like dance halls and the skating rink, they were indulging in the same kind of flânerie as the rich young dandies represented in the ballet. As the growing literature on flânerie attests, the flâneur is a marginal figure whose class position was steadily being eroded by modernity. Many middle-class French men in the early 1920s felt demoralised by the experience of war – Léger served in the trenches – and by the social and economic changes that followed it, including women's new found independence. While finding modernity strange, such men nevertheless sought to compensate for their sense of loss through refining their ability to enjoy the spectacle of the city's streets.

In the ballet, the disturbing qualities of these modern spaces are articulated through the use of the 'modern', abstracted qualities in the movement material and by the stylised planar movements dictated by the costumes' construction. In this are references to the mechanised motion of the roller skate and to the modern popular entertainment form, the cinema. Léger's design, by causing groups to visually merge with one another into the backdrop, de-individuated characters, making them into an equivalent to the de-individuated anonymous modern masses that the flâneur observes on his wanderings. The modernist abstraction of *Skating Rink* is contemporaneous with that of other modern ballets and movement experiments – in particular biomechanics developed by the Russian theatre director Meyerhold, Russian machine ballets by Goleizovsky and others (see Souritz 1990), and the theatre works of Oscar Schlemmer that have already been mentioned. These works should be seen in the context of left-wing interest by Soviet Russians and Weimar Germans in Taylorism – F.W. Taylor's theories of scientifically managed industrial efficiency. In France the group of artists, architects and writers associated with the periodical *L'Esprit Nouveau* subscribed to Taylorism. Léger's writings, including pieces on ballet, regularly appeared in *L'Esprit Nouveau*, and one of his paintings was hung in Le Corbusier and Pierre Jeanneret's L'Esprit Nouveau pavilion at the 1925 Exposition des Arts Decoratif in Paris.

The role of the Poet or Madman can be related to the political beliefs of *L'Esprit Nouveau*. The origin of his role is that of the Charlot character played by Charlie Chaplin in *The Rink* but transformed into a quasi-Futurist hero in Canudo's poem. At the rink Charlie is characteristically inept and clumsy, leaving an inevitable trail of collisions in his wake. When he spies The Girl (Edna Purviance) receiving unwanted attention from Mr Stout (Eric Campbell), he surreptitiously trips the latter up and engages in a stunningly choreographed fight with him. During the actual fight itself, Charlie is no longer inept and clumsy but amazingly well co-ordinated and polished on the roller skates: no matter how precarious a situation he gets into he doesn't once fall over. This sequence of course ends with Charlie skating happily away with The Girl. Canudo jettisons all the clown elements of the Chaplin role in the film and amplifies its heroic and imperturbable side.

> All of a sudden a man appears. Tall, straight-backed, lean. Ineluctable like the will to rhythm
> in the hands of the conducteur. A man alone, on his skates.
> Like the actors in ancient Greece in their buskins. The end of the red scarf at his neck
> flutters, like the flame of a candle that is shaken. . . .
> He is the leader of the skating dance. He captures in his swirling motion the metallic glare of the fairground organ, and all the movement.
> His bones vibrate like an instrument. Visible, tangible, cords stretched beneath supple muscles.
> In his open arms he holds the rhythms of the couples
> who spin the desperate meaning of life. Frenzied Corybant. Poet. Madman.
>
> > (quoted in Håger 1990: 162)

Canudo and Léger were both members of the group which published *L'Esprit Nouveau* as was Elie Faure. As Richard Brender explains:

> Elie Faure laid the foundation for the theory of the collective spectacle by postulating the alternation between 'symphonic' or 'ecumenical' social periods, when the needs, hopes, and desires that animated a populace were more or less homogenous, and more individualistic periods, when the traditional social order is destroyed and gradually replaced by the ideals of a hero (called 'constructeur'), who thoroughly transforms the way people look at the world. When these latter periods play themselves out, creating dissension and anarchy in their wake, a new unifying, organic social order grows up. According to Faure, World War I signified the complete destruction of the old individualist order, and any modern order would have to be more organic, with its subjects thinking of themselves as cogs in the wheel of a larger society.
>
> > (Brender 1986: 137)

The Poet/Madman is a 'conducteur' who transforms the way people do the skating dance. What evolves during the ballet is the dissension and anarchy – 'the complete destruction of the old individualist order' – out of which it was hoped the new utopian order would emerge. The notion of subjects as cogs in the wheel of society is of course Taylorist. The puppet-like character of the dancers in the ballet should therefore be seen as a fusion of Taylorist and utopian socialist ideas.

In 1922, the year of the ballet, Le Corbusier and Jeanneret exhibited designs for a 'Ville Contemporaine' capable of housing three million people which they controversially proposed should be built on a site on the Parisian left bank made by demolishing existing housing there. Planning the modern city, Le Corbusier argued, necessitates such drastic measures. '[To] desire to rebuild a great city in a modern way is to engage in a formidable battle . . . in order, as it were, to hold a wild beast at bay. That beast is the great city' (Le Corbusier 1996: 369). Despite being one of the most positive advocates of modern urbanism, Le Corbusier betrays here an underlying horror of the disturbing nature of modernity. Such fears are repressed but return as symptoms through projection onto the geography of the city itself. Just as most twentieth-century choreography is an externalisation through time and space of the interior and private – the world of feelings – so the (masculine) flâneur externalises his private, repressed anxieties through his obsessive cruising of public spaces. It is my contention that, in *Skating Rink*, masculine anxieties evoked by the disturbing new spaces of metropolitan modernity are disavowed through projecting them onto the figure of the Young Woman who is the source of conflict between the Poet and Apache Man. She represents the City itself which, as the term metropolis – mother city – suggests, is of course feminine.

The ballet ends with a sentimental image of the woman's dead or unconscious body being carried off by the Poet while the Apache Man succumbs to lonely despair amidst the callously indifferent revels of the anonymous metropolitan crowd. Sentimentality is invariably a reassuring emotion. In this case it is masculine egos that are reassured and the social tensions revealed in the ballet resolved by the collapse – almost a sacrifice – of the Young Woman. Yet the final image need not only be read in a sentimental way. On a choreographic level, the ending presents a richly complex and dynamic tableau of 'skating' movement. As such it contrasts with the insecurity and uncertainty that the skaters initially exhibited at the beginning of the ballet. It is the Poet who, according to Canudo's poem, has introduced a new standard of skating. Like Chaplin in *The Rink*, the Poet is an absolutely brilliant skater who never falters or wavers but precipitates several spectacular collisions amidst the crowd and several times floors his rival the Apache Man. If at the end of the ballet the crowd have attained the Poet's new standard of skating, this seems to have been acquired over a woman's passive or dead body.

The Big City

Another ballet which evoked the anonymous scale and monotony of city life through references to popular dance movement is Jooss' *The Big City*.[11] Like

Skating Rink, it shows contemporary social dancing and has a cast of generalised city types which span similar wide cross sections of class and
occupation to *Skating Rink*. The two ballets were created ten years apart in
different countries. I am not aware of any evidence to suggest that Jooss
knew of *Skating Rink*[12] yet, interestingly, both ballets have similar simple,
incidental story lines in which a working-class man loses his sweetheart to a
wealthy libertine. Both ballets end by emphasising the isolation of the poor
loser alone amidst the swirling indifference of a crowd of dancers or skaters.

Jooss choreographed *The Big City* in 1932 when, following his success in
the International Choreographic Competition, he was putting together an
evening-length programme of works to take on tour.[13] Whereas *Skating
Rink* has only one scene with a painted back cloth, *The Big City* has three (or
four) scenes with no set at all. It opens with a busy street scene, full of all
sorts of different people – factory workers, clerks, typists, tramps, busi-
nessmen, a newspaper vendor, nursemaids, women of different classes. There
a young man meets his sweetheart and then sees her stolen away by a rich
libertine. The young woman and the libertine are then seen in the back
street of the poor neighbourhood where she lives as she goes home to change
into a smart evening dress that he has given her. Mothers and children react
suspiciously towards the libertine as he loiters waiting to take her off to a
night club. Some accounts imply that the rest of the action takes place in
one dance hall. Reviewing the Joffrey Ballet's 1975 production of *The Big
City* (mounted by Anna Markand with coaching by Jooss himself), Jack
Anderson says that light changes and different styles of dancing shift the
action between a posh night club and a working-class dance hall; the libertine takes the young woman to the former while in the latter the jilted lover
searches in vain for his sweetheart (Anderson 1975: 363). Marcia Siegel
observes that Jooss has both rich and poor groups dancing simultaneously on
stage but that they are distinguishable because one group is dancing to a
three/four rhythm while the other is dancing in four/four. 'The people don't
clash,' she observes, 'their rhythms do' (Siegel 1976: 147). It is possibly this
innovative 'cross cutting' between the two night spots that made A. V.
Coton liken an earlier production of Jooss' *The Big City* to the experimental
documentary film *Berlin: Symphony of a City* (1927) by Walter Ruttman
(1887–1941). Jooss, he writes, gives 'a pictorial diagram of living in the
modern industrial city' (Coton 1946: 44).

The fact that Jooss' company did not use any scenery but instead made
innovative use of lighting allowed both the pace of modern living and its
anonymity to be evoked. (Crucially for dancing, a stage unencumbered with
scenery allows greater freedom of movement.) An electrician was on the
company payroll and they took a complete lighting system with them on
tour (Kersley and Kersley 1986: 17). The lighting conventions employed in
works like *The Big City* and *The Green Table* were those developed by
German Expressionist theatre directors in the first quarter of the century.

The elaborate scenery used in nineteenth-century theatre, ballet and opera productions had sometimes taken so long to change that a meal could be consumed during the interval between acts. To represent the hectic pace of modern living required new, less cumbersome theatrical means. The new electric lighting equipment enabled progressive theatre directors in the early twentieth century to utilise a subtly responsive and easily changed succession of expressive lighting states. As W. H. Sokel commented:

> The lighting equipment behaves like the mind. It drowns in darkness what it wishes to forget and bathes in light what it wishes to recall. Thus the entire stage becomes a universe of the mind, and the individual scenes are not replicas of three-dimensional reality, but visualised stages of thought.
>
> (quoted in Patterson 1981: 54)

A. V. Coton's description of the ending of *The Big City* suggests that lighting design was used to do precisely this, heightening the jilted lover's sense of isolation in the indifferent crowd of dancers:

> The Youth presses through the crowd, both sorts of dancers [rich and proletarian] weaving a complex pattern through which he pushes vainly trying to reach her [his sweetheart]. Then the groups change patterns, and the poor people slide away, the other dancers move altogether up stage; the Youth is left quite alone, isolated in a pool of soft light while the others fade into shadows. The lights dim more and more, the maddening stupid rhythm goes on and on, marked by the even stamp and shuffle of the dancing automatons who are happily ignorant and uncaring of the drama that is passing amongst them. The Youth, crushed with misery, stands alone staring blindly into the night, still faintly visible at the downrush of the curtain.
>
> (Coton 1946: 44)

It is through these pools of light and their surrounding shadows – these visualised stages of thought as Sokel put it – that *The Big City* evoked the disturbing spaces of modernity just as *Skating Rink* had done through its depersonalised, mechanistic movement. It is in their endings that *Skating Rink* and *The Big City* seem most closely related. Each shows the characteristic indifference of the metropolitan crowd to the plight of the working-class loser, and both mediate notions of feminine weakness and vulnerability that were current in the nineteenth century.

Where *The Big City* differs from *Parade* and *Skating Rink* is in its attitude towards modernity and nationalism. As Huyssen observes, the trust of artists and intellectuals (like Léger, Börlin and de Maré) 'that capitalism's power to modernise would eventually lead to its breakdown was rooted in a theory of economic crisis and revolution which, by the 1930s, had already become obsolete' (1986: 14). By 1932 Jooss and his audiences had learnt from bitter experience that economic crisis, far from provoking revolution, had strengthened the far right. Far from celebrating modernity therefore, Jooss' *The Big City* draws to the spectator's attention its social inequalities and problems. *Parade* and to a lesser extent *Skating Rink* take as their setting modern France: both show a fairly homogenous community that corresponded to the extent of the knowable and imaginable national community. *The Big City* shows class differences that transcended national boundaries. As Jooss towards the end of his life told Michael Huxley, during the early 1930s he subscribed to a left-wing partly satirical journal *Die Weltbühne* which published pieces by Kurt Tucholsky. The latter, Jooss recalled, 'wrote about secret things which were going on – about preparations for a new war and that nobody noticed. . . . It was then, already directed against Nazism and all that' (Huxley 1982: 9). Tucholsky was also internationalist. His last piece of writing before his suicide was 'What we are proud of in Europe': 'This continent is proud of itself and it can well be proud of itself. In Europe one is proud: Of being German; Of being French; Of Being English; Of not being German; Of not being French; Of not Being English' (Tucholsky et al. 1969: 13). It was growing alarm about the increasing dangers of extreme right-wing nationalism that led to so many artists and intellectuals espousing a left-wing anti-fascist internationalism both in Europe and, as we shall see in Chapter 6, in the United States.

The big city at night

While *Skating Rink* and *The Big City* were set in the relative neutrality of skating rinks and dance halls, many evocations of the metropolis were set in the city's night clubs and brothels.[14] The seamier side of metropolitan night life was a subject explored by many artists, film makers and writers, particularly in Weimar Germany.[15] Here is a description by Rudolf Laban from his 1936 autobiography of his 1927 dance-play *The Night* (*Die Nacht*).

> The play opened with a crowd of mechanically grinning society men and women, followed by all I had experienced and felt when I first met life in the big city. It was built round a fantasy on work which showed money being earned without work. Greed, covetousness, adoration of three idols: dollars, depravity and deceit. The whole wild orgy found no solution and ended in madness. The music was a caricature of jazz.
>
> (Laban 1975: 43–5)

In the piece Laban set out to show:

> the violent storm and evil spirits of our time. What the revues and films of our days made out to be charming and chic, sophisticated and smart, what people took for terribly sweet and amusing, I portrayed here with its true bitter aftertaste, with its obnoxious flavour and its degrading nastiness.
>
> (ibid.: 43)

Beyond the few sentences Laban writes about his dance play in his 1936 autobiography, little else is known of *The Night*. As is the case with much lost choreography, it is more or less impossible to discuss how particular qualities of movement signified the thematic material indicated in the documentary evidence that is available. The depravity of the big city was however a theme that many German artists, writers and film makers explored during the 1920s, and indeed the Neue Sachlichkeit paintings of the city's night life and its mean streets by George Grosz and Otto Dix have become virtually icons of the Weimar period. Otto Dix's triptych *The Big City* (*Grosstadt*) painted in 1927–8 presents a central panel where blasé, cosmopolitan habitués of night life sit in a curiously opulent yet uncomfortably garish night club seemingly unaware of or indifferent towards the spectacle of poverty – prostitutes and disabled war veterans – outside on the streets that are depicted in the two flanking panels. The contrast between an opulent night club and a disabled war veteran that Dix presents in this triptych was used earlier by the progressive theatre director Erwin Piscator in his *Red Revel Revue* (1924). A photograph of this is reproduced in Peter Jelavich's book *Berlin Cabaret*. This shows a 'revue within a revue' in which bourgeois spectators sit watching female dancers while in front of them lies a crippled war veteran with a stick (Jelavich 1993: 212). The indifference of these bourgeois spectators is characteristically metropolitan and a quality that, as I have argued, was evoked in both *The Big City* and *Skating Rink*.

Many of these representations of metropolitan night life focused on the figure of the prostitute. In the absence of further information one can only speculate as to whether Laban included prostitutes in *Die Nacht*, but they do appear in some pieces by his pupil, Kurt Jooss and in the repertoire of the dancer Valeska Gert. Indeed prostitutes were such a common theme in German cultural texts of the 1920s that when an exhibition of work by Dix, Grosz and others was shown in Moscow, the critic Fedorov-Davidov commented:

> When you come down to it the social protest of the German artists is directed exclusively against prostitution. . . . Undoubtedly prostitution is among Germany's most flagrant problems but is it the most important, let alone the only one?
>
> (quoted in Willett 1978: 114)

Gert also went on a concert tour of the Soviet Union at this time. A critic in the newspaper *Izvestia* said this of her:

> The city is the source of her social fantasy. The dregs of humanity provide her with material. The fantastic shapes of procuresses, drug addicts and cast-offs of society distort themselves in terrifying forms before the deeply stricken audience. The entire century of Capitalism dances in her dances.
>
> (quoted in de Keersmaeker 1981: 58)

What this critic recognised but Fedorov-Davidov seems to have missed is the fact that artists used prostitution as a metaphor for what they felt was happening to their society. As Dieter Scholz puts it in his discussion of Dix's *The Big City*:

> The compulsion to prostitution means putting up the body for sale and thus refers to a basic fact of capitalistic societies in particular. In such a perverted system, those people are the most honest who do not attempt to cover up reality by fleeing into a dream world. Prostitutes cannot conceal themselves and must draw attention to their bodies for 'professional' reasons. They demonstrate an interplay of concealment and exposure, just as Dix shows in his paintings.
>
> (Scholz 1989: 80)

The prostitute in many paintings and drawings, 'street movies' and even a few dance pieces during the Weimar period can be interpreted as standing for the modern city as a whole. The city is a place that doubly feminises workers: first, through capitalist economic relations at work and second, through extravagant, sensual, feminine consumption. Such an interpretation, however, reinforces a normative notion of femininity as passive, vulnerable and corrupting. To interpret the figures of prostitutes in these paintings and dance pieces in this way is only to see them as addressing the point of view of a male spectator. Furthermore the theme of prostitution in the metropolis is one which, as Patrice Petro observes, 'displaces male anxieties about class identity onto anxieties about women and sexual identity' (Petro 1989: xxii). Impotent, passive, and objects of pity, such images speak of the sense of male loss that was being experienced as a result of 'changes in the definition of male cultural and economic authority in the wake of the lost war, inflation, and developments in the industrial division of labour' (ibid.: 25).[16]

One of the scenes in Jooss' *The Green Table* is set in a brothel. This ballet starts and ends with the Gentlemen in Black who are negotiating from two sides of a long green table. The breakdown of their discussions precipitates the outbreak of a war. In the next few scenes the men say farewell to their loved ones, there is a battle, the women left behind grieve, a female saboteur works behind the lines while in the background of each scene the figure of Death (initially played by Jooss himself) lurks waiting to take away a victim, making each one dance with him in a different way. Finally he leads all his captives in a dance of death after which the Gentlemen in Black ominously reappear to repeat the opening scene. Also in each scene is the shifty figure of the Profiteer who, like Death and the Gentlemen in Black, gains from the war. In the brothel scene the Profiteer forces the Young Woman to dance with one soldier after another while all around them identical couples sway from side to side suggestively to the dance music, the women staring brazenly at the audience. The Young Woman resists one soldier on leave after another until the Profiteer arranges for her to be left alone with a client. As they dance together Death interposes himself, subtly taking the man's place. Then, as if her resistance has at last been broken, she finally allows herself to be intimately held and sinks amorously to the floor pulling him down after her. As she arches her back and Death crouches, burying his head in her breasts, he pauses and chillingly throws an impassive glance at the audience.

While ostensibly it is the war that drags the Young Woman into prostitution, she is clearly also a victim of modernity. The impersonal speed and repetitiveness of her encounters with the men evoke the alienating pace of the American-style efficiency improvements introduced into factories along with American capital during the 1920s. The Young Woman is trapped in a system of economic exchange from which she herself does not profit. While standing in this way as a symbol for the alienating effects of modernity and capitalism, the Young Woman conforms to conventional notions of feminine purity, passivity and vulnerability. By showing her sad demise in this way, however, Jooss, like Dix, is displacing male anxieties about men's place in an increasingly alienating social environment onto anxieties about women and sexual identity. Similarly *Skating Rink* and *The Big City* also explored the theme of heterosexual male anxiety at supposed female vulnerability. That neither painter nor choreographers were representing women's actual historical experiences of the period can be shown by comparing their representations of prostitutes with that of Valeska Gert.

Whereas Jooss and Dix both used the figure of a prostitute to make a general criticism of capitalist society as a whole, Valeska Gert danced the role of a prostitute and similar characters as an act of defiance in order to draw attention to aspects of feminine experience that were generally hidden and ignored.

> Since I didn't like the bourgeois, I danced these people dismissed by them, whores, procuresses, cast-offs, those who had slipped. . . . It

was from the beginning to the state of being 'broken'. In the beginning energy and youth, and then more and more 'kaputt'.

(quoted in de Keersmaeker 1981: 58)

In *Canaille*, Gert showed a prostitute on the street, walking in a provocative and suggestive way, attracting a customer, having sex with him and then afterwards either acting satisfied, dissatisfied or angry with him. Kurt Tucholsky described the piece in 1921 in *Die Weltbühne* like this:

> In the circle of light, a shabby figure in black slinks across the stage adjusting the folds of the red collar which cover her head – a depraved head with messy, louse-ridden hair. Who is it? What kind of a face is there? 'The prostitute of the faubourgs' by Toulouse-Lautrec would look like a countess compared with this whore. Indifferently she shrugs her shoulder blades, indifferently she pushes her commodified body, that piece of venal meat, through the streets. A guy clutches her – and she accomplishes the most daring thing ever seen so far on stage. Her legs open and close. And bored indifference, a cramp – a little spasm at least – and the greed for money shakes up the ravaged body: syphilis and the Salvation Army are both fighting with the same ardour to conquer this poor soul. If anyone has ever wanted to see the 'famous naked dances of Berlin', here it is. Never before have I understood so well how closely pleasure and pain can come out of the same flute, out of the same hole. Then the body exhales the last remaining physical sensation, she spits without actually doing so and sinks backwards into the darkness.

(Tucholsky quoted in Peters 1987: 44–5)

Photographs of Gert in this role show her making lascivious facial expressions and taking up suggestive poses. She is wearing a plain black dress with a short skirt but long sleeves and a high neck. Although she apparently lifted her skirt to show the fringes of her black garters, she didn't display her body in the kind of eroticised manner of some dancers of the 1930s, like Anita Berber or the nude dancers of the Ballet Celly de Rheidt to which Tucholsky refers (see Jelavich 1993: 154–65). Gert's aim was to shock rather than to titillate. Thus she explicitly mimed the movements of sexual intercourse and then commented on her imaginary male partner's performance. As Gert herself explained in 1931:

> One day this girl enjoys her work, another day she despises it, yet another day she does her work out of desperation or indifference, or even out of spite. There is a different emotion behind the dance each time it is performed, the character of the steps changes as well.

Figure 3 'Her legs open and close. And bored indifference, a cramp – a little spasm
at least – and the greed for money shakes up the ravaged body.'
Kurt Tucholsky on Valeska Gert in *Canaille*

Source: Theaterwissenschaftliche Sammlung, University of Cologne

> This makes them appear improvised, the same steps that yesterday were performed with hesitation and resentment the next time are performed quickly and with enjoyment.
>
> (Gert 1990: 14)

By allowing herself this freedom to choose how to end the piece, Gert allowed herself to stay in control of a piece which might otherwise have been about submission and victimisation. She was also drawing attention to female sexuality, through giving expression to the prostitute's enjoyment or lack of it. Some men, she was implying, aren't very competent sexually. In Germany in the 1920s there was considerable debate about male sexual performance, as a result of anxieties provoked by the rise of the 'new woman'. To put it perhaps over-simply, if young women could now support themselves financially in blue or white collar jobs, would they need men at all any more? Added to this was the apparent rise or increased visibility of lesbianism. In this climate there was an increase in the publication of sex manuals (for men). In an atmosphere of male anxiety about sexual performance, Gert's *Canaille* would have been likely to exacerbate rather than allay heterosexual male anxieties about male sexual performance.

Jooss, when he created the brothel scene for *The Green Table*, was drawing on an existing repertoire of images of women within which, as I have outlined, the figure of the prostitute carried a complicated series of meanings and associations. These were so strong that they inescapably carried with them notions of the pathos of feminine vulnerability and weakness which bore little relation to women's actual lived experience during the Weimar period. Gert however made a shocking intervention within this repertoire by desentimentalising the image of the prostitute and through it attacking bourgeois sexual hypocrisy.

The comparison of Gert's *Canaille* and the brothel scene in Jooss' *The Green Table* is not an advantageous one for Jooss from the point of view of sexual politics, and this is not fair to Jooss. The Young Woman is not the only female role in *The Green Table* but one of a number of characteristically modern female types including the old Mother and the female Saboteur. The overall effect of these various roles is not therefore to present all women as weak, vulnerable and inferior to men. *The Green Table* was created a decade after *Canaille* and each was formed in a different political landscape. In Tucholsky's review, Gert's prostitute is specifically German. Her grotesqueness is inimitably gothic, she is compared to the famous Berlin nude dancers and Tucholsky implies that she is far more corrupt and degenerate than any Parisian prostitute that Lautrec might have drawn. She is a symptom of a social and political problem that is a product of the devastating inflation of the early Weimar period and her presentation on stage constituted an attack by Gert that was aimed in particular at the provincial conservatism of Wilhelmine bourgeois society. Jooss' Young Woman driven to prostitution is a more generalised figure, as are all the roles in *The Green Table*. The spectator is not encouraged to identify with them as individuals but to recognise the universality of their behaviour or their plight. The situation Jooss' prostitute faces transcends national barriers. Like the Gentlemen in Black who negotiate around *The Green Table*, her precise identity is not fixed but left open so that she becomes a symptom of problems that exist in every country, while *Canaille* referred to a more specifically German issue. These differences can also be identified on the level of performance style. Critics invariably described Gert's performance as grotesque in its over-exaggeration and histrionics. Jooss' ballets were much cooler. Choreographically they were indebted to Laban's understanding of dance's potential to signify meanings in an expressive way that underlay the development of early modern dance in Germany; but they combined this with the more internationally recognised vocabulary of classical ballet technique.

Conclusion

Although it is difficult to judge just how a ballet like *The Green Table* was performed in the 1930s, a film of the Folkwangschule performance group during the 1960s performing the ballet with Pina Bausch as the Old Woman has a sharpness, precision and lack of emotionalism that is the antithesis of the short film clips of Gert dancing in the 1920s. As Iso Partsch-Bergsohn has shown, ballet rather than modern dance enjoyed an almost exclusive state patronage in West Germany between the end of the Second World War and the emergence of Tanztheatre in the early 1970s. This was the result of a shift from a nationally focused pre-war modern dance which explored specifically German cultural values, to an internationally focused, apolitical ballet that sought to attain and surpass technical and artistic standards set by British, French and American ballet companies. It is this post-war European historical situation that is the context which Susan Manning was seeking to explain when she proposed that in the twentieth century 'Modern dance became an arena for the forging of national identity, while 20th-century ballet became an arena for international competition' (Manning 1988: 36). The story of how American modern dance was exported in the post-war period as an international, apolitical art form is beyond the scope of the present study, but these post-war ideologies of apolitical international modernism need to be seen as a reaction formation against the horrors of the Second World War and the Holocaust. What this chapter has shown is that these ideologies of nationalism and internationalism were present in ballets and modern dance pieces of the 1920s and 1930s which addressed the vision of the utopian world that modernity would make possible. The gap between this utopian ideal and the actual experience of modernity as ambiguous, threatening and disturbing was largely disavowed and displaced through projection onto the idea of the modern metropolis.

The First World War inspired a nationally-focused isolationism in both ballet and modern dance. In France Diaghilev and de Maré responded in varying ways to the French 'rappel à l'ordre'. *Parade* and to a lesser extent *Skating Rink* sought to align the avant-garde with notions of French tradition perceived as the legitimate descendant of the Renaissance and classical tradition. Broad sections of the avant-garde came to support the 'rappel à l'ordre' particularly around the notion of Cubism as a new classicism which was mediated through these two ballets. Meanwhile, in a defeated and isolated Germany, dance artists like Gert, Laban and Wigman explored philosophical, aesthetic and social themes that concerned German artists and writers.

Nevertheless, America fascinated Europeans as an exemplar of a modernity manifested in jazz, *The Perils of Pauline* and Chaplin's *The Rink*, and through the advanced methods of industrial efficiency developed by F. W. Taylor. During the 1920s American modernity came increasingly to erode the distinctive ideologies and material conditions on which European differentials of national and class identities were maintained. While the arts were an area through which these identities were defined and affirmed, artistic modernism, particularly in its avant-garde guise, also contributed to this erosion. The utopian socialist vision was of the better future modernity could help bring about through the collapse of the existing bourgeois order. This utopian vision had its repressed other in the metropolis. For Laban and Le Corbusier the city appeared as a threatening beast, and for many its luxuriousness was marked as gendered, sexualised and a threat to notions of national and racial identity. This disavowed and sublimated unease with modernity was projected onto others. In dance terms the alien bodies of these others became the Others of modernity in terms of race and gender. It is with the relationship between these alien bodies and ideologies of national identity and of internationalism that the rest of this book is predominantly concerned. The next three chapters look at this relationship within the historical development identified in this chapter of the decline of the utopian ideals of the avant-garde in response to the financial collapses following the Wall Street Crash and the rise of fascism. What it traces are the contradictory associations between modernity as ultra modern – the future now – and modernity as renewal that embraces the primitive. At issue is how the themes of the city, the machine and the primitive/modern became the subject and inspiration of dance and of dance criticism. The last three chapters focus on modern dance in America and on the same themes – the city, the machine and the primitive/modern – which were explored by American modern dance artists.

The next two chapters examine differing responses to dance as mass entertainment, focusing on jazz – jungle music and the song of the machine. Josephine Baker's first appearance in Paris was under the management of Rolf de Maré. For many who were associated with the avant-garde, her dancing offered a vision of a utopian alternative to what they perceived to be a moribund and degenerating society. Siegfried Kracauer's essay 'The Mass Ornament' develops a left-wing view of the Tiller Girls and is informed by avant-garde ideas about the potential of modernity to create a revolutionary collapse of capitalism. This chapter has traced the decline and transformation of the utopian hope that avant-garde artistic practices could bring about a better life through a fusion of mass culture and high art. It is this historical process that forms the context for the ideas discussed in the next three chapters.

3

'SAVAGE' DANCER:
TOUT PARIS GOES TO SEE
JOSEPHINE BAKER

When Josephine Baker and the other African American dancers and performers arrived at the Opéra Music-Hall des Champs Elysées with their show, the management found that their performance didn't fit their idea of what a 'revue nègre' should look like. As Baker put it later: 'We had thought our show was marvellous and Monsieur Rolf's verdict – "Catastrophic" – struck us like a thunderclap. But he was an able and agreeable taskmaster and we did what he wanted although it meant working night and day' (Baker and Bouillon 1978: 50). Monsieur Rolf was of course Rolf de Maré, who had recently liquidated the Ballets Suédois. A new final number was devised for the *Revue Nègre* – a 'savage' pas de deux in which Baker and Jo Alex wore nothing but red and blue feathers around their waists and ankles. This was the first of a small number of 'savage dances' for which Baker became famous. Although in 1930 she substantially changed her image for her appearance at the Casino de Paris in *Paris qui Remue*, singing French songs and dancing on pointe in choreography by Georges Balanchine,[1] she nevertheless went on doing variations on her 'savage' numbers into the late 1930s.

The two best known of these are this 'savage' pas de deux from the *Revue Nègre* 1925 and the 'banana' dance, sometimes referred to as 'Fatou', which she first performed in the revue *La Folie du Jour* at the Folies-Bergère in 1926–7. A film version of the latter has recently been found which apparently shows Baker dancing this number on the Folies-Bergère's stage in 1926. Baker's Paris debut in the *Revue Nègre* and her overnight ascent to international stardom is one of the more fascinating stories of Paris in the 1920s. It was as a dancer that Baker first took Paris and other European capitals by storm, although she soon became an all-round performer and later concentrated on singing. Yet Baker has appeared in very few dance history books. Because she was based in Paris from the age of 19 (and perhaps because she was a woman) she isn't generally seen as an important figure in the development of African American dance. Only her career prior to 1925 is covered by Jean and Marshall Stearn (1968), though Lynn Fauley Emery devotes a few pages to her (1988: 228–31). Like most African

American dancers pre-1960, she doesn't appear in general books on modern dance,[2] not least because she is not classed as a 'serious' dancer, having appeared only on the commercial stage. Since Baker's death in 1975 and the publication of her last autobiography (Baker and Bouillon 1978),[3] a number of biographies have been published in response to curiosity about the exotic and glamorous myth that has grown up around her memory (Haney 1981; Hammond and O'Connor 1988; Rose 1990; Baker and Chase 1993). Her life has even been the subject of a feature film *The Josephine Baker Story* (1991) directed by Brian Gibson with Lynn Whitfield as Baker and dances choreographed by Georges Faison.

There is a wealth of information and discussion of Baker, attesting to the fascination she exerted over audiences throughout her life, and to the powerful hold that the exotic myth of 'la Bakaire' still has on the popular imagination. But if one wants to progress beyond the sensational aspects of her life and career, Baker is not an easy person to write about because of the fact that a whole mass of ideologically over-determined discourses have been inscribed around her blackness. At the heart of the myth is the image of Baker as a naked 'savage'. This conjures up for the white male imagination a stereotypical image of the mysterious black female as 'other' – the sensual feathers that concealed her sex, the allure of her beautiful naked breasts, the erotic attraction of her rhythmically shaking buttocks. Many people in the United States, Britain and elsewhere who are of African descent, feel a pride in the memory of Baker's glamour, her erotic power, her personal and professional success; the recognition and serious critical appreciation her dancing received together with the huge salaries she commanded – all this and more have made her, as Michel Fabre has put it, 'an international beacon of African American memory' (1995: 122).

In many ways the myths that surround Baker, especially those concerning her initial rise to stardom, have created an essentialised and mystified image of her that gets in the way of understanding her history and appreciating her achievements. Essentialising any black person, particularly a woman, runs the risk of stereotypically associating them with the body, and thus with (an ideologically constructed idea of) nature rather than with culture. This is especially true for black female dancers, and I return to the problem of essentialism later. To dwell on Baker's achievements and see them as attributes of genius is to imply that her qualities are timeless – as if such talents would have ensured success at any period. Attractive as such ideas are, they can have the effect of contradicting important issues. Making her exceptional, a genius, can have the effect of raising her above and beyond her racial origins, as if she was somehow not like other black women, almost a token white. Or it can have the opposite effect, so that her skills and the hard work she put into developing them are made invisible, and her 'magic' is seen as somehow innate, a capacity that all 'black' people have and therefore not a measure of personal achievement. By seeing her as timeless she is of course ahistoricised. The ways in which she was the right person in the right place at the right time are lost. (When de Maré chose to make her a star there were undoubtedly many other women of her age with similar abilities and qualities whom he could have chosen, but she was there and she fitted into his avant-garde sensibility.) What is lost above all is the fact that stars and their mythologies are constructed. It is with the context and process of this construction that I am primarily concerned in this chapter, and the key role of the 'savage' dances in articulating her star persona.

Richard Dyer has argued that stars embody important ideas about freedom and individuality, and points out that their appeal is contingent on the way individuals within their audiences feel social and economic pressures on them at the time:

> Stars matter because they act out aspects of life that matter to us; and performers get to be stars when what they act out matters to enough people. Though there is a sense in which stars must touch on things that are deep and constant features of human existence, such features never exist outside a culturally and historically specific context.
>
> (Dyer 1987: 19)

Baker's singing and dancing, and her revelation of her naked body epitomised the idea of natural, vital sexuality in a way that captivated modern audiences in Europe in the 1920s and 1930s. In saying this it is necessary to qualify what is meant by natural in relation to sexuality. On the one hand Baker's blackness – her African descent – allowed her naked, exuberant performance to be interpreted in relation to Rousseauesque ideas of the noble savage: her 'primitiveness' making her, in social Darwinian terms, closer to 'nature'. At the same time Europeans have often projected sexual fantasies onto various colonised peoples who are supposed to be free of restrictive white, European codes of sexual morality in terms either of supposed innocence, or greater sexual licence, or even in terms of a capacity for sexual violence. On the other hand there is a sense in which Baker's 'naturalness' can be seen not as racially specific, but can be compared with the naturalness of stars like Marilyn Monroe. Both Baker and Monroe developed star personas that mediated notions of 'natural', innocent sexuality that were in each case socially and historically specific. Another point of comparison is the star persona developed by MGM for Lena Horne. Like Baker, Horne's performances in the 1940s and 1950s were objectified into eroticised spectacles of exotic, black sexuality. Horne herself has more recently spoken out about how these made her feel, of her anger at the way her image was used and the pain and tensions she experienced in hiding her feelings about this (see Kakutani 1981; Dyer 1987). By all accounts Baker was happier with her image than Horne. The latter's image was created under the totalising control of MGM, while Baker's image was initially formed under the auspices of Rolf de Maré and artists and intellectuals associated with the Parisian avant-garde. Chance seemingly having brought her to Paris and stardom, Baker's autobiographies attest to her conscious decision to do all she could to remain in France. But that doesn't mean that one can forget that her star persona was a construction and not the 'real Joséphine'. Baker was as aware as Horne of the problematics of being identified with white-defined stereotypical notions of black female sexuality. Baker herself once commented: 'The white imagination sure is something when it comes to blacks' (quoted in Rose 1990: 81).

It is perhaps Phyllis Rose's failure to pay attention to signs of Baker's awareness of herself as an American Negro[4] and the specificity of her experiences as a black woman, that has prompted bell hooks to criticise Rose's biography *Jazz Cleopatra*. While hooks rebukes Rose for assaulting Baker's life and works she does allow that now and then Rose 'offers tidbits of useful information ... particularly so in the passages that address Baker's theorising of the body and its relation to eroticism' (hooks 1992: 141). hooks draws attention to the following discussion from *Jazz Cleopatra* of Baker's bottom:

She handled it as though it were an instrument, a rattle, something apart from herself that she could shake. One can hardly overemphasise the importance of the rear end. Baker herself declared that people had been hiding their arses too long. 'The rear end exists. I see no reason to be ashamed of it. It's true that there are rear ends so stupid, so pretentious, so insignificant that they're good only for sitting on.' With Baker's triumph, the erotic gaze of a nation moved downward: she had uncovered a new region for desire.

(Rose 1990: 24)[5]

hooks comments as follows:

Rose lacks the knowledge of black culture that would enable her to decode the subtext of Baker's comments as well as an informed perspective on race that would have enabled her to understand that 'arses' have always been eroticised in black sexual iconography, that within black folk culture the arses that are ridiculed and mocked are those of whites, called names like 'ironing board butts'. Hence, only the gaze of the white segment of the nation was transformed by Baker's assertion of bodily passion in dance.

(hooks 1992: 141)

Like Rose, I undoubtedly lack the kind of knowledge of black culture on which black intellectuals on both sides of the Atlantic can draw. However, my decision to look at both black and white artists in this book derives from a recognition of the importance of theorising the cultural politics of race and ethnicity as these effect representations of the dancing body and to acknowledge the generally unacknowledged debts that modern (and postmodern) dance owes to African American cultural traditions.

It is important to recognise, when considering Baker's star persona and the ways in which this was mediated through her dancing, that tensions existed between her own identity and aspirations as an American Negro woman and the image created for her initially by members of the Parisian artistic avant-garde. Indications of these tensions can be glimpsed in Baker's own comments on some of the reviews of her appearance in the *Revue Nègre*. Baker later wrote that she collected these reviews and used them to learn French. One of these was by André Levinson:

> In the short pas de deux of the savages, which came as the finale of the Revue Nègre, there was a wild splendour and magnificent animality. Certain of Miss Baker's poses, back arched, haunches protruding, arms entwined and uplifted in a phallic symbol, had the compelling potency of the finest examples of Negro sculpture. The plastic sense of a race of sculptors came to life and the frenzy of the African Eros swept over the audience. It was no longer a grotesque dancing girl that stood before them, but the black Venus that haunted Baudelaire. The dancer's personality had transcended the character of her dance.
>
> (Acocella and Garafola 1991: 74)

Baker, observing that a reviewer had said she was 'a black Venus' commented: 'It was true that everyone seemed to love me, but I had heard no talk of marriage. Venus, yes. But the black part didn't seem to help' (Baker and Bouillon 1978: 53). Here Baker is wryly subverting Levinson's talk of erotic frenzy and his high cultural references, by pretending that Venus is the goddess of loving marriages rather than of sexual love. She isn't denying altogether the erotic impact of her act but drawing attention to the warmth of her personality and the fact that everyone seemed to love her. Then she ends up, though still in a light-hearted manner, by gently alluding to the realities of racism through commenting that her colour 'didn't help'.[6]

Levinson, in calling Baker a black Venus, was referring to the tradition of European visual art, to the Venus de Milo and Botticelli's *Birth of Venus*. This goes with his references to the finest African sculpture and thus to what he sees as a distinct but admirable aesthetic. Baker's own dancing he admires intensely. By referring to Baudelaire – the original 'poet maudit' – Levinson, however, conjures up the threat of contamination, the moral and physical decay Baudelaire famously went through as if infected by his Creole mistress Jeanne Duval – his black Venus.[7] There are references to infection in

Levinson's essay, not in relation to African and African American dancers as such but in the context of the fashion for jazz dancing. Thus Levinson states that Negro dance 'as it is found in our present-day dance halls . . . may appear as a symptom of an epidemic contagion which should concern the pathologist' (Acocella and Gararafola 1991: 70), and: 'The really devil-ridden today are those European idlers who passionately give themselves up to an enjoyment of Negro dancing without setting up any barriers to its atavistic, demoralising appeal' (ibid.: 75). Levinson is an idealist, and for him Baker's dancing has a passion and idealism that transcends the merely physical character of the dance – in Levinson's original French the last sentence quoted above reads: 'Sa personnalité dépasse le genre', her person-ality exceeds the genre (1929: 277). It is the dilution of what Levinson saw as separate African and European aesthetic ideals through the mixing of black and white that he abhors. Arnold Haskell, another balletomane reviewer, criticised Baker for doing precisely this. To him she appeared too tainted by white culture when compared with Florence Mills who also danced in the *Revue Nègre*:

> Josephine Baker . . . always seems to me to be playing up to what the public wants the negress to be. She has become totally Parisianised. The case of the late Florence Mills was entirely different. She was an admirable artist, always true to herself, proud of the true Negro origins of her art.
>
> (Haskell 1930: 456)

Haskell, as I shall argue later, is right about Baker playing up to white audi-ence's expectations. However, he wanted Baker to be 'authentic' where being inauthentic is defined as loss of origins as these were determined by domi-nant white, colonial ideologies. In these extracts Haskell and Levinson are reinforcing what bell hooks has called 'colonial imperialist paradigms of black identity which represent blackness one-dimensionally in ways that reinforce and sustain white supremacy' (1990: 28). What Haskell, Levinson and indeed many white commentators on both sides of the Atlantic, feared was cultural contamination. Haskell asked readers of *The Dancing Times* to:

> Imagine a performance of *Les Sylphides* danced by loose-limbed, 'coal-black mammies'! Such a thing seems utterly ridiculous, and yet we are perfectly used to seeing our pink and white girls charlestonning and blackbottoming – (I am not discussing the ball-room versions). To me both sights seem very much the same. I am a great admirer of Negro dancing, but only when danced by Negroes.
>
> (Haskell 1930: 455)

In looking at Josephine Baker's dancing it is necessary to read Levinson and

Haskell against the grain and not reinscribe within the discourse of dance history the racism that informs their aesthetic judgements. To acknowledge that Baker was a great dancer must not be to see her as someone who transcended and exceeded the character of 'Negro' dance. Rather, the notion of racial purity that Levinson and Haskell articulate needs to be placed within its social and political context and identified in its diverse variations. It needs to be located within the context of the 'borrowing' from Black American dance and music by white performers during the last two centuries, and the situation where African American performers for commercial reason, have had to imitate white imitations of black performers. As Paul Gilroy observed, it is important not to deny, and therefore oversimplify 'the volatile dynamics of the on-going processes that are half-grasped by incomplete concepts like creolisation, syncretism and "hybridity" ' (Gilroy 1996: 14). Levinson and Haskell's notion of racial purity also needs to be located in relation to the modernity that was the everyday experience of Baker's European audiences. The jazz music to which Baker danced was perceived both as jungle music and the song of machines – simultaneously the most up-to-date modern style and an absolutely primitive one. Both were qualities that Europeans perceived themselves to lack in their culture. For those Parisians (and Berliners and audiences in other major capital cities)[8] who went to Baker's performances and witnessed her night club acts, part of the enjoyment of dancing to jazz music at that time was a temporary, ritualised blurring of the difference between self and 'other' through losing themselves in the strong, 'primitive' rhythms of jazz music. Baker's supposedly African dancing – particularly when seen from a French utopian socialist point of view – also evoked an image of a mythical organic community, one that was in touch with 'primitive', natural essences with which over-civilised modern Westerners believed they had lost touch. From a more conservative point of view, contamination from contact with non-Western art was taken as a sign of the erosion and degeneracy of specifically national and racial identities.

The imagined dangers of blurring the boundaries between individual or cultural identities, and of diluting racial purity are particularly pertinent to dancing. When a white person dances a black dance style, or when a black person dances in a style like ballet that has its origins in European culture, each is taking into their body a stance and way of moving that is associated with a cultural tradition other than their own. Haskell's revulsion at the idea of loose-limbed black dancers performing *Les Sylphides* is founded on essentialist notions of racial identity, and fear of the loss of distinctness that comes through the blurring of boundaries. In this unwillingness to own up to this fear about the instability of his own, white identity, he projects what he fears about himself onto the body of another, stereotypically conceived as 'other'. As a consequence he only sees colour and body types and cannot or will not realise that any one can do any movement vocabulary or style if given the appropriate training.[9] One aim of this chapter is to present readings of Baker's 'savage' dances that recognise the extent to which Baker was able use the fluid, boundary-lessness that contemporary European audiences associated with her dancing to create an integrationist intervention within the discourses of race and modernity in which her image was located.

In order to locate Baker's 'savage' dance routines within these social and political discourses, this chapter therefore proceeds as follows. First, it considers the relationship between the 'African-ness' of Baker's dancing and Baker's identity as an American Negro – her experience as a performer within the jazz dance tradition and her cultural inheritance of memories of an African past. Then it examines the process through which Baker was commodified as a star and locates this within notions of primitivism that were current within the Parisian avant-garde of the early 1920s, particularly those developed in the circles within which Rolf de Maré moved. Third, the ways in which some women may have viewed her image is considered through an examination of a contemporary female description of her body by the novelist Colette. Molly Haskell suggested that female Hollywood stars are 'the vessels of men's and women's fantasies and the barometers of changing fashion'. As such, they have 'reflected, perpetuated, and in some respects offered innovations on the roles of women in society' (1974: 12). Though Baker was primarily a star of live shows rather than movies, I shall argue that her star image offered a progressive image of women's roles in society. Because these three different strands were enmeshed within her 'savage' dances, each takes these as their starting point but then develops in entirely different directions. In the last part of the chapter a reading is presented which suggests that these embodied important ideas about freedom and individuality that moved her audiences because of the way they articulated aspects of their experience of the social and economic pressures on them at that time.

Baker's Africa

When Baker and the other African American dancers and performers arrived at the Opéra Music-Hall des Champs Elysées with their show, their performance didn't fit the management's idea of what a 'revue nègre' should look like. As Baker put it later: 'We had thought our show was marvellous and Monsieur Rolf's verdict – "Catastrophic" – struck us like a thunderclap. But he was an able and agreeable taskmaster and we did what he wanted although it meant working night and day' (Baker and Bouillon 1978: 50). A new 'African' number was devised, and it was this dance that made Baker famous overnight. Although Baker had been gradually working her way up the showbiz ladder in the United States, too often her 'savage' dances are seen as entirely invented for the occasion in Paris and without precedent or connection with any previous dance. It is as if, when asked by Monsieur Rolf and the management of the Opéra Music-Hall des Champs Elysées to do an 'African' dance, Baker was able to pull out from somewhere a sensational improvised dance that was immediately recognised as a work of inspired genius. What Baker herself later wrote of this first dance seems to support this view:

> Driven by dark forces I didn't recognise, I improvised, crazed by the music, the overheated theatre filled to the bursting point, the scorching eye of the spotlights. Even my teeth and eyes burned with fever. Each time I leaped I seemed to touch the sky and when I regained earth it seemed to be mine alone. I felt as intoxicated as when, on the first day I arrived in Paris, Douglas had given me a glass of anisette.
>
> (Baker and Bouillon 1978: 51–2)

What I want to argue here, however, is that Baker's dancing should be seen as rooted within African American traditions and that it exemplified what Brenda Dixon Gottschild (1996) calls an Africanist aesthetic. Even Baker's statement here about her improvisation and her feelings of intoxication on stage are within this tradition. When she was asked by Monsieur Rolf to dance in a more 'African' way, he may on the one hand have been asking her to do something that conformed more closely to his idea of Africa, but she too had an idea of Africa. Music and the body were crucial to the ways in which African Americans have had access to a shared, communal memory of Africa before the Diaspora, together with the accounts of slavery that some African American children have heard in the form of stories from the older generation. It is thus possible to tease out the parameters of what African-ness meant to Baker.

Baker had not been hired as an 'African' dancer but as a highly sophisticated, up and coming young performer who had appeared in two high-profile all-black Broadway musicals *Shuffle Along* and *The Chocolate Dandies* and at the prestigious New York night club The Plantation. Before this she had toured with the Dixie Steppers, a company on the racially segregated TOBA vaudeville circuit. When she arrived in Paris she had therefore undergone a practical education in the performing traditions of African American music and dance. Improvisation was an important part of these traditions, a skill that she had learned and which had developed with experience. When Baker says she improvised on stage at the Opéra Music-Hall des Champs Elysées this should not be taken to mean that she just made something up out of her head on the spur of the moment. Dancers who improvise generally do so with rehearsed material. Baker's improvisation will have derived from a specific and codified movement vocabulary, and she will also have shared with Jo Alex and the musicians some general rules and an agreed idea of the dance's structure.

This is how she had been performing in the States. The blues singer Ethel Waters who was ten years older than Baker, encountered her more than once before the latter departed for Paris and stardom. In the summer of 1925 they were appearing together at the Plantation Club in New York, where they shared a dressing room.

> Josephine was in the chorus, but she stepped out of the line to do her speciality once during each show. Josephine was a mugger with a great comic sense, and she had a beautiful form. She could dance and she could clown joy into you.
>
> (Waters 1983: 249)

Mugging meant improvising. Others who knew Baker at that time also remember her ability to do this. It was as the funny chorus girl in *Shuffle Along* that Baker had her first Broadway success. Eubie Blake, who composed the music for *Shuffle Along* and conducted the orchestra, recalled Baker would come on stage dancing at the end of the chorus line and then start to do 'crazy things': 'no routine – just mugging, crossing her eyes, tripping, getting out of step and catching up, doing all the steps the rest were doing, but funnier' (quoted in Stearn and Stearn 1968: 134). What both Waters and Blake value is Baker's freedom and imagination, but the comic girl on the end of the chorus line was an established convention and Blake significantly mentions that Baker did all the steps the rest were doing.

Some photographs from Baker's American acts show her in blackface, and Baker's clowning will have drawn on African American versions of minstrelsy. It is tragic that more or less the only way African Americans were able to earn any money as performers from the end of the civil war right up until the early 1900s was through acting out white, racist stereotypes of black people. This painful adoption by African American performers of a blackface mask nevertheless allowed the possibility for subversion. Paul Gilroy observes that the use of a mask afforded opportunities to refine 'the ability to manipulate the expectations of whites who are conditioned and misled by the consistency with which those whom they dominate (and on whom they depend) deploy the mask effect' (Gilroy 1996: 16). Baker's 'savage' dances were not done in blackface but her adoption of a savage persona nevertheless constituted a sort of mask. When writers like André Levinson (but not Haskell) seemingly took them entirely seriously they were probably being misled about their authenticity.

The extent to which Baker was clowning during her 'savage' dances can be seen in a sequence from the surviving film of her 'banana' dance in *La Folie du Jour*, and this can also serve to demonstrate how her dancing corresponds to Brenda Dixon Gottschild's very useful characterisation of distinctive elements of the Africanist aesthetic of African American dance. The 'banana' dance is so called because of the famous gilded girdle of bananas which Baker wears. In the film she also wears a white bra, although in most photographs connected with this dance number the bananas are all she has on.[10]

Although this dance has gone down in history as a solo, one part of the film shows a volatile interaction between Baker and an unidentified drummer (he is not mentioned in any English language source). He carries his drum under one arm and lightly shifts around, intently following her every move while Baker, for her part, seems driven by his drumming. Throughout, Baker's dancing is fast, strong and involves every part of her body in a flexible and sensitive way. She slowly turns round on the spot shaking her bottom – the bananas rattling and flying as if they had lives of their own – while in response the drummer circles round the outside so that they remain facing one another and in eye contact, his fingers beating away at the drum head. Later he initiates a move round the outside and she follows him, shoulders hunched and head on one side like a boxer shadow boxing an opponent. Her face is active and changing all the time, calling, laughing, pursing her lips and then smiling. Her arms pump up and down. Her fingers are sometimes limp, sometimes delicately splayed. Everything about her is energetic and continually mobile, with sudden, unexpected changes from one movement idea to another. Thus she rustles her girdle of bananas like an Arabic 'belly' dancer, then, with knees bent, slides her feet sideways, zigzagging across the floor, then quite unexpectedly turns around and makes a high kick as if booting an imaginary ball high into the wings. In one section she can be seen opening and closing her knees with her hands on her knee caps, swapping the hands alternately from one knee to the other and back – a classic Charleston move. As she does this she smilingly faces the camera then quickly turns her head and shouts to someone off screen to her right – presumably the drummer – then quickly smiles forwards again, the rhythmic repetition of this suggesting call and response. Baker's smile couldn't be more different from the polite self presentation of the ballerina 'showing her teeth'. Throughout the film, Baker projects herself straight towards the camera's lens and smiles (at posterity) what has to be described as an infectious smile. She is 20 years old and, despite the fragmentary nature of the film, enough of her extraordinary stage presence – her warm spontaneity and vitality – comes across to corroborate the many superlatives that were used to describe her performances during her first few years in Europe.

There are some elements here that can be identified as African – such as the call and response. Others specifically referred to topical European ideas and misconceptions about African Americans: the reference to boxing would have reminded Europeans of the relatively new phenomenon of African American heavyweight boxing champions; while the belly dancing motif may indicate ignorance about African dance among the producers of *La Folie du Jour*. The high kicks and the opening and closing of the knees would have been recognised at the time as Charleston moves, a dance which Baker is credited with introducing to Paris. These motifs and elements would therefore have signified 'Africa' to European audiences. But what can be seen on this film is neither the Charleston itself nor an authentic African dance but a wonderfully, inauthentic, misleading and mischievous performance. It is full of irony, multiple meanings and innuendo which, as Brenda Dixon Gottschild points out are:

> three interrelated attributes of the Africanist aesthetic that have been worked, reworked, and brought into high relief because of the need of diasporan African peoples to simultaneously conceal and reveal, disguise and display themselves in alien, if not hostile, New World environments.
>
> (1996: 12)

It is these attributes that de Maré and members of the Parisian avant-garde appreciated, as I shall show shortly, together with the fact that Baker's dancing was informed by an aesthetic which decisively contradicted the dominant white aesthetic.

Three qualities that Gottschild identifies as characteristic of an Africanist dance aesthetic are clearly present in Baker's 'banana' dance: polycentrism/ polyrhythm, ephebism, and high affect juxtaposition (1996: 11–19). What Gottschild calls polycentrism/polyrhythm is the most generally recognised characteristic of African dance – dancing with two or more centres operating simultaneously and each moving to a different rhythm. Thus Baker shakes her girdle of bananas to one rhythm centred on the pelvis while her feet mark out a separate beat as she slowly turns around on the spot. By ephebism Gottschild means youthful energy and dynamism that shows off both supple flexibility and stamina. This, she points out, is the opposite of the comparatively muted sensitivity and control of traditional European ballet. Ephebism is exactly what distinguishes Baker's dancing from, for the sake of comparison, the film of Pavlova dancing *The Dying Swan*. The 'banana' dance is also full of high affect juxtaposition – the sudden changes of dynamics like her sliding zigzag across the floor, which is unexpectedly followed by a high kick.

If the aesthetic qualities of Baker's dancing were African, they not only came from her experience dancing on the TOBA circuit and on Broadway but from her deeper African roots. An important way through which she would have tapped the shared, communal knowledge of Africa was almost certainly from her experience of going to church. Black churches have played a central role in the buffers that African American people created to ward off the nihilism of giving in to despair in response to the experience of slavery and racism. These buffers, as Cornell West has put it, 'equip black folk with cultural armour to beat back the demons of hopelessness, meaninglessness, and lovelessness' (West 1992: 40). Baker was religious. For example, she writes of kneeling in her dressing room to pray before each performance:

> I believe in the importance of prayer. It's the best way to draw strength from heaven. One day as I was praying, someone opened the door. Since I was busy talking to the Lord, I didn't look up. The intruder, who turned out to be the stage manager, lost no time in telling the entire cast that I had been worshipping stark naked. Why not? That was the way God made me.
>
> (Baker and Bouillon 1978: 61)

Rose says that as a child Baker attended a spiritualist church – the Holy Rollers (1990: 26–7). Some of her experiences there seem to have helped form her identity as a dancer. Baker wrote:

> One of the critics compared our movements [in the *Revue Nègre*] to St Vitus's Dance. 'What kind of dance is that?' I asked. 'It's a nervous disorder that makes you tremble all over.' 'That's not a sickness,' I retorted. 'It's the way we act in church back home.' 'Here in France, God likes us to kneel quietly.' Why didn't God demand the same behaviour in France as in Harlem? It would make things so much easier.
>
> (Baker and Bouillon 1978: 53)

Reading between the lines, Baker clearly felt a connection between the spontaneous, 'ecstatic', bodily worship in the spiritual churches she had attended and her improvised dancing on stage.

The great Gospel singer Mahalia Jackson, who was six years younger than Baker,[11] said the Sanctified or Holiness Churches were a great influence on her singing (although she herself was a Baptist). She gives this description of the Sanctified Church next door to the house she lived in as a child:

> Those people had no choir and no organ. They used the drum, the cymbal, the tambourine and the steel triangle. Everybody in there sang and they clapped and stomped their feet and sang with their whole bodies. They had a powerful beat, a rhythm we held on to from slavery days, and their music was so strong and expressive it used to bring tears to my eyes.
>
> I believe the blues and jazz and even rock and roll stuff got their beat from the Sanctified Church. We Baptists sang sweet, and we had the long and short meter (sic) on beautiful songs like 'Amazing Grace, how sweet it sounds', but when those Holiness people tore into 'I'm so glad Jesus lifted me up!' they came out with real jubilation.
>
> (Jackson 1983: 293)

Ralph Ellison has also commented on the roots jazz has in such church groups: 'Most of all [jazz] is an art which swings, and in the South there are many crudely trained groups who use it naturally for the expression of religious feeling who could teach the jazz modernists quite a bit about polyrhythmics and polytonality' (Ellison 1972: 216–17). Katherine Dunham, who found Charleston steps in folk dances in Haiti, also wrote that she had seen 'possessed devotees in "store-front" churches propelling themselves up and down the aisles with a practically pure Charleston step' (1978c: 73). In traditional African societies no distinction is made between dance and religion. White plantation owners in the late eighteenth and early nineteenth centuries seeing the 'ring and shout' dance did not realise it was a form of worship. If Baker made a connection between dance and worship, she is not the only African American dancer to do so in the twentieth century. Alvin Ailey's *Revelations* (1960) and Bill T. Jones' *The Last Supper in Uncle Tom's Cabin/The Promised Land* (1990) both in different ways blur the distinction between dance and ceremony, audience and congregation.

What I am arguing is that, when asked by the management of the Opéra Music-Hall des Champs Elysées to do an 'African' dance, Baker was able to pull out from somewhere an almost innate memory not just of the idea of Africa but some residual experience of it that had been passed down to her within her family and within the African American community. (In Chapter 8, I return to the concept of African retentions in African American memory when discussing Katherine Dunham's ethnographic research.) The problem here with arguing this is that it seems to support an essentialist view of racial identity as somehow innate. bell hooks' observations on the problem of essentialism offer a possible solution. 'There is a radical difference,' she argues, 'between a repudiation of the idea that there is a black "essence" and recognition of the way black identity has been specifically constituted in the experience of exile and struggle' (hooks 1990: 29). While recognising that essentialist thinking can support a racist stereotyping whereby all black people are reduced to the same pre-existing pattern, hooks nevertheless argues for a pragmatic acceptance of essentialism if it opens up the possibility of recognising the 'multiple experiences of black identity that are the lived contradictions which make diverse cultural productions possible' (ibid.).[12]

One of Baker's lived contradictions was that she was recreating her own imaginary 'Africa' out of her African American heritage for Europeans who were telling her what African American dance should and should not look like. Joe Alex and Louis Douglas, with whom Baker danced in the *Revue Nègre* had both performed in Europe before. They undoubtedly understood what Europeans expected of black dancers and it is not impossible that they might have seen some 'authentic' African dancers performing in Europe. The unidentified drummer in the banana dance might have been African rather than African American, but I am not aware of any evidence that Baker in 1925 had had any direct contact with Africa or African people. Rolf de Maré, however, was a keen collector of 'primitive' art who had travelled extensively all over the world and, according to Bengt Håger (1990), had a house in Africa. He would almost certainly have told Baker about African dancers he had seen in their own countries. Somewhere along the line, someone may have told Baker about Arabic women's dances, or she may have seen an Arabic dancer (or a European woman doing her impression of 'belly' dancing). Nevertheless what 'Africa' meant to Baker was different from what it meant to de Maré and his friends and associates. If it is difficult to make any definitive statements about what it meant to her, that must remind the reader of the extent to which the Africanist dance aesthetic has been consistently marginalised, misunderstood and only appreciated when appropriated by white practitioners. Baker, after all, only became an international star under the management of white impresarios and directors.

Baker and Parisian negrophilia

When Josephine Baker and the other African American dancers and performers arrived at the Opéra Music-Hall des Champs Elysées with their show, their performance didn't fit the management's idea of what a 'revue nègre' should look like. A new final number was devised – a 'savage' pas de deux – and the rest, as they say, was history.[13] Baker achieved a status that has gone down in history because initially she was the right person in the right place at the right time. Since Picasso and Braque had started appropriating imagery from African sculpture in Cubist painting around 1907, and since Raymond Roussel's 1910 novel *Impressions of Africa* (1966) and Jean Paulhan's first book of translations of Madagascan 'poetry' in 1913, the Parisian literary and artistic world had been fascinated with the idea of 'Africa' as a source of the primitive, wild and elemental. In the 1920s, as James Clifford has pointed out, 'a series of stereotypes [of black people] long associated with backwardness and inferiority acquired positive connotations and came to stand for liberation and spontaneity, for a simultaneous recovery of ancient sources and an access to true modernity' (Clifford 1989: 901). This negrophilia – this love of 'Africa' – was at its peak by the mid-1920s when Baker arrived. The 1925 Exposition Internationale des Arts Décoratifs in Paris translated elements of advanced Cubist and abstract painting, including appropriations from African sculpture, into the decorative style subsequently known as art deco. Georges-Henri Rivière, disappointed in the lack of primitive bite he found in this exhibition, found what he was looking for in the *Revue Nègre* instead.

It is surely no coincidence that the art deco exhibition, the Paris performances by the Southern Syncopated Orchestra, and the *Revue Nègre* should have taken place the same year with the publication of Paul Guillaume and Thomas Munro's book *Primitive Negro Sculpture*. In 1925 the avant-garde

71

artist Man Ray was one of many professional photographers who took photos of Baker. Many of his photographs at that time appropriated an African aesthetic, such as his portrait of Nancy Cunard wearing African bracelets or his photograph *Noire et Blanche* published in *Vogue* in 1926 showing his model Kiki with an ebony Baule mask (see Chadwick 1995). Around these borrowed signs of African (and African American) culture, high fashion, popular culture and the avant-garde were becoming blurred. While she was rehearsing the *Revue Nègre*, Baker was photographed by Roger-Viollet on the roof of the Opéra Music-Hall des Champs Elysées, sticking her bum out and crossing her eyes. On that same roof, about a year earlier, Erik Satie, Francis Picabia, Marcel Duchamp and Man Ray had been filmed doing equally silly things by René Clair for the film *Entracte* that was shown in the interval of the ballet *Relâche*, the Ballets Suédois' last ballet. De Maré's decision to disband his ballet company and rename the theatre an Opéra Music-Hall may have been expedient – he had been losing money on the company and his lease on the theatre had one year to run – but there are nevertheless continuities between the avant-garde orientation of the ballets and the *Revue Nègre*. The Africanist aesthetic in Baker's dancing was the complete antithesis of the European ballet tradition and hence of the ways ballet mediated civilised European values. The avant-garde fascination with jazz depended in part at least on their own project to desecrate traditional, civilised European values.

Fernand Léger, writing in 1924, praised *Relâche* for aiming 'a lot of kicks in a lot of backsides, whether hallowed or not' and claiming that because of this:

> The watertight compartment separating ballet from music hall is broken through. The author, the dancer, the acrobat, the screen, the stage, all these means of 'presenting a performance' are integrated and organised to achieve a total effect. One single aim: to bring the stage to life. All prejudices come crashing down.
>
> (Léger 1968: 169)

It is Léger who is sometimes credited with first suggesting to de Maré that he hire real black dancers from Harlem, after the lukewarm reception of the Ballets Suédois' attempt at a 'ballet nègre', *Création du Monde* with set and costumes by Léger. What Léger admires in *Relâche* is its blurring of high and popular culture. The Italian Futurists had presented music hall performances while the Zürich Dadaists had run a cabaret. The blurring of boundaries between art and life was a central tenet of the historical avant-garde. *Relâche* is generally seen as the 'one last posthumous fling', as John Willett (1978: 93) has put it, of Paris Dada. Willett points to 'the ineffectiveness of the political Left [in Paris], combined with the dependence of the arts on the patronage of a still largely aristocratic Parisian élite' (ibid.: 92). Avant-gardism was undoubtedly highly attractive to the very rich, providing them with a distinctive form of anti-bourgeois, cultural experience. The crossing over of certain avant-garde preoccupations into more popular forms was precisely what Léger saw in *Relâche*. It was a logical development for de Maré, having been involved in producing an avant-garde ballet that was almost a revue, to go on to produce a revue whose African American dancers and musicians corresponded to an avant-garde sensibility.

Accounts of the preview and first night of the *Revue Nègre* stress that 'tout Paris' was there, but it is hardly surprising that those listed are primarily associated with the Parisian avant-garde's taste for 'Africa'. Paul Guillaume, the art dealer who sold African sculpture and had just published the book mentioned above, was there along with Kees Van Dongen who with Guy Fauconnet had designed costumes and decor for Guillaume's 'Fêtes Nègre' in 1919. This earlier event was devised by the poet Blaise Cendrars, a close friend of Léger's. Ornella Volta (1991–2) points out that its scenario was a precursor for that which Cendrars devised for the Ballets Suédois' 'ballet nègre' *La Création du Monde*. Paul Poiret, later to design dresses for Baker, had gone to the 'Fêtes Nègre' with an entourage of his models all in black-face. At the fête, Van Dongen had painted tattoos directly on people's bare skin, while Fauconnet had devised grass skirts and girdles made of bunches of bananas – surely a precedent for Baker's famous costume. Léger, who designed the set and costumes for *La Création du Monde*, was at both the preview and the premiere of the *Revue Nègre* along with Darius Milhaud who had composed the ballet's music. Cendrars wasn't there, being away on an expedition into the Amazonian jungle. Jean Cocteau, who back in 1917 had suggested including jazz music in the score for *Parade*, came to the Revue's premiere.

The two people most involved in creating Baker's star image are Paul Colin, the graphic artist who designed posters and programme covers for the revue, and Rolf de Maré, the impresario who had leased the Théâtre des Champs Elysées. The story of Baker's encounter with Colin is told in all the biographies and is shown in Brian Gibson's film. Baker demurred when asked to pose for him in the nude, artists' use of life models being outside her experience. Pressure was put on her to undress for him and after a few days she complied. 'I spent many happy hours in his quiet studio,' she later wrote. 'Paul gave me self confidence. For the first time in my life, I felt beautiful' (Baker and Bouillon 1978: 50). He played an important role in defining her image, not just in the poster but in other areas as well. It was he, for example, who took her to Paul Poiret to dress her in Parisian haute couture. Colin therefore played the role of Professor Higgins to Baker's Eliza Doolittle; but whereas Eliza was changed from a working-class flower seller to a radicalised and politicised member of the intelligentsia, Baker was turned from a talented comedienne into a self-confident, glamorous and thus commercially much more valuable performer.

Baker's nude appearances undoubtedly appealed to European curiosity about the naked black female body. Brenda Dixon Gottschild, Phyllis Rose and Andrea Stuart all account for the popularity of Baker's nude dances by referring to Sander Gilman's work on stereotypes and in particular his essay on Saartje Baartman, the so-called Hottentot Venus (Gilman 1985; Rose 1990: 275; Stuart 1994; Gottschild 1996). Parts of Baartman's body were embalmed after her death and put on display along with a plaster cast of her body. As a student I saw this at the Musée de l'Homme at the Trocadero and I believe the cast is still there on display. Gilman shows how her steatopygic buttocks and 'primitive' genitalia were taken by nineteenth-century Europeans as proof of 'scientific' ideas about racial difference. When one looks at Colin's poster for the 1925 revue and his design for the programme cover, these show no evidence of his needing to draw Baker in the nude. While drawn in an art deco style, they are a caricature of blackface minstrels (though his posters of her in the 1930s were less crudely stereotypical). In his 1925 poster there is a large, ill-defined egg shape under her dress around her pelvis. It is as if Baker might have buttocks like Baartman's, or as if African women are possessed of archetypal wombs blessed with primeval fertility. Although Colin was privileged to know that Baker's body was not different, when creating the 'right' image with which to market the revue, he perpetuated the stereotype.

Colin seems to have been a longer on of the Maré's for some time. He designed a poster of Jean Börlin in 1925, and back in 1920 he had designed Börlin's costume for the latter's solo *Sculpture Nègre* premiered in his first solo show at the Théâtre des Champs Elysées. The success of this solo show had convinced de Maré that it was worth starting his own ballet company, the Ballets Suédois. The circumstances surrounding the collapse of this company explain why de Maré brought over the company of African American dancers and musicians for the *Revue Nègre*.

In 1923–4 the Ballets Suédois made a financially disastrous tour of the United States. De Maré was a wealthy man and up until then the theatre and the ballet company had more or less broken even financially. On his return to France he found serious financial irregularities at the theatre. De Maré was a shy, vulnerable man and up until then most Parisians had not realised he was behind the theatre and the ballet, believing these were run by Jacques Hébertot, de Maré's theatre manager. De Maré dismissed Hébertot but didn't him take to court so his exact involvement in the affair is not known, but a lot of money from theatre receipts had gone missing. These, taken together with the losses from the American tour, caused de Maré to start to sell off some of his large collection of modernist paintings in order to go on financing the ballet. At the end of 1924, the controversial and provocative ballet *Relâche* received a mixed reception and de Maré's finances did not seem to be improving. Added to this, Börlin was becoming ill through overwork – he had created fourteen ballets in four years as well as dancing the principal role in all of them and thus giving thousands of performances. He had also been de Maré's lover but in 1925 left him to get married. De Maré therefore decided to disband the ballet company. This was partly for financial reasons and partly because, after *Relâche*, to try to do anything else artistically seemed, in Bengt Håger's words, 'retrogression or stagnation' (1990: 57). But in January 1925 de Maré still had a year's lease left on the theatre. He therefore issued a manifesto to the press announcing his decision to change its name to the Opéra Music-Hall des Champs Elysées and to show work that was as popular as music hall but of the quality of opera. Supporting this were also a series of lectures on 'primitive' dance, and in the programme of performances were appearances by a number of 'exotic' or non-Western dancers.

De Maré had become interested in ballet around 1919. Before that he had been a knowledgeable collector of modernist paintings – he had for example started to buy Léger's work in early 1915 (see Freeman 1995) – and on his protracted world tours collected ethnographic artefacts. This interest in folk art and ethnography informed his decision to found the ballet company. Part of the original intention was that the company would present Swedish folklore just as the Ballets Russes had presented Russian folklore in ballets like *Firebird* and *Sacre du Printemps*. In 1927, after de Maré's lease on the theatre had expired, he went on a long journey to the Far East where he made some documentary films about dancing in Cambodia and elsewhere, recording indigenous dance material which he believed to be dying out.

Bengt Håger comments that the Opéra Music-Hall was never intended to be permanent, and that the programmes de Maré devised 'were ruinously expensive – even though the shows were regularly performed to a full house. . . . Parisians were to remember his music hall as the most brilliant, the most lavish entertainment they had ever known' (ibid.: 58). De Maré is mentioned several times in Baker's last biography though Rose and Haney seem not to realise his importance. For example Baker wrote:

> On October 16 we began our third week of our engagement at the Champs Elysées. Monsieur Rolf is still making changes. The latest was a line of chorus girls, dressed in transparent white sheaths, parading to the music of tom-toms. On October 23, the newspapers announced that the amazing troupe currently brightening the Parisian scene' had even more surprises in store.
>
> (Baker and Bouillon 1978: 54)

Baker was therefore very lucky to have been hired by de Maré. He was passionately interested in dance and had the resources, and by 1925 the experience, to produce and promote dancers. And he clearly recognised her talents: before the premiere of the revue he repeatedly told her 'You're going to be famous, young lady' (ibid.: 51). When the revue was premiered her dancing received serious critical attention from leading writers. At this time this would never have happened in New York. Graham in 1925 did not receive the kind of serious critical attention that Baker received.[14]

In arguing that Baker 'landed on her feet' when she was booked for the *Revue Nègre*, I do not wish to underestimate the extent to which European intellectuals misrecognised her blackness. What attracted these intellectuals to Baker (and to other African American dancers, singers and musicians) were her supposedly authentic African roots and what these meant in the context of French social and intellectual currents in the 1920s. Some of the critics who were most violently opposed to Baker's performance in the *Revue Nègre* felt that what she represented was a degenerate threat, and that enjoyment of her dancing was acquiescence in a process of moral decay. Thus Robert de Flers, writing in the *Figaro* called the show a 'lamentable transatlantic exhibitionism which makes us revert to the ape in less time than it took us to descend from it' (quoted in Rose 1990: 32). In response to Flers' article, Paul Guillaume wrote in the revue's defence, citing a check-list of all the painters and writers who had been inspired by African art: Picasso, Derain, Matisse, Segonzac, Laurencin, Braque, Léger and Modigliani, and among the writers Cendrars, Apollinaire, Breton, Eluard and Cocteau. He then made the strange remark that 'we who think we have a soul will blush at the poverty of our spiritual state before the superiority of blacks who have four souls, one in the head, one in the nose and throat, the shadow, and one in the blood' (quoted in Rose 1990: 45). Guillaume acknowledges in this article that European culture might be a dying civilisation.

Writing in 1939, Michel Leiris characterises the taste for jazz in the 1920s in similar terms:

> In the period of great licence that followed the hostilities, jazz was a sign of allegiance, an orgiastic tribute to the colours of the moment. It functioned magically, and its means of influence can be compared to a kind of possession. It was the element that gave these celebrations their true meaning, with communion by dance, latent or manifest exoticism, and drinks the most effective means of bridging the gap that separates individuals from each other at any gathering. Swept along by violent bursts of tropical energy, jazz still had enough of a 'dying civilisation' about it, of humanity blindly submitting to The Machine, to express quite completely the state of mind of at least some of that generation: a more or less conscious demoralisation born of the war, a naïve fascination with the comfort and the latest inventions of progress, a predilection for a contemporary setting whose insanity we nonetheless vaguely anticipated, an abandonment to the animal joy of experiencing the influence of a modern rhythm, an underlying aspiration to a new life in which more room would be made for an impassioned frankness we inarticulately longed for. In jazz, too, came the first appearance of *Negroes*,

the manifestation and the myth of black Edens which were to lead
me to Africa and, beyond Africa, to ethnography.

(quoted in Clifford 1989: 902)

In Leiris, as in de Maré, one can discern a coming together of three strands:
an interest in jazz, an interest in ethnography, and a taste for modernism.
From a modernist point of view, exotic people, objects and styles of performance were consigned to the past. Baker's 'African' dance (like the
Cambodian dances de Maré filmed) was therefore valued as a purer and
more rare cultural expression than those at the time available within the
over-civilised, dehumanised and decaying culture of modern Europe (see
also Clifford 1988). Thus, even though many Europeans admired what they
took to be 'African' culture, the manner in which they interpreted it tells us
more about Europeans in the 1920s and 1930s than it does about the lived
experience of Africans and African Americans during the same period. They
saw in Baker's dynamic spontaneity and wild abandon[15] a pure spark of
vitality of the kind they believed was needed to inspire a longed-for cultural
renewal.

Baker and the slender modern body

When Josephine Baker and the other African American dancers and
performers arrived at the Opéra Music-Hall des Champs Elysées with their
show, their performance didn't fit the management's idea of what a 'revue
nègre' should look like. In the new final number Baker danced for the first
time naked. Perhaps the most interesting and beautifully written description of Baker's nude performances is by Colette, in her preview of Baker's
1936 appearance in the Folies-Bergère show, *En Super Folies*.

> The hard work of the company rehearsals seem to have made her
> slimmer, without stripping the flesh from her delicate bone struc-
> ture; her oval knees, her ankles flower from the clear, beautiful,
> even-textured brown skin with which Paris is besotted. The years,
> and coaching, have perfected an elongated and discreet bone-
> structure and retained the admirable convexity of her thighs.
> Joséphine's shoulder-blades are unobtrusive, her shoulders light, she
> has the belly of a young girl and a high-placed navel. Naked except
> for three gilt flowers, pursued by her four assailants, she assumes
> the serious, unsmiling look of a sleepwalker, which ennobles a
> daring music-hall number. Her huge eyes, outlined in black and
> blue, gaze forth, her cheeks are flushed, the moist and dazzling
> sweetness of her teeth shows between dark and violet lips – her face
> shows no response to the quadruple embrace under which her pliant
> body seems to melt. Paris is going to see, on the stage of the Folies,

how Joséphine Baker, in the nude, shows all other nude dancers the meaning of modesty.

(quoted in Hammond and O'Connor 1988: 142–3)

This is a remarkable piece of writing for several reasons. First, apart from the mention of Baker's even-textured brown skin, there is no suggestion that she was in any way different from anyone else on account of her colour. Baker is what she is as an individual, not as a member of any particular race. Second, this is an extremely intimate piece of writing about a body that is nevertheless not eroticised for the delectation of a male reader. It describes a boyish or androgynous body. Patrick O'Connor, who quotes the passage, takes it as evidence that Baker's performances were open to a lesbian interpretation. This may well have been the case, but what is perhaps more significant about Colette's description is that it suggests how women in the 1920s and 1930s, regardless of their sexuality, may have responded to the spectacle of Baker's nude, dancing body. Colette's appreciation of Baker's body is informed by her experience of her own body. She does not see Baker's body as natural and essential but as the product of hard work. She knows from her own experience what it is like to try to create and maintain such a slender body. Colette also appreciates, from her own nude performances at the Folies-Bergère in 1907, that it is not just Baker's body that is a construction but also her skill as a performer.

As is increasingly being recognised by cultural theorists at the end of the twentieth century, the shape of bodies and of female bodies in particular, are historically and culturally specific. What Colette refers to in her description of Baker's performance is the form of the modern body of the 1920s and 1930s. One of the reasons why Baker attained and maintained her status as a star was surely the fact that in the form of her body as well as in her singing and dancing, female spectators could read important aspects of their historically specific experiences of modernity.

Susan Bordo argues that the Western fashion for the slender body has its origins at the end of the late nineteenth century:

> Social power had come to be less dependent on the sheer accumulation of material wealth and more connected to the ability to control and manage labour and resources of others. At the same time, excess body weight came to be seen as reflecting moral or personal inadequacy, or lack of will. These associations are possible only in a culture of over-abundance – that is, in a society in which those who control the production of 'culture' have more than enough to eat.
>
> (Bordo 1993: 192)

She also points out that it is at times when women have been challenging men in the public sphere and competing with them for jobs in the world of work – in the 1890s, 1920s and from the mid-1960s to the present – that slenderness has become a fashion norm. By contrast, in periods when women have been encouraged to return to the home and adopt more traditionally subservient feminine roles, the fashion silhouette has become more lush and curvaceous – for example the figures of Marilyn Monroe and Sophia Loren in the 1950s. The boyishness of the slender body, Bordo suggests, can be read as a way of reducing the psychological threat to the men with whom working women compete. From a female point of view, a preoccupation with slenderness that can verge on the anorexic can be seen as a denial of signs of maternity. Thus, for women: 'Disidentification with the maternal body, far from symbolising reduced power, may symbolise . . . freedom from a reproductive destiny and a construction of femininity seen as constraining and suffocating' (ibid.: 209).

Colette's description of Baker presents a body that is stripped of signs of maternity. When Colette says Baker has the belly of a young girl she is referring to the fact that Baker has had no children. For those female viewers in the 1920s and 1930s who enjoyed new female consumer lifestyles, the revelation of Baker's body in performance must thus have evoked an ideal of liberation from women's traditional domestic, reproductive destiny.[16] The advertising endorsements that Baker made for a number of beauty products and her assignments modelling couture fashions for fashion magazines like *Vogue* and *Harpers Bazaar* attest to the centrality of Baker's image within the marketing of consumer lifestyles for such 'new women'.

Baker's image was of course not static but highly mobile. By introducing the Charleston to Paris, Baker defined the core movement experience of the so-called jazz age. Haskell, Levinson and others, as we have seen, abhorred jazz. The bright young things, of course, didn't take any notice. Jazz gave young people in the 1920s an experience that, as we have seen, Michel Leiris characterised as 'an abandonment to the animal joy of experiencing the influence of a modern rhythm, an underlying aspiration to a new life in which more room would be made for an impassioned frankness we inarticulately longed for' (quoted in Clifford 1989: 902). One small part of a Charleston step that I identified in Baker's 'banana' dance sums up what was at stake here. During this step, the dancer places her weight forwards over her toes and alternately slides her heels towards and away from one another, causing her knees to move in the opposite direction. Take the moment when the heels are furthest apart and the knees almost knock together: this momentary position is the complete antithesis of the turned-out stance that is at the heart of ballet and was central to formal, respectful deportment in the higher levels of European society. In ballet and the traditional social dances of middle- and upper-class European society, the torso and pelvis area move as one – almost as if fused together – while in African and jazz dances the legs, pelvis, and upper torso can of course move independently of one another, each marking out a different rhythm – what Gottschild calls polycentrism/polyrhythm. In abandoning herself to the experience of modern rhythms, the 'new woman' dancing the Charleston was therefore abandoning codes of self-presentation through respectful deportment that had mediated important social distinctions upon which the social structure of European society up until the First World War had depended. It was that war and the turmoil of the modernisation and industrial restructuring that followed it, rather than the Charleston, that undermined and did away with older forms of social hierarchy. Haskell, Levinson and their ilk may have deplored their passing but what reason had the 'new women' of the 1920s for wanting to hang on to them? Those women who envied Baker's boyish figure and the impassioned frankness of her performances were registering their longing for a 'new life'. For them, the wild energy, disruption and frenzy of Baker's 'savage' dances meant progress.

Dislocation, disruption and frenzy

So far I have examined a number of different points of view from which Baker's 'savage' dances were interpreted by her contemporaries. Baker's performances had a broad appeal because they dealt with aspects of the experience of modernity which were of wide concern at that time. Baker in the 1920s and 1930s typified the transcendency of the star over the ordinary and wearisome nature of the everyday. André Levinson wrote of her that her personality exceeded her genre. Her star sign was undoubtedly the sign of excess. Baker's acts were extremely and exquisitely glamorous and spectacular. Her sequinned cache-sexes, her dyed ostrich feather tail-pieces, and her gilded, diamante-studded girdle of bananas were the stunning costumes she wore for dazzling entrances in, for example, the celebrated, giant Fabergé-style egg in *La Folie du Jour* or the gilded bird-cage in the film *Zouzou*, or down the grand staircases that were the indispensable prop of the leading revue theatres of the day. Baker was, in a word, charismatic.

Charisma is the very essence of showbiz stardom. It is also a notion that the sociologist Max Weber developed in the field of political theory to account for the authority of political leaders. Richard Dyer, while acknowledging that there are problems in transferring the notion of charisma from political to film theory, suggests that there are nevertheless useful correspondences between political and showbiz charisma, particularly with regard to 'the question of how or why a given person comes to have "charisma" attributed to her or him':

> Charismatic appeal is effective especially when the social order is
> uncertain, unstable and ambiguous and when the charismatic figure
> or group offers a value, order or stability to counterpoise this.
> Linking a star with the whole of society may not get us very far in
> these terms, unless one takes twentieth century Western society to

have been in constant instability. Rather, one needs to think in terms of the [various kinds of] relationships . . . between stars and the specific instabilities, ambiguities and contradictions in the culture (which are reproduced in the actual process of making films and film stars).

(Dyer 1979: 35)

I am extending Dyer's comments on film stars to include stars like Baker who were primarily live entertainers. Baker and her audiences in the 1920s were living through a period of social instability, ambiguity and contradiction. When critics ended up describing Baker's performances with words like dislocation, disruption and frenzy, these were words that might otherwise have summed up the social experiences of metropolitan modernity. Her dancing must have seemed to embody so much of what was strange and worrying in her audiences' everyday lived experience; yet she herself was able to use these qualities, as Ethel Waters put it, 'to dance joy into you'. Baker's star image was a means through which concern about social and cultural instabilities, ambiguities and contradictions was ameliorated or defused. The 'savage' dances used the signs and forms of modernity to represent freedom from the puritan moralising of nineteenth-century bourgeois culture. By creating a positive image of personal enjoyment, Baker in effect supported the modernist myth of social, scientific and technological progress.

Apart from commenting that Paris was besotted with Baker's clear, beautiful, even-textured brown skin, there is nothing in Colette's beautiful review to suggest that Baker was different from anyone else on account of her colour. By 1936, Baker's nude appearances had done much to correct notions of racial difference based on misinformation about steatopygia and 'primitive' genitalia. Back in 1925 the fear and fascination, the pleasure and disgust that her racial difference evoked for white Parisian audiences was undoubtedly a key factor in the success of the *Revue Nègre* and with it Baker's ascent to stardom. It was a time when older social structures and hierarchies were breaking down or becoming blurred. It could be said that individuals who, for whatever reasons, felt undermined by 'progress', feared that their sense of their own distinctness and individuality was being erased. What were being blurred were the differences between self and 'other'. Enjoyment of the spectacle of Baker's 'savage' dances made the erasure of difference fun. Jazz was the music of a group deemed 'other'. To lose oneself in it was an abandonment to animal joys that, as Michel Leiris put it, were inarticulately yearned for. Dancing to jazz music in a dance Baker introduced to Paris was for white Europeans a temporary, ritualised blurring of the difference between self and 'other' through losing themselves in the strong, 'primitive' rhythms of the music. This is what Baker articulated in her dances.

Two more incidents that exemplify this yearning conclude the chapter: first, from Baker's autobiography:

> As opening night [of the *Revue Nègre*] approached, our rehearsal schedule grew more and more hectic. Some of the troupe were so disgusted they were ready to take the boat home. Not I. I felt happy and free. Sensing that the organisers liked my work made me blossom like a flower. If it had been December I would have called Monsieur Rolf my Santa Claus. He liked to put his index finger on the top of my head (he was very tall) and twirl me around like a top. When I had stopped spinning he would say in a serious voice: 'You're going to be famous, young lady'.
>
> (Baker and Bouillon 1978: 51)

The second incident can be reconstructed from a scene captured in a photograph of Baker at her Paris night club 'Chez Joséphine'. She is posing on the dance floor with an unidentified but deliciously embarrassed male customer. She wears a beautiful white silk, full-length dress and has paused while dancing alone with her partner whose arm tentatively circles her waist. Behind them the other customers sitting at tables are laughing, looking at Baker with obvious, but warm amusement. This is because she has gracefully lifted her arms and delicately placed one finger of one hand on her own head and one finger of her other hand on her partner's head. It is as if she is about to twirl them both around like tops, just as she says de Maré had twirled her around. At the moment the photograph was taken she has just crossed her eyes. The man, wearing a sober lounge suit, is standing with knees slightly bent and his feet pointing in, probably in a stance from the Charleston. He is smiling sheepishly and his eyes have a surprised expression as if caught by the photographer's flash at a moment when he is not at all certain what he must look like. His one hand tentatively touches her waist while the other has instinctively risen to half cover his embarrassed, smiling mouth. He has probably had too much to drink, or perhaps eaten some of the petits pain fourrés au hachis – hash brownies – that were a speciality of the house. He is entirely in her hands. He probably suspects that she is making him look ridiculous, and later may mock him, calling his bottom something like 'ironing board butt'. But for this one moment, caught by the camera's lens, he's deliriously happy. Touching and being touched, out of his head, rubbing up against stardom, he is letting a little of that glamorous 'otherness' onto the other side of the boundary that separates inside and out so that those awkward and problematic binaries are perhaps, just for the moment, dissolving into wholeness.

Figure 4 Josephine Baker posing on the dance floor of Chez Jospéphine with an unidentified but deliciously embarrassed male customer

Source: National Archives, Washington

4

THE CHORUS LINE AND THE
EFFICIENCY ENGINEERS

Performing with Josephine Baker in the revue *La Folie du Jour* at the Folies-Bergère in 1926–7 were a troupe of Tiller Girls. Those that Doremy Vernon interviewed for her book, *Tiller's Girls*, remembered Baker as unusually friendly for a leading star. If Baker had started touring on an American vaudeville circuit at the age of 13, the Tiller girls had often started dancing for John Tiller at the age of 8 or 10 in Manchester or Blackpool. Baker was the same age as many of them, and as Vernon notes:

> They were filled with admiration for her highly individual personality; they had been trained to sink their personalities into the line and were happy to do so. Although they were in the same show and of the same age, they were worlds apart as women and performers.
>
> (Vernon 1988: 78)

John Tiller (1854–1925) was a successful Manchester cotton broker who, as Vernon recounts, had always been attracted to the theatre and, having devised in 1890 a successful children's dance number, went on to apply his business skills to building up a successful production company specialising in children's and women's chorus line dance acts. The company recruited young Lancashire girls from working-class inner city Manchester and later from other Lancashire towns. It was initially Tiller himself who trained the dancers, demanding a precision that in its day was called military, and up until his death it was he who arranged the dances. One former Tiller recalled a gruelling rehearsal with him in Blackpool before the First World War:

> We went on for what seemed hours and still none of us understood. Eventually he bent over and told the Head Girl [the leading dancer in the troupe] to kick him; she was amazed but she did so – just stepped forward and kicked him and that was exactly the step he wanted. They call it the strut now.
>
> (ibid.: 64)

At first this appears to suggest that Tiller wasn't good at communicating with his dancers, but it probably also indicates the problems of working with dancers who are narrowly trained from a young age to submerge their personalities in order to achieve uniform precision. This chapter is not primarily concerned with the Tiller Girls as such, but with what their precision dancing and with it this submergence of individuality signified to German intellectuals in the 1920s, and in particular to Siegfried Kracauer.

John Tiller had been dead two years but his company was still at the height of its success when in 1927 Siegfried Kracauer wrote a now famous essay 'The mass ornament'. In this, Kracauer proposed that the anonymous precision of the Tiller Girls' dancing (which he also linked with mass gymnastic displays) was not only an expression of the rhythm of modern times, but also filled a gap that was created by modern metropolitan life. What Kracauer identified in the dancing of the Tiller Girls was an image of social totality for which the individual yearned because of her or his experience of the fragmentation and alienation of metropolitan existence. He called their dancing Taylorist, referring to the scientific approach to industrial efficiency developed by F. W. Taylor. (The popularity of Taylor's ideas among European artists and intellectuals was referred to in Chapter 2). Kracauer saw in the phenomenon he called the mass ornament an instance in which the individual could lose her- or himself, blurring the distinction between self and Other by becoming part of a coherent, unitary mass. In 1927 Kracauer saw this in philosophical terms as an undermining of the rational unitary subject of the Enlightenment. Initially Kracauer saw the dancing of the Tiller Girls both as a sign of the fragmentation and the approaching demise of capitalism, and as a utopian glimpse of new possibilities of social harmony. By 1931 this hope for a new social order had turned sour with the rise of fascism. By 1947 Kracauer viewed the mass ornament as a symptom of German society's slide towards totalitarianism and fascism. As his political analysis altered with changing circumstances, so did his view of the relationship between the subjective experience of embodiment and the holding of moral and political values. It is this issue around which I am focusing my discussion of Kracauer's discussion of the Chorus Girl phenomenon and rhythmic gymnastics.

Kracauer's essay is useful for a number of reasons. Published in 1927 in the *Frankfurter Zeitung*, it was written at the height of an economic boom in Weimar Germany and thus before the rise of the National Socialists and the subsequent association of fascism and body culture. Far from being a keen dancer or an advocate of body culture, Kracauer was an 'up tight', Jewish, left-wing intellectual who was neither knowledgeable about nor sympathetic towards dance or body culture. He was, however, an acute and fascinating commentator on cultural trends. Kracauer's insights into the social and cultural context of the rise of body culture during the early years of the twentieth century and his sceptical critique of its ideological premises make this essay a useful vantage point from which to evaluate subsequent uses of body culture within National Socialist propaganda. In this chapter and the next I follow the changing political meanings that Kracauer articulated when he discussed the mass ornament, between its first expression in the article of that name in 1927 and its later use in his 1947 book *From Caligari to Hitler*. By the mass ornament Kracauer meant both the precision kick dancing of chorus girl troupes like the Tiller Girls and mass spectacles of a theatrical and sporting nature in outdoor theatres and stadiums. This chapter examines Kracauer's social and philosophical thesis and places this in the context of Weimar society. It is also concerned with the connections Kracauer made between jazz dancing and modernity. The next chapter starts with a discussion of a film extract showing a gymnastic display which comes from Leni Riefenstahl's documentary film of the 1936 Olympic Games. This is then used as a basis for interrogating the uses that the National Socialists made of the mass ornament and of Weimar body culture.

Kracauer and the mass ornament

Until recently Siegfried Kracauer (1889–1966) was best known for his work in the United States, in particular his two books *From Caligari to Hitler* (1947) and *Theory of Film* (1960). Of all his writings from the 1920s and early 1930s for the *Frankfurter Zeitung*, it is 'The mass ornament' that has attracted the most comment. When in the early 1960s Kracauer prepared a collection of his early essays for re-publication in German, the book was called *Das Ornament der Masse* (1963) after the essay, and the recent English translation of Kracauer's Weimar essays by Thomas Y. Levin is also called *The Mass Ornament* (1995). The original essay has of course attracted attention for its combination of philosophical and sociological methods of analysis, rather than for what it reveals about dance and body culture. As Karsten Witte observes, it 'contains *in nuce* all the key categories of his method and his critique' (Witte 1975: 59, emphasis in the original). It is almost programmatic in the way that it lays out Kracauer's approach to the interpretation of ephemeral manifestations from popular, mass culture. It is in the unconscious nature of these, Kracauer asserts at the start of the essay, that the underlying meanings of an epoch can be most clearly glimpsed. In applying this approach to the dancing of the Tiller Girls and to various forms of body culture, Kracauer applies an ideological critique of capitalist society that combines Marxism with the German sociological tradition of Max Weber and Georg Simmel (Kracauer having studied with the latter).

'The mass ornament' also marks a turning point between Kracauer's early writings about religious and mystical thought and his later more politicised writings. Where the two seem to overlap, as Miriam Hansen observes, is in his 'apocalyptic sense of withdrawal of meaning from the world, which blends contemporary theories of alienation and reification (Weber, Lukács) with the imagery of Jewish Messianism and Gnosticism' (Hansen 1992: 64). In essays like 'The mass ornament', the way in which Kracauer theorises the impact of modernity on the individual as a diminution of the rationally constituted subject (as Kant defined it), is seen as a precursor for the negative dialectics of Theodor Adorno (1903–69) and Max Horkheimer (1895–1973). The group of Jewish intellectuals who in the early 1920s used to meet in a café near the Opera House in Frankfurt subsequently became key figures in the field of post-Second World War philosophy (see Lowenthal 1991), and current interest in Kracauer has a lot to do with his role in the origins of what is now called the Frankfurt School. Somewhere along the line, however, the original dance and movement that inspired Kracauer to write 'The mass ornament' have got lost. My intention here is to bring dancing bodies back into the discussion. As well as providing a useful overview of the context of performances of mass ornamental movements, Kracauer discusses these in terms of groups, gymnastics, and bodies as machines; in doing so he develops concepts of distraction, abstraction, spatiality and subjectivity that he applies to the analysis of the cultural forms within which the mass ornament occurs. It is these notions and concepts that I shall use to interpret the film extract of mass gymnastics with which the next chapter starts.

The following briefly summarises Kracauer's essay. Within the domain of body culture and dance, the mass ornament produced by groups like the Tiller Girls exemplifies through its abstractness and precision the rationalising process of the capitalist system. The project of the Enlightenment is one of increasing the human capacity for reason and thus freeing individuals from the irrational fear of nature. Capitalist modernity constitutes a particular form of abstract rationalisation, which Kracauer calls the *Ratio*. Through reification, the capitalist *Ratio* increases wealth without having to increase the human being's capacity for reason and thus does nothing to free humanity from an irrational dependency on nature. Capitalist modernity, Kracauer pronounces, 'rationalises not too much but rather too little' (1995: 81). In some forms of body culture human beings express a yearning for a mythical organic past: this is irrational because it regresses to a dependence on and awe of nature. The mass ornament, however, is produced by the *Ratio*, and is therefore less natural and less retrogressive than other forms of body culture. It therefore has the potential to increase humanity's capacity for reason.

Context

In 1927 Kracauer was not the only or the first intellectual to discuss chorus line dancers in revues. Fritz Geise had discussed them in his 1925 book *Girlkultur*, while in Paris, André Levinson wrote an article 'The Girls' in 1928. In this Levinson comes to very similar conclusions about the meaninglessness of their precise, abstract, machine-like choreography to those Kracauer expressed. Levinson and Kracauer, Jewish intellectuals born within two years of each other, were both admirers of classical rationality and its expression in formalism, both being close readers of Kant. (Where they differed was in politics: Levinson a passionately anti-communist refugee from communist Russia, Kracauer a Marxist and subsequently a refugee from National Socialist Germany. Levinson's article 'Girls' is discussed in the next chapter.) Another intellectual who subsequently wrote about the chorus line dancers was Walter Benjamin in a fragment from his unfinished *Arcades* project. Benjamin was an acquaintance of Kracauer's in the 1920s who became closer to him when both were refugees in Paris in the 1930s. Benjamin makes a connection between Baudelaire's poem 'The Seven Old Men' and chorus line dancers. In his poem, Baudelaire expressed his horror while out wandering the new boulevards at seeing, one after the other, seven disreputable old men. Benjamin interprets this, as Susan Buck-Morss points out, as horror at mass production. Hence he makes a connection between chorus line dancers and the seven old men: both seem uncannily, unnaturally identical, just as mass produced goods are identical (Buck-Morss 1989: 190–3). Benjamin here was almost certainly following Kracauer who saw the Tiller Girls as embodying the logic of mass production through the precision of their dancing.

Kracauer doesn't initially define what he means by the mass ornament. The precision kick dancing of the Tiller Girls is just one aspect of what he discusses. He starts off by referring to the domain of body culture and its representation in the illustrated papers; he singles out mass spectacles in sports stadiums which can be seen in weekly newsreels even in the tiniest villages, but he leaves his category open to other unspecified occurrences. (Many of the types of stadium sports displays to which Kracauer refers will have been produced under the auspices of left-wing workers' sports associations.) By coining the phrase 'the mass ornament', Kracauer was referring to a widespread phenomenon with which he assumes his readers in the *Frankfurter Zeitung* would be familiar. Kracauer was no dance writer and he gave no description of any of the movement material to which he referred. John Tiller had come up with the definitive kick line around 1910 when he first directed his dancers to link their arms around each other's waists. This added proximity enabled their kicks to be more precisely co-ordinated. Essentially this set the pattern for the familiar chorus line that is probably familiar to the reader: a line of female dancers (generally eight or sixteen) who enter the stage in a long line, facing front and smiling. In the 1920s they generally wore shorts or short skirts that allowed their whole leg to be seen, since this was the primary focus of their performance. The steps consisted of precisely co-ordinated kicks in various directions with or without bending the knee, either with all the dancers performing in unison or with a ripple effect where a movement starts at one end and moves along the line like a wave. Arms may also be co-ordinated in a similar way. The line of dancers may break up into segments which then move into sequences of simple, symmetrical geometric floor patterns. The main feature of this kind of dancing is the effect that is achieved through precise co-ordination. It was this geometric rationality that principally interested Kracauer and which he linked with gymnastic and other spectacular displays in outdoor stadiums.

The fact that there was popular fascination at this time with this kind of imagery is supported by Maud Lavin. In her study of the artist Hannah Hoch's work, Lavin analyses the scrapbooks that Hoch kept during the Weimar period. Among the photographs Hoch cut out of popular illustrated magazines are many pictures of mass ornaments. Lavin, for example, discusses a photograph of women in a Moscow cinema college, sunbathing under the studio lamps: they are arranged in a perfect circle with feet all radiating from the centre. Next to it Hoch had stuck a very similar circle showing women in a modern dance class in Hanover (Lavin 1993: 70). Another couple of scrapbook pages include an aerial shot of a synchronised swimming display, women sunbathing on a beach, lying again in a circle with their feet radiating out, but this time making up a clock face with numbers on their swim suits and in the middle of the circle, giant clock hands (ibid.: 88–9). The range of images in Hoch's scrapbooks show how international this taste for the mass ornament was: although they don't feature in these, Busby Berkeley's spectacular dance sequences were an American example of the phenomenon. Lavin points out that almost all these images of mass ornaments are of women. She argues that from a male point of view, the mass ornament is 'desired but perhaps also feared, a fantasy of women embodying industrial technology, a condition specific to 1920s attitudes towards technology' (ibid.: 86). From the point of view of women in the 1920s, Lavin points out the continuity between images of mass ornaments and commodified images of women in advertising material:

Women were encouraged to aspire to the status of mannequins with the help of commodities, and the commodity itself was offered as an ideal with which to identify. Fascination with the mass ornament meant, however, that not all inducements to conform to a techno-cratic modernism were necessarily individualistic but could also have spoken to a desire to be part of a smoothly functioning collec-tive unit or a unified 'class' of modern women. In addition, the interest of a female viewer in the public nature of the mass orna-ment presentation could be interpreted allegorically as a desire for the creation of a legitimate female public sphere.

(ibid.: 93)

Groups

Kracauer used presentations of mass ornamental movements as a way of discussing what to him was the central problematic of modernity. He contrasted it with other forms of dancing and body culture that did not for him touch upon 'the unconscious nature of modernity'. Ballet and military displays he dismissed as survivals from the past.[1] Other newer areas of body culture constituted different types of reactions against the dehumanising aspects of modernity that were, in Kracauer's view, romantic and reactionary. One of the types of performance that Kracauer refers to were communal groups of the people (*Völk*) who make performances: 'A current of organic life surges from these communal groups – which share a common destiny – to their ornaments endowing these ornaments with a magical force and burdening them with meaning' (Kracauer 1995: 76). Kracauer relates this type of group performance with that by 'those who have withdrawn from the community and consider themselves to be unique personalities with their own individual souls' (ibid.). Again these rituals or performances are not identified specifically and Kracauer may have assumed that his readers would be familiar with the sorts of performances to which he was referring. He might be referring here to the medievalising cults initiated by the Stefan George circle, or to Eurythmy performances by the Anthroposophists – the followers of Rudolf Steiner. Both groups are referred to in Kracauer's 1922 essay 'Those who wait'. Within the same broadly defined genre were the *bewegungschore* or movement choirs of Emile Jaques-Dalcroze and Rudolf Laban. Though I am not aware of references to either of these two figures in Kracauer's writing of the time, Kracauer might also be referring to these types of performance; by 1924 there were twelve Laban movement choirs in existence including one in Frankfurt run by Sylvia Bodman and Lotte Müller which Kracauer might perhaps have come across (Preston-Dunlop and Hodson 1990: 129). There were a variety of large scale community performances in Germany. As Henning Eichberg has observed: 'Amateur plays, open-air theatres, scenic stage, drama for the masses . . . had been growing since 1900, and . . . had taken shape in the ethnic (völkish), catholic social democratic, communist and locally commercial spheres' (Eichberg 1977: 147). For Kracauer, it is the organic, magical, or mythical types of meanings that distinguish these group performances from those presenting mass ornaments. The latter, however, far from being burdened with meaning, has none at all. Kracauer himself is critical of any quasi-mystical or cult-like group, having himself renounced an earlier adherence to Messianic Jewish beliefs. This leads Thomas Levin (in the 1995 edition of *The Mass Ornament*) to describe some of Kracauer's more metaphysical thinking as lapsarian (Kracauer 1995: 13; see also Lowenthal 1991).

Gymnastics

The other areas of body culture that Kracauer referred to in 'The mass ornament' are various types of gymnastics. Of rhythmic gymnastics, Kracauer
commented with characteristic acerbity that their teachers go 'beyond
personal hygiene' to 'the expression of spruced-up states of the soul – to
which instructors of body culture often add world views' (1995: 85). Here,
as elsewhere, it is the relationship between rationality and modernity with
which Kracauer is primarily concerned.

> These instructors seek to recapture the organic connection of nature
> with something the all too modest temperament takes to be soul or
> spirit – that is, exalting the body by assigning it meanings which
> emanate from it and may indeed be spiritual but which do not
> contain the slightest trace of reason.
>
> (ibid.: 86)

Like the communal magical or mythical performances discussed above, it is
the pretension to conveying meanings that Kracauer is attacking here. From
Kracauer's point of view such gymnastic and dance instructors are deluding
themselves and their pupils about the withdrawal of meaning from the
modern world. Compared with such 'meaningful', organic (and thus irrational) movement activities, the mass ornament made by the Tiller Girls'
dancing and in displays at huge sports stadiums were not only more rational
but did not claim to mean anything at all.

There is perhaps an inconsistency here in Kracauer's notion of the mass
ornament. He lumps together the precise kick dancing of the chorus line
with the mass gymnastic display in the stadium. Yet surely the stadium
display consists of gymnastic movements which Kracauer denounces elsewhere for their organic connection with nature. It seems likely that Kracauer
hadn't actually seen a mass gymnastic display live but only within a newsreel film, as it is in this form that it is mentioned in the essay. Filmed from a
distance, such stadium presentations become detached and dehumanised;
they thus exhibit the abstracted precision that Kracauer identified within
the dancing of the Tiller Girls. The presence of the body itself is lost on
film. Experienced as a live event, however, the stadium display would not
have entirely corresponded to the rational (unnatural, inorganic) qualities
Kracauer attributes to the mass ornament.

Bodies as machines

It is the precision of the Tiller Girls that Kracauer discusses as his main
example of the mass ornament. A cartoon by Paul Simmel from the *Berliner
Illustrirte Zeitung* in October 1926 which shows Tiller Girls coming out of a

factory on a conveyor belt, bears the caption 'Ford takes over the production of Tiller Girls'. Published before Kracauer's essay, this anticipates one of its jokes – that the Tiller Girls are mass produced in 'American distraction factories' (Kracauer 1995: 75) by which Kracauer means factories that manufacture forms of commodified distraction[2] – and his main theme: 'The structure of the mass ornament reflects that of the entire contemporary situation' (ibid.: 78) and: 'The mass ornament is the aesthetic reflex of the rationality to which the prevailing economic system aspires' (ibid.: 79). In a later essay 'Girls and Crisis', in which Kracauer looked back in 1931 at his earlier essay, he explored this theme in a lighter and more fanciful way. Stating that the 'girls' were mass produced in the USA and exported to Europe in waves', he proceeds:

> They were not merely American products but a demonstration at the same time of the vastness of American production. I clearly recall seeing such troupes in the season of their fame. When they formed themselves into an undulating snake, they delivered a radiant illustration of the virtues of the conveyor belt; when they stepped to a rapid beat, it sounded like 'business, business'; when they raised their legs with mathematical precision over their heads, they joyfully affirmed the progress of rationalisation; and when they continually repeated the same manoeuvre, never breaking ranks, one had the vision of an unbroken chain of automobiles gliding out of the factory into the world and the feeling of knowing that there was no end to prosperity.
>
> (Kracauer 1994: 565)

When Kracauer writes of an unbroken chain of automobiles gliding out of a factory, he is probably thinking of the fact that in Europe in the late 1920s it took eight workmen to make seven cars in the same time that five American workmen produced fifty-five cars (Wollen 1993: 40). The retrospective tone of this article indicates that by 1931 Kracauer had realised that there was after all an end to the prosperity which the Tiller Girls' dancing had exemplified. In the light of the economic depression and the rise of fascism,[3] the mass ornament appeared to him a delusion. What earlier had been informed by an avant-garde sensibility was now described with a witty cynicism. Back in 1927 he asserted that 'the aesthetic pleasure gained from ornamental mass movements is legitimate' and 'No matter how low one gauges the value of the mass ornament, its degree of reality is still higher than that of artistic productions which cultivate outdated noble sentiments in obsolete forms – even if it means nothing more than that' (Kracauer 1995: 79).

Distraction

Some clues as to why Kracauer believed this was the case can be found in another slightly earlier essay, 'Cult of distraction' (published in March 1926). In this Kracauer argued that intellectuals, like everyone else in the big city 'are being absorbed by the masses, a process that creates the *homogenous cosmopolitan audience* in which everyone has the *same* response' (ibid.: 325, emphasis in the original). So, to put it simply, if Kracauer as an intellectual could see the meaninglessness of mass cultural products, so should everyone else. Writing about Berlin cinemas that offered programmes combining films with live revue acts, Kracauer proposed:

> Indeed the very fact that the shows aiming at distraction are composed of the same mixture of externalities as the world of the urban masses; the fact that these shows lack any authentic and materially motivated coherence, except possibly the glue of sentimentality, which covers up this lack but only in order to make it all the more visible; the fact that these shows convey precisely and openly to thousands of eyes and ears the *disorder* of society – this is precisely what would enable them to evoke and maintain the tension that must precede the inevitable and radical change. In the streets of Berlin, one is often suddenly struck by the momentary insight that someday all this will suddenly burst apart. The entertainment to which the general public throngs ought to produce the same effect.
>
> (ibid.: 327, emphasis in the original)

Kracauer hopes that the masses will recognise the meaninglessness of mass culture and thus become radicalised and engage in political action. This avant-garde hope is repeated at the ending of 'The mass ornament':

> The process leads directly through the centre of the mass ornament, not away from it. It can move forward only when thinking circumscribes nature and produces man as he is constituted by reason. Then society will change. Then, too, the mass ornament will fade away and human life itself will adopt the traits of that ornament into which it develops, through its confrontation with truth, in fairy tales.
>
> (ibid.: 86)

Abstraction

Kracauer's hope that society will progress through transcending the mass ornament has resonances within European architecture in the early twentieth century, with which Kracauer, who worked as an architect from 1916 to 1922, would almost certainly have been familiar. The conclusion of 'The mass ornament' echoes a similar sentiment expressed by the Viennese architect Adolf Loos in his controversial essay of 1908, 'Ornament and Crime'. In this essay, with which Kracauer must surely have been familiar, Loos defends his practice of designing unornamented buildings by adopting what is perhaps a self-mockingly ornamental, Nietzschean literary style:

> Weep not. Behold! What makes our period so important is that it is incapable of producing new ornament. We have out-grown ornament, we have struggled through to a state without ornament. Behold, the time is at hand, fulfilment awaits us. Soon the streets of the cities will glow like white walls! Like Zion, the Holy City, the capital of heaven. It is then that fulfilment will have come.
>
> (Loos 1985: 100)

Kracauer's notion of the development of body culture from organic, mystical forms to abstract, modernist ones can also be seen as paralleling developments in modern architecture. A crystalline and organic style of expressionist architecture, found for example in the work of Poelzig and Bruno Taut, had its origins before the First World War. After the war, the Weimar Bauhaus also exemplified this with its tendency, under the influence of Johannes Itten, towards mysticism and cults. All of this gave way in the mid-1920s to the international, modernist style of architecture and design exemplified by the Dessau Bauhaus and the work of architects who taught there, like Mies van der Rohe[4] and Herbert Bayer. Loos' unornamented buildings and the Bauhaus' International style of architecture unproblematically signified artistic progress. In Kracauer's view, however, the mass ornament represented a highly circumscribed glimmer of hope in a situation which signified the imminent demise of the project of the enlightenment.

Space

The fact that Kracauer worked as an architect undoubtedly gave him a particular sensitivity to space, as several writers have commented. Anthony Vidler points out that spatial metaphors were an important and idiosyncratic manner of characterising and criticising the social impact of modernity which Kracauer inherited from his teacher Simmel:

> Starting with the spatial sociology of Simmel, and developing in the paradigmatic spaces identified and described by his student, Kracauer, a unique sensibility of urban space is worked out, one that is neither used as an illustration of social history nor seen as a

mechanical cause of social change, but rather a conception of space as reciprocally interdependent with society. This sensibility was by its very nature attached to certain kinds of social spaces that were, for social critics, inherently related to the social estrangement that seemed to permeate the metropolitan realm.

(Vidler 1991: 32)

The social space articulated through performing in mass ornamental movements is one in which Kracauer saw such signs of social estrangement. The precise dancing of the Tiller Girls presented Kracauer with a spatial image of the way the capitalist economic system reduced subjectivity and embodiment to minimal dimensions. Alternatively, its scale and repetition evoked what was disturbing about the new spaces of modernity, fears which Simmel connected with agoraphobia (see Vidler 1991). Faced with the social estrangement of metropolitan modernity, the modern subject therefore either experiences a nervous reaction such as agoraphobia or hardens him- or herself and becomes blasé and indifferent.

Benjamin's linkage of the modern impact of seeing chorus line dancers and Baudelaire's horror at the seven old men is one that links a nervous response akin to agoraphobia with the alienation of the modern subject. Describing employment exchanges in 1930, Kracauer wrote: 'Spatial images [*Raumbilder*] are the dreams of society. Wherever the hieroglyphics of these images can be deciphered, one finds the basis of social reality' (quoted in Witte 1975: 63). With spectacles like the mass ornament, the masses were so distracted that, to extend Kracauer's metaphor, there was no room for dreams within the rationally defined spatial and temporal co-ordinates of the choreography even though their spatial co-ordinates – the mass scale – were generally of a proportion likely to provoke an agoraphobic reaction.

As Susan Bordo points out, hysteria and agoraphobia were characteristic nineteenth-century female maladies. Referring to the large feminist literature on hysteria, she points to the close correspondence between socially constructed, European upper- and middle-class feminine norms and the compendious list of often contradictory or conflationary symptoms associated with hysteria and neurasthenia. These, she argues, can be seen as 'concretisations of the feminine mystique of the period, produced according to rules that governed the prevailing construction of femininity' (Bordo 1993: 168). The nineteenth-century gentlewoman was so limited in her lifestyle that, Bordo proposes, she used physical symptoms as a form of protest, which as a consequence further circumscribed and limited her ability to live a healthy and satisfying life. What was new about the 'new woman' of the Weimar period was the extent to which she broke out of these social constrictions and re-entered the public sphere that, for the last hundred years, had been the exclusive preserve of men. Performances by women of mass ornamental movements expressed ideals of enjoyable, healthy, physical activity that were the antithesis of notions of the delicacy of nineteenth-century feminine health. Mass spectacles by women gymnasts in particular demonstrated a freedom from the types of peculiarly modern and largely feminine nervous fears loosely grouped under the label agoraphobia.

Subjectivity and space

Adorno once recalled that when he was a teenager Kracauer, who was fourteen years older than him, used to read Kant's *Critique of Pure Reason* with him.

> As he presented it to me, Kant's critical philosophy was not simply a system of transcendental idealism. Rather, he showed me how the objective-ontological and subjective-idealist moments warred within it, how the more eloquent passages in the work are the wounds this conflict has left in the theory.
>
> (Adorno 1991: 160)

For Kracauer, the rational subject that Kant had proposed was disintegrating under the impact of the alienating experience of modernity. In Kant's writings, the subject's knowledge of the world includes knowledge of its position in space and time. It is within space and time in particular that Kracauer perceived signs of the process of the subject's disintegration. Dance is an art form in which the body makes material its subjective experiences of space and time. Kracauer acknowledges these dimensions when he writes about dance (although this is not out of an interest in dance as such but because of its potential to reveal to Kracauer the unconscious nature of modernity).

In his 1925 essay 'Travel and dance', Kracauer describes the disintegration of the modern subject in spatial and temporal terms. Tourism seems to him to reduce travel to a meaningless experience of space while, through jazz, 'dance has been transformed to a mere marking of time' (1995: 66). The result is that the subject disintegrates to a one-dimensional existence in space and time. Kracauer betrays a cultural conservatism when he regrets in this essay the passing of nineteenth-century social dances like the waltz. For Kracauer, these at least signified something – 'pleasant flirtation, a tender encounter in the realm of the sensuous' (ibid.), ideas that were expressed in time. Jazz dance however signifies nothing and reduces the experience of time to nothing more than rhythmic pulsion:

> The secret aim of jazz tunes, no matter how Negroid their origins, is a tempo that is concerned with nothing but itself. These tunes strive to extinguish the melody and spin out ever further the vamps that signal the decline of meaning, in that they reveal and perfect the mechanisation already at work in the melody.
>
> (ibid.: 66–7)

Kracauer was therefore just as conservative as Levinson and Haskell (see the previous chapter) were in their response to jazz dance, although Kracauer was of course not overtly racist. If Kracauer ever tried dancing to jazz music he didn't seem to have felt anything – certainly nothing like the passionate, intoxicated frenzy that Michel Leiris described in the previous chapter.[5] Kracauer is not writing as a participant but as a spectator, and he judges jazz dances with the same detached, critical disposition which Kant ascribes to the process of aesthetic judgement. Kant believed aesthetic judgements to be universal experiences about which everyone must agree. Thus if Kracauer felt nothing while watching jazz dance, it never occurred to him that anyone else might feel any different. For Kracauer, of course, the alienated modern subject who makes such aesthetic judgements 'is reduced to an unreal, purely formal relation that manifests the same indifference to the self as it does to matter' (ibid.: 177). It is this wholly intellectualised response Kracauer had to jazz dancing that underlies his concept of the disintegration of the modern subject.

In 'Travel and dance', Kracauer argues that the modern subject is reduced in leisure (watching dances and being a tourist) and at work to 'a mathematical given in space and time':

> His [sic] existence disintegrates into a series of organisationally dictated activities, and nothing would be more in keeping with this mechanisation than for him to contract to a point, so to speak – into a useful part of this intellectual apparatus. Being forced to disintegrate in this direction is already enough of a burden on people. They find themselves shoved into an everyday life that turns them into henchmen of the technological excesses. Despite or perhaps precisely because of the humane foundations of Taylorism, they do not become masters of the machine but instead become machine-like.
>
> (ibid.: 70)

Efficiency engineers

The idea of Taylorism occurs both in the essay 'Travel and dance' and in 'The mass ornament'. It was the name given to the scientific approach to industrial management proposed by Frederick Winslow Taylor (1856–1915). Taylor devised a method of studying the physical movements of workers in factories in order to find the most efficient movements and gestures for each particular activity. As Mel Gordon explains:

> Calling his study *motion economy*, Taylor had soon to take into account such non-linear and unmechanical factors as work-rhythms, balance, muscular groupings, fatigue, and 'rest minutes'. Through trial and

error, Taylor developed a system of *work cycles*, each involving a whole network of movements and pauses, allowing the worker to produce the greatest work output with the least amount of strain.

(Gordon 1974: 75, emphasis in the original)

The ideas of Taylor and his successors had considerable social and political consequences when they became widely known in Europe. Efficiency engineers applied scientific management in ways that had consequences for social and economic planning. As Charles Maier has pointed out:

Generally during the early post-war years technocratic or engineering models of social management appealed to the newer, more syncretic, and sometimes more extreme currents of European politics. Italian national syndicalists and fascists, German 'revolutionary conservatives' and 'conservative socialists', as well as the so-called left liberals who sought to mediate between bourgeois and social democracy, and finally Soviet leaders, proved most receptive. Later in the decade, as the American vision of productivity was divested of its more utopian implications, it came to serve a useful function for business conservatives.

(Maier 1970: 28)

American models of social engineering were thus a key factor in the process of industrial rationalisation that was being introduced in Germany at the time Kracauer wrote these essays (see Law and Gordon 1996). His attitude towards them was clearly a sceptical one.

In 'The mass ornament', Kracauer writes that the Tiller Girls' dancing 'is conceived according to the rational principles which the Taylor system merely pushed to their ultimate conclusion. The hands in the factory correspond to the legs of the Tiller Girls' (1995: 78–9). The modern rationalisation of such dancing, in Kracauer's metaphor, produces a system in which the dancers' performance is broken down and dehumanised in a rational, scientific way:

The ornament, detached from its bearers, must be understood *rationally*. It consists of lines and circles like those in textbooks on Euclidean geometry, and also incorporates the elementary components of physics, such as waves and spirals. Both the proliferations of organic forms and the emanations of spiritual life remain excluded. The Tiller Girls can no longer be reassembled into human beings after the fact. Their mass gymnastics are never performed by the fully preserved bodies, whose contortions defy rational understanding. Arms, thighs, and other segments are the smallest component parts of the composition.

(ibid.: 78, emphasis in the original)

Here again Kracauer refers to a spatial experience that is rationally ordered, scientific and mathematical. The Tiller Girls, here as elsewhere in Kracauer's writings, resemble puppets. Their de-individuated, mindless, puppet-like movements signify a reconciliation between the human worker and the industrial process: the state of de-individuated mindlessness being defined in minimal spatial and temporal terms.

Conclusion

Kracauer's ideas about the Tiller Girls' dancing (and of mass rhythmic gymnastics displays) are factually inaccurate. The Tiller Girls were not from ultra-modern, industrialised America but from declining cotton spinning towns in the north of England. Kracauer should not therefore have associated them with everything America signified to German intellectuals during the 1920s, and their precision dance routines had no material or logical link with the work of F. W. Taylor. Although Kracauer dismissed military displays as survivals from the past, it was military precision that John Tiller had sought to emulate. The continuities between Kracauer's ideas about dancing in the essay 'Travel and dance' and in 'The mass ornament' suggest that he was unaware of the origins of jazz dance in African American culture and of the chorus line in the different traditions of British popular entertainment. While the factual detail of 'The mass ornament' is therefore askew, it is on a theoretical level that the essay is valuable. Kracauer has an avant-garde sensibility and finds qualities appreciated by modernist artists – abstraction and the fragmented quality Kracauer calls distraction. On the face of it his notion of the mass ornament as something which chorus line dancing and stadium gymnastic displays (together with other unspecified performance forms) have in common seems an unwieldy combination lacking in stylistic homogeneity. But by reading an historically specific social phenomenon on an aesthetic level Kracauer offers unusual insights into the ways in which the performance of mass ornamental movement material mediated the way subjectivities were embodied and produced in that particular historical, social and psychological context.

Chapter 2 looked at the decline and transformation of the utopian hope that avant-garde artistic practices could bring about a better life through a fusion of mass culture and high art. What Kracauer analyses in 1927 are the means through which modernity produces alien bodies by undermining the rational unitary subject of the Enlightenment. Kracauer's avant-garde sensibility underlies his hope in 1927 that the mass ornament is a symptom of the demise of capitalism and of the libertarian utopia that should replace it. By 1931, when he wrote 'Girls in crisis', Kracauer no longer held such libertarian views. Whereas in 1927 Kracauer was particularly critical of the contradiction within many forms of gymnastics, group activities and body culture, by 1947 he attributed the same negative effects to the mass ornament as he had earlier attributed to these other forms, seeing them all as having contributed to the German people's acceptance of fascism. By 1947 the dancing bodies themselves have been dropped from Kracauer's theorisation, presumably as a result of the appropriation by Nazi German eugenicists of what had up until then been a largely left-wing, working-class body culture movement. In turning in the next chapter to the mass ornament and body culture under the National Socialist regime, it is the fact that Kracauer's critique of Weimar body culture was written before the rise of Hitler that makes it a useful reference point for evaluating Nazi uses of body culture.

5

TOTALITARIANISM AND THE MASS ORNAMENT

As I initially remembered the film extract, it started with a close-up of a smiling young woman doing a gymnastic exercise swinging clubs, and then the camera pulled back so that the spectator could see more and more women all doing the same exercise. When I looked at it again, however, I found that there was always more than one woman visible on screen and it didn't start with the smiling woman at all. However, even if its construction is more complex, the dynamic of the sequence is that it goes from the individual to the mass with the smiling woman as the key performer. What the extract actually starts with is a mobile close-up shot taken from above and slightly behind another young woman who is bending slightly forwards kneeling on the grass. She is performing a cyclical exercise where she swings around to one side and reaches up and out so that at the furthest stretch she is upright at the top of her circling movement. This then carries on round and down the other side, getting smaller and less extended until she is back down and curled forwards again. As she moves, the camera also moves around from behind to one side, and when you see her face, her eyes seem to be almost closed, her head back almost as if in prayer or meditation. The music accompanying this is quiet – high, piping woodwinds in a lilting, folksy melody. This shot quickly fades into another and then another showing that this woman is part of a line of young women – all of whom are perfectly synchronised – and that there are other rows in front and behind. The camera angles for these are steep, so that in one shot the lines of women cut in sharp diagonals across the rectangle of the screen; in others the camera is low so that the young women are shown as strong shapes against the clouds which have been photographed (the film is black and white) with a filter so that they stand out sharply against the darker cloudless parts of the sky. Again the women's faces are neutral, and if their eyes are not entirely closed then their focus is inwards. These women are concentrating on the physical experiences of the flow of momentum and breath that make up the movement sequence. This scene fades into a shot of another gymnastic exercise done by women standing with bent knees and consisting of lateral stretches. Then there is a more definite cut to the exercise with the clubs featuring the woman with the lovely smile. The progression in the extract is therefore from an exercise kneeling, through one with bent knees to one standing upright.

This woman is the only one who is smiling: everyone else has directed their focus internally. Her smile suggests that she knows the exercise well and finds the repetition of its familiar, well-rehearsed pattern of movements pleasurable. Her enjoyment is infectious. She makes it look so easy and such a pleasure that one almost wants to join in. The music has moved to a slightly lower register and strings have been added, but the simple, lilting tune is still the same. The camera is once more low, with clouds again behind her and the other women around her – the torso of one who is nearer the camera cutting briefly into the frame, partially obscures the woman who is smiling. When the latter is visible again, the shot fades into another where the camera is high up looking down on maybe twenty or thirty women, and then quickly fades again into a view from further away showing perhaps a hundred all still swinging clubs. Finally we see an aerial view looking down on a huge field with thousand upon thousand of women in precise ranks all swinging their clubs in unison with, in the background, the

Figure 5 The smiling gymnast in Leni Riefenstahl's *Fest der Schönheit*
Source: Leni Riefenstahl Productions

stadium for the 1936 Berlin Olympic Games. The music for this last shot is a development of the original tune only now far more martial with a full orchestra, and lots of brass and drums. The whole sequence has lasted about one and a half minutes. It shows part of a mass gymnastic display directed by Heinrich Medau[1] and comes from *Fest der Schönheit* (*Festival of Beauty*), the second of Leni Riefenstahl's two *Olympia* films.

Looking at the young woman who is smiling, one is convinced of her pleasure in her physical accomplishments through being reminded of one's own muscular memories of the physical sensations of doing similar exercises or activities. The film invites the spectator to make a connection between her or his own subjective experiences of embodiment and those of this young woman. It seems a particularly easy connection to make as she herself is sharing these muscular sensations with so many thousands of others. Her individuality thus appears merged within this mass with whom her momentum and breath are in perfect synchronisation. One suspects that although she cannot see the visual effect to which she is contributing, she must nevertheless feel it. Her smile thus not only signifies her enjoyment of harmonious motion but also her pleasure at belonging and being incorporated within the massive group. The film therefore also invites the spectator to at least approve of this group if not actually want to join in and become part of it, the group being defined in exclusive national terms.

Riefenstahl's practice of restaging events from the Olympic Games to obtain better pictures of them is well documented (Hinton 1978; Downing 1992). One suspects that Riefenstahl could easily have restaged part of the mass display with a group of specially picked gymnasts so as to get the close-up shots, and may have directed the performers to assume those neutral expressions and told the woman whose 'naturalness' and beauty best exemplified a Nordic ideal, to smile. Alternatively, she could have achieved this effect at the editing stage through the way she selected the film material for the final cut. Whatever was the case, the effect is constructed in order to create here as elsewhere in the film the effect of putting the spectator into 'the mind and body of the participants' (Hinton 1978: 75).

Seen close up, the gymnastic exercises in the extract from *Olympia* have an organic quality. Their use of the body's momentum to phrase curving movements gives the impression of natural cycles such as growing and subsiding, or the succession of in-breath and out-breath. However, the further away from the women the camera is placed, the more mechanical the exercises look. Another important difference between close-up and distance is in the way the women appear spatially. Close-up, their bodies are solid and substantial, and their limbs and torsos dip into and through the space around them in every direction. From afar, however, they are reduced to two dimensional, animated pictograms whose perfectly synchronised, stick-like limbs describe a flat moving pattern within their allotted section of the overall grid. These long shots turn the women into a mass ornament – a term which Siegfried Kracauer first applied to these and other performances in the key essay discussed in the previous chapter.

There is something about the sheer scale of the gymnastic display, together with its anonymous precision, that identifies it as a product of the twentieth century and of modernity. The seventeenth-century painter Breughel also showed massive crowds of anonymous but individuated people by using a similarly high viewpoint. But Breughel's masses always sprawl in ragged disorder across an untidy landscape. It is only a capitalist and rationalised industrial society that requires and therefore produces standardised, docile and disciplined bodies of the sort shown in this film extract. The film also shows a type of display that, as Walter Benjamin pointed out, looks better on film than in real life:

> Mass movements are usually discerned more clearly by a camera than by the naked eye. A bird's-eye view best captures gatherings of hundreds of thousands. And even though such a view may be as accessible to the human eye as it is to the camera, the image received by the eye cannot be enlarged the way a negative is enlarged. This means that mass movements, including war, constitute a form of human behaviour which particularly favours mechanical equipment.

> (Benjamin 1970: 253)

Seen with the help of this modern equipment, such a display of modern, controlled, rationalised movement can appear beautiful, although its vertiginous view point and agoraphobia-inducing scale is in itself potentially threatening in the way it reminds the spectator of what is disturbing about modernity. Healthy exercise compensates and revitalises bodies that have been exhausted and misused within scientifically rationalised industrial production. The film presents a utopian image of ideals of health and wholeness which modernity seemed to undermine, yet this image is inconceivable without modern technology and modern social developments. Both the film itself and these docile bodies are modern products. The way the event has been filmed and edited both evokes and counteracts the threatening aspects of modernity.

Forms of body culture including modern dance were important areas within which the individual's lived experience of modern life – how the individual relates to the mass and to the mechanisation and bureaucratisation of work and leisure – was explored in critical and often antagonistic ways. Far from denying modernity, this film extract recognises its ubiquity while also endorsing the values which modernity seems to threaten. Uneasiness about modernity is registered in the film extract only to be dispelled. Thus the editing establishes the reassuring three dimensionality of the women before reducing them to a two dimensional mass ornament. It asserts the 'naturalness' of the movements so that spectators can then also admire their formal precision; and it shows the woman happily smiling before presenting a spectacle of so many who, it implies, are equally happy in their disciplined roles. The filmic links between the smile and the disciplined mass are made as smooth as possible: the montage of images contains only one cut amid several slowly faded superimpositions. The film, like the display, thus reproduces contradictions that existed within modernity itself because that is the context of their production.

Chapter 3 ended with a description of a white man whose dancing with Josephine Baker, it was suggested, constituted a blurring of boundaries between binary opposites – black and white, male and female, European and American. This chapter has started with a woman whose participation in a mass gymnastic display involves a blurring of boundaries between herself and the others in the group. The difference between the two instances of blurring are ethical in a political way: whereas Baker's dancing partner is erasing boundaries that have been produced by a racist way of thinking, the German gymnast is only erasing boundaries within a larger field that is already ethnically cleansed. The threat of the erosion of national sovereignty by modernity results in a reaction formation where national boundaries are reasserted in embodied terms as an imaginary, 'purified' community of healthy Aryan bodies. The filmed extract showing the mass gymnastic display therefore poses an ethical question. By ethics I mean the kind of relationship one ought to have with oneself which, as Michel Foucault has put it, 'determines how an individual is supposed to constitute him [or her] self as a moral subject of his [or her] actions' (Rabinow 1986: 348). *Olympia* is a seductive film that convinces the viewer that the smiling woman really is enjoying herself and makes her or him want to join in and experience the same delight in physical movement. What makes this delight problematic is its association with the National Socialists' eugenic policies. The sort of links that existed I shall discuss shortly. What is at issue is the degree of complicity that connects participation in and pleasure at viewing the presentation of this mass performance with the eugenic policy of the Nazis. Were other related kinds of performances of such mass spectacles also complicit? The answer to these questions lies in understanding the continuities between the subjective experience of embodiment and politics as ethics.

What I shall argue in this chapter is that confusion about the ethics of performing such mass gymnastic exercises within a politicised propaganda context are caused by misunderstandings in theorising the social construction of embodiment. The chapter proceeds as follows. First, I place dance within the cultural contexts of the Weimar and National Socialist periods and look at the continuities between dance and physical culture during the period as a whole. In doing this I also take into account the extent to which the institutions of the National Socialist state used physical culture as part of a process of indoctrination for eugenic ideas. Kracauer's 1927 essay 'The mass ornament', which was introduced in the previous chapter, is informative about the ways in which such performances were perceived at the time as cultural products that mediated the experiences of modernity, and is useful for Kracauer's critique of contradictions within Weimar physical culture. It is also important as an attempt to develop a materialist account of the social experience of embodiment within a fragmented and alienated society. This provides me with a frame within which to re-examine issues of the embodiment of ethics exemplified within the extract from Riefenstahl's film.

The politics and modernity of mass gymnastics

Taylor Downing, in his discussion of Riefenstahl's two *Olympia* films, tries not to get involved in the debates about their relationship with National Socialist ideology. He thus merely comments that this type of display of women's group gymnastics 'has fallen out of fashion because it is indelibly associated with the health and beauty, open-air philosophy of National Socialism' (Downing 1992: 74). Clearly this type of response did not exist in the 1930s and, furthermore, only exists now in Western Europe and the United States: until recently large-scale precise spectacular performances in stadiums continued to be produced in some socialist countries and in countries where a personality cult has developed around a totalitarian political leader. In considering how the movement in the gymnastic display in this film extract related to lived experience of modernity, it is particularly important to place it in its historical and political background and not reduce such spectacular productions to a generalised notion of totalitarianism.

It would be wrong to associate the performance of mass ceremonial and ritualised acts, and the use of flags and uniforms, solely with the National Socialists. These were in fact, as Henning Eichberg (1977) has pointed out, an aspect of much of the political culture across a broad political spectrum during the first few decades of the twentieth century. As was noted in the previous chapter, mass spectacles in sports stadiums were often produced under the auspices of left-wing workers' sports associations. In this they were imitating the ceremonial and ritual acts that were developed between 1912 and 1936 to accompany the opening of the Olympic Games. In 1912 there were the marching athletes, opening ceremonies, choruses and cannon salutes. In 1920 there were Olympic flags, symbols and oaths. In 1924 flag ceremonies and Olympic fires were introduced and in 1932 hymns. The 1936 Olympics was the first to start with the lighting of the Olympic torch (ibid.: 148). In the aftermath of the 1914–18 war, Germany and the Soviet Union were excluded from the Olympic Games and alternative Workers' Olympics were held – the first in Frankfurt in 1925, the second in Vienna in 1931. Both included the performance of mass festival plays. The opening of the 1936 Olympics included the premier of a 'Thingspiel' performance 'Das

Frankenberger Wurfelspiel' ('Frankenberg Dice Game') and a mass dance performance 'Olympische Jugend' ('Olympic Youth') in which many German modern dancers led by Mary Wigman performed. 'Das Frankenberger Wurfelspiel' was almost cancelled, according to some sources, because of its use of dramatic devices associated with left-wing mass theatre (Gadberry 1980: 112). Laban had also produced for the opening of the games a large-scale *bewegungschore* (movement choir) piece 'Vom Tauwind und der neuen Freude' ('The Warm Wind and the New Joy') which Goebbels cancelled at the last minute (Preston-Dunlop 1989). Eichberg points out that the types of mass ceremonial and ritual performances that have subsequently been associated with Hitler and the National Socialist regime were not their exclusive invention but were a much more widespread phenomenon at the time. What is significant about their use of them, he argues, is the fact that they found them difficult to control and ineffective. The near cancellation of 'Das Frankenberger Wurfelspiel' and the cancellation of Laban's *bewegungschore* and Laban's subsequent dismissal from his post in Goebbel's Ministry of Propaganda need to be seen in this light.

Group gymnastic displays by women like the one in Riefenstahl's film were an international phenomenon.[2] A photograph which was printed in *The Times*, 14 August 1936 – coincidentally towards the end of the last week of the Berlin Olympic Games – shows a women's gymnastic display.[3] About a hundred women, arranged in rows that form a solid square, are kneeling on the ground performing an exercise that looks in this photograph remarkably similar to the one at the start of the extract from *Olympia*. The caption reveals that it is a display by women gymnasts from all parts of the world who are attending the English Scandinavian Summer School at Milner Court, Sturry, Kent. Behind the women can be made out the shape of the pitched roof and half-timbered walls of a typical Edwardian country house. It is quite a large group, though not on the scale of the display Riefenstahl filmed in Berlin. If the exercise is not the same one then it must be very similar. As Downing rightly observes, these kinds of gymnastic displays are, at the end of the twentieth century, associated solely with the National Socialists while all the other instances of these and similar performances and activities that were not associated with them seem to have been forgotten. It is undeniable that these activities were appropriated and used by the National Socialists for political indoctrination. To assess whether, as Eichberg implies, the effectiveness of these propaganda uses of body culture has been overestimated by post-war historians, it is necessary to understand the ways in which the modern body of the 1930s was socially and historically constructed and subject to what Michel Foucault called the investment of power.

Susan Sontag in 'Fascinating fascism', her brilliant invective against those who would unthinkingly rehabilitate Riefenstahl, makes one striking observation:

In dealing with propagandistic art on the left and on the right a double standard prevails. Few people would admit that the manipulation of emotion in Vertov's later films[4] and in Riefenstahl's provides similar kinds of exhilaration. When explaining why they are moved, most people are sentimental in the case of Vertov and dishonest in the case of Riefenstahl.

(Sontag 1983: 95)

The National Socialists used art for propaganda purposes. Fascism, as Walter Benjamin observed in 1936, aestheticises politics. Since the end of the Second World War and the awful discoveries in the concentration camps, there has been a tendency, as Sontag herself recognises, to exclude fascist cultural products from the sort of critical scrutiny that is applied to other works of the period. It was thus all right to look at German Expressionist painting and Dada and Constructivist art because the National Socialists had banned these and declared them 'entartete kunst' (degenerate art), but the realist paintings that the National Socialist regime sponsored, along with Riefenstahl's films, were kept securely out of circulation.

The American critic and commentator Clement Greenberg was the first to formulate the theoretical premises that subsequently underpinned this approach. In his 1940 essay 'Avant-garde or kitsch'. In this he argued that progressive modernist art can only be made in free, democratic countries while the realist propaganda art of both the National Socialist and Stalinist regimes is mere kitsch. Recent art historical research has shown that such comfortably clear cut distinctions between 'good', progressive modern and 'bad' retrogressive realist art do not fit the facts. The painter Emil Nolde, a member of the pre-First World War Brücke group of Expressionist painters, became a member of the National Socialist party in the early 1920s. Although condemned as a degenerate artist his work still seems to have been appreciated by Goebbels (see Speer 1970: 27). Not only were some Expressionist painters sympathetic to aspects of National Socialist ideology, but modernist art by Russian Constructivist photographers and designers was used for propaganda purposes by Stalin's communist regime in the late 1920s and early 1930s at the same time that Mussolini's fascist regime in Italy was favouring Futurist painters, Modernist graphic artists, and International-style modernist architects in official government commissions (see Buchloh 1981).

Although the fact that German Expressionist painters were declared degenerate by the National Socialists seems to indicate a neat break between art in the Weimar and National Socialist periods, there were in fact continuities between the art of both periods which can be seen most clearly in the case of early European modern dance. Wigman and dancers from the Laban School in Zürich (though not Laban himself) danced in Dada Soirées organised by the Zürich Dadaists, and both Laban and Wigman were centrally involved in preparations for the dance festival accompanying the 1936 Berlin Olympic Games. Film of some of the dance festival was included in *Olympia*. Recognition of these continuities in the field of modern dance and the related field of body culture has led to an ongoing debate among dance historians. Many questions are still to be answered about how far key figures like Laban and Wigman became involved with the National Socialist regime, to what extent modern dance artists were able to continue working under the Nazis, and to what extent they were restricted and stifled by them.[5]

When I have shown and discussed this extract from *Olympia* with students, what seems to disturb them are not the confusions and complications within the cultural history of the period, fascinating though these may be. What is troubling is the seductive, aesthetic appeal of the bodies it shows and the association that can be made, with hindsight, between these and the horrors of fascism. As Wilfred van der Will has observed, the notion of the ideal Aryan body as shown in photographs of nude sunbathers or in gymnastic displays lay behind the eugenic policies of the National Socialists:

> With the hindsight of historical knowledge the sheen on the bodies of Fascist nudes was that of the pretension to master-race status which carried a death-warrant for those who could not satisfy the legally and bureaucratically enshrined criteria of racial conformity.
>
> (van der Will 1990: 43)

Van der Will conclusively shows that both in proletarian and bourgeois nudist groups in Germany there was widespread interest in and acceptance of eugenic ideas. This interest was politicised by the National Socialists through emphasising the way in which the body represented a politicised image of the nation. Thus members of Bünd Deutsches Mädel – the National Socialist women's organisation – were told in 1935 as part of National Socialist indoctrination that they should undertake sport because of 'the duty woman owes to her body, and within it to her descendants' (quoted in Richardson 1990: 76) where female bodies were reified as national assets.

It is in this context that the mass gymnastic display shown in Riefenstahl's film takes on political associations. With hindsight, the image of the smiling woman in the film seems implicated with the terrible programme of systematic collection and murder of several million Jewish people together with smaller numbers of communists, socialists and other political opponents of National Socialism, gypsies, homosexuals and people with mental and physical disabilities. From this point of view, the docility of the mass of women gymnasts appears disturbing because it seems somehow connected with the docile acceptance by the German people of Hitler's anti-Semitic policies. Someone must have co-ordinated the women to enable them to perform with such accurate co-ordination – like some piece of precision engineering. Their individuality seems therefore not just merged into the massive group but also subordinated to the person who is in control of this overall design. For the spectator who knows about the concentration camps, the idea that anyone could accept leadership in this way in such a design is disturbing.[6] All in all, the mass ornament of the gymnastic display appears inextricably and troublingly linked with mass exterminations in the concentration camps. It is surely a mistake, however, to uncritically reduce all images of healthy white bodies involved in body culture that date from the 1920s and 1930s to a generic notion of a fascist body which is totally different from 'our' democratic, free bodies. This does not fit the historical facts. The type of body culture that is shown in Riefenstahl's film was neither exclusively German nor confined to those sympathetic to right-wing nationalist ideologies.

Some aspects of Weimar body culture were more popular with those on the left than those on the right. As van der Will has shown, there was a German left-wing, proletarian nudist movement during the 1920s which advocated that:

> People should not just discard their clothes but with them the whole armour-plating of authority-fixated conditioning which held proletarians in deference to their masters, parental authority, the paternalism of school and church, the mass media, and the organs of law and order. . . . Proletarian nudity was intended as a purgative of deep-seated anti-sensual prejudice and a rational method of discarding the chains of bourgeois ideas around proletarian minds.
>
> (van der Will 1990. 31)

Many middle-class bohemians and artists saw nudism in similarly libertarian, countercultural terms – including members of the Brücke group. It was Emil Nolde who first told Wigman about Laban who, in the years immediately preceding the First World War, held dance summer schools at a vegetarian nudist colony in Ascona on the Swiss shores of Lake Maggiore. Van der Will says that in 1933 all the proletarian body culture organisations including the nudist groups were disbanded and their property confiscated. Henceforth any involvement in body culture had to be made through the organisations that were under National Socialist control. Similarly the modern dance movement that Laban and his ex-students had developed in Germany became in 1933 a recipient of state subsidy with Laban himself working as a paid official of Goebbels' Reich Chamber for Culture. This must be seen as part of a larger process of 'gleichschaltung' or ideological incorporation that was applied to many areas of German public life under the National Socialists (see van der Will 1990: 110–16).

As van der Will points out, the National Socialists maintained their position in Germany by appealing to notions of 'a new racial harmony of the body and the reintegration of the individual in a pacified society' (1990: 46). Claudia Jeschke has also commented upon the way that, on the level of ideas, the National Socialists took over and subtly altered existing conceptions as well as practices. She describes the 'cultural space' of German dance as follows:

> This 'cultural space' was nurtured by a variety of philosophical, even cosmological, ideas about nature, body, rhythm and women, which, as early as the second half of the nineteenth century, were meant to help people overcome social alienation. The cosmological ideas alone, however, failed to alter the social alienation. The National Socialists finally adopted certain aspects of the existent philosophies and interpreted them as practical social devices and direct prescriptions. They thereby elevated, or 'empowered', these ideas to 'dominant structures'.
>
> (Jeschke 1995: 35)

It was by projecting such ideologies within rallies and propaganda films like those by Riefenstahl that the National Socialists were able to absorb many members of left-wing proletarian body culture associations and Laban's conservative, but arguably not fascist, modern dance movement within the hegemony of the National Socialist state.[7] This goes some way towards explaining the continuities between early modern dance in the Weimar Republic and modern dance under the National Socialist regime. Whereas modernism in various forms was publicly supported in many ways under Weimar, the National Socialists were strongly opposed to modernism in the arts. Early modern dance had its origins in modernism: while the National Socialist regime initially supported modern dance, it undoubtedly became increasingly antagonistic towards it after 1936.

The gymnastic display in *Olympia* expressed libertarian ideas about the body which, as Jeschke points out, developed in Europe during the late nineteenth and early twentieth centuries as forms of criticism and resistance against alienating and dehumanising aspects of the social experience of modernity. These ideas were perhaps more defined in Germany than in other Western countries because of the late, but alarmingly rapid transformation of Germany into a modern, industrialised nation. Similar libertarian ideas about the body were expressed in other areas of physical culture including European modern dance. What is at issue is how far these libertarian ideas contributed to the acceptance in Germany of National Socialist ideology. My aim here is to argue against a crudely deterministic notion of a generic fascist body which, as I shall show, underlies Sontag's critique of *Olympia*. This notion of a generic fascist body is in my opinion based upon a dualistic misconception about the nature of embodiment. Distaste at the notion of fascist corruption of the body draws on Judaeo-Christian ideas that see the body as a sinful source of temptation which it is a moral duty to resist and repress. In this view the irrational, physical and sensual appeal of National Socialist ideology is contrasted with the rational, disinterested disposition from which the subject as pure disembodied consciousness makes judgements. This is dualistic in the way the body is seen as irrational while only the mind is capable of moral and ethical intentions. Likewise, fascism is seen as an irrational aberration that was opposed to modernity and progress which, as 'we' all know, is based upon rational, scientific premises.

To argue that holding libertarian ideas about the body necessarily led to an irrational submission to fascism is to misunderstand and oversimplify the complex set of factors, circumstances and ideological investments that led to the German people's acceptance of fascism. There is a vast range of existing literature and ongoing research on how National Socialism became so popular among Germans.[8] As someone primarily concerned with dance history, the contribution I want to make in this chapter is a clarification of the ways in which the subjective experience of embodiment in the 1920s and 1930s related to this social, political, economic and cultural context. At issue is how the bodily practices of performing mass ornamental movements related to politics, morality and ethics. In this context, it is necessary to distinguish between libertarian ideologies of the body that were prevalent during the Weimar period and subsequent propaganda uses of these by the National Socialist regime. Riefenstahl's film of the gymnastic display was released over a decade later than the newsreel film of a stadium display that Kracauer wrote about. The young women who became members of organisations like Bünd Deutsches Mädel were a different generation with different aspirations from those Kracauer was writing about in 1927.

In my discussion of the extract from *Olympia* I have argued that the mass gymnastic demonstration was not entirely anti-modern but in fact articulated a cluster of varying and contradictory responses to modernity. My contention is that it is whether and how these contradictions were recognised and acknowledged that distinguishes Weimar body culture from National Socialist uses of it for propaganda purposes.

The mass ornament, National Socialism, and docile bodies

Siegfried Kracauer's insights into the social and cultural context of the rise of body culture during the early years of the twentieth century and his sceptical critique of its philosophical and ideological premises (discussed in the previous chapter) offer a framework for contextualising the short extract from *Olympia* introduced at the beginning of this chapter. As a mass gymnastic display, it is clearly a continuation of a type of gymnastic activity that was popular during the Weimar period and which Kracauer refers to in 'The mass ornament'. It is a film of such an event, and it is newsreel film of gymnastic displays that Kracauer refers to. Seen close-up in Riefenstahl's film, the exercises that make up the mass ornament are burdened with what Kracauer felt were retrogressive, natural meanings; seen from a distance, however, these exercises turn into rationalised, abstracted patterns. In 1927, Kracauer related these retrogressive, natural meanings to yearnings for a return to a mythical, organic community that arose because capitalist modernity does not rationalise too much but too little. In 1936 Riefenstahl's film aimed to demonstrate the existence of a mythical, organic community and to show what National Socialism had done for Germany.

Maud Lavin has suggested that Weimar women's involvement and plea-sure at images of the mass ornament was 'a desire to be part of a smoothly functioning collective unit or a unified "class" of modern women' (1993: 93). The younger generation of German women who became keen members of the National Socialist women's organisation, Bünd Deutsches Mädel, rejected their parents' acceptance of the sort of contradictions within Weimar culture that Kracauer identified in German body culture. For this new generation, the National Socialist party offered a positive call to serve Germany. Thus, whereas Weimar journalists discussed 'girlkultur' (see Berghaus 1988), the magazine of the Bünd Deutsches Mädel was called *Fräuen-Kultur*. What many of the women who were members of this organi-sation remembered later was a positive feeling of community well-being, of togetherness and belonging, and it was in communal rituals that these feel-ings were engendered (Koonz 1987; see also Thamer 1996). For women in Germany and elsewhere in the 1920s sport activities had emancipatory connotations, but, as we have seen, members of Bünd Deutsches Mädel were told that, through engaging in sports activities, they were fulfilling 'the duty woman owes to her body, and within it to her descendants' (quoted in Richardson 1990: 76).[9]

These then are the main differences in context between the mass orna-ment that Kracauer wrote about in 1927 and that Riefenstahl filmed in 1936. Kracauer criticised Weimar body culture because its practitioners were not aware of its underlying contradictions. National Socialist propa-ganda and indoctrination tried to convince German citizens that under Hitler these contradictions had disappeared, and attempted to conceal any indication that they still existed. Thus Riefenstahl presents gymnastics in such a way as to blur and hide these inherent contradictions. The difference between Kracauer's reading of the mass ornament and Riefenstahl's presenta-tion of it in *Olympia* is clearest on an aesthetic level: Kracauer looks as a modernist and finds qualities appreciated by modernist artists – abstraction and the fragmented quality Kracauer calls distraction. Riefenstahl is anti-modernist. Her editing eschews the fragmented montage beloved of avant-garde film makers, and instead of abstraction and distraction, she creates out of her footage of the mass gymnastic display an image of harmony and clarity. Riefenstahl's film does not, therefore, seek simply to articulate desires and yearnings but to channel them. The 1936 Olympics and Riefenstahl's films of it were intended to present to both the international community and the German public a positive image of Hitler's Germany. The film constructs an impression of a meaningful community as a way of presenting National Socialism in the best possible light. The newsreel that Kracauer watched in the 1920s showed a mass display which utilised reduced temporal and spatial dimensions of bodily expression. He argued that these were so efficiently devised out of abstract, geometric shapes that there was no room for them to mean anything. Through Riefenstahl's editing, however, the film of a similar display in 1936 conveys what Kracauer would have described as regressive, organic meanings. Such meanings are reinscribed onto the display's vacant, meaningless mass patterns. Rather than showing the disorder of society, a revelation which Kracauer in the late 1920s believed should create the circumstances that must precede inevitable and radical change, the film creates an image that signifies an ideal, ordered society. If, following Benedict Anderson (1991), film technology is an important means through which the idea of the national community is imagined, then the image of the mass gymnastics spectacle in Riefenstahl's *Olympia* suggests an imaginary community that is well co-ordinated, happy and healthy.[10]

For Kracauer, the mass ornament is Taylorist. The choreographed movements of disconnected body parts are so tightly defined in terms of the performer's subjective experience of time and space that there is no spatial or temporal dimension for the ornament to signify anything. For Riefenstahl and other propagandists of National Socialism the meaninglessness of the mass ornament allows the propagandist to superimpose on it political meanings appropriate to National Socialism. When the viewer of Riefenstahl's film is presented with the gigantic image of the field of perfectly synchronised women gymnasts, she or he has already been convinced that at the centre of each unit in the grid there lies a happy face. Kracauer asserts that within a Taylorist regime, individuals do not become masters of the machine but machine-like. Riefenstahl suggests that within the rational and scientific grid of the mass ornament, the individual gymnast nevertheless maintains her humanity. At issue here are questions of how to theorise the way power and control is exerted over the individual subject's body.

In 1947 when Kracauer wrote about 'Triumph of the Will' in his book *From Caligari to Hitler*, he said that the marching party members appeared as mass ornaments to Hitler and his staff 'who must have appreciated them as configurations symbolising the readiness of the masses to be shaped and used at will by their leaders' (1947: 302). In 'Fascinating fascism' Susan Sontag argues that the objectification of the massed participants in both *Olympia* and *Triumph of the Will* is about sexual domination. In *Olympia* she says: 'one straining, scantily clad figure after another seeks the ecstasy of victory, cheered on by ranks of compatriots in the stands, all under the still gaze of the benign Super-Spectator, Hitler, whose presence in the stadium consecrates this effort' (Sontag 1983: 87). She finds the same process in *Triumph of the Will*: 'Like Nietzsche and Wagner, Hitler regarded leadership as sexual mastery of the "feminine" masses, as rape. (The expression of the crowds in *Triumph of the Will* is one of ecstasy; the leader makes the crowds come)' (ibid.: 102). It is through this process of sexual mastery that the individual's body is transformed into a fascist body, a transformation that is achieved through repression. Sontag believes that the narratives Riefenstahl creates about bodies in *Olympia* and in her later photographs of the African Nuba tribespeople are about repressed sexuality. For her, it is this repression that creates a generic fascist body:

> Nazi art is both prurient and idealising. A utopian aesthetics (physical perfection; identity as a biological given) implies an ideal eroticism: sexuality converted into the magnetism of leaders and the joy of followers. The fascist ideal is to transform sexual energy into a 'spiritual' force, for the benefit of the community. The erotic (that is, women) is always present as a temptation, with the most admirable response being a heroic repression of the sexual impulse. . . . Fascist aesthetics is based on the containment of vital forces; movements are confined, held tight, held in.
>
> (Sontag 1983: 93)

While Nazi sculptures of nude athletes and warriors represent tight, armoured bodies which might be said to embody such an aesthetic, this is not the case with movement in the mass gymnastic display. The latter has a free flowing quality that surely has nothing to do with repression of sexual impulses. Nevertheless, Sontag argues that Nazism has become associated with sado-masochism because the National Socialist propagandists theatricalise rituals of domination and enslavement, evident in films like *Olympia* and *Triumph of the Will*, which, in Sontag's view, have an erotic surface.

As far as sexuality is concerned, Kracauer considered the mass ornament operated in a completely different way. In his 1927 essay he proposed that whereas ballet was 'a plastic expression of erotic life' the dancing of the Tiller Girls was not erotic: 'They are a linear system that no longer has any erotic meaning but at best points to the locus of an erotic' (1995: 77). André Levinson, in his 1929 essay 'The Girls' concurs with this judgement and his description could be applied equally to the women in *Olympia*:

> In these young girls there is nothing but an excess of health and the consequent absence of everything morbid or passionate which might give them mystery. The soul is skin-deep: they are bodies full of a joy of life expressed in feats of strength and skill. Pretty? Judged by the canons of sculpture, no, probably not; but in point of

sportsmanlike 'form' [leur 'forme sportif'], yes, emphatically yes. That 'form' serves to safeguard their sex. There is no perverse impli- cation or equivocal appeal in the chastity of their half-naked limbs.

(Acocella and Garafola 1991: 93)

The history of middle-class dance criticism is full of men judging the formal beauty of female dancers in rarefied terms in order to claim that their appre- ciation of dancing is entirely aesthetic and therefore innocent of any erotic motivation.[11] This, however, is not in my opinion the case here. When Levinson mentions the dancers' 'forme sportif' he is surely alluding to the slender female body that was fashionable in the 1920s and 1930s and is exemplified by the Tiller Girls, the women filmed by Riefenstahl and, as was noted in a previous chapter, Josephine Baker.

It would clearly be in line with some feminist readings of images of women to see the objectivisation of female bodies in revues and films of gymnastic events as an eroticised spectacle designed to satisfy voyeuristic male heterosexual desire. While I don't want to deny that such vicarious pleasure might be derived by male viewers from such displays of female bodies, I feel it would be a mistake to reduce the phenomenon of the mass ornament to nothing more than an eroticised display – be it titillating or only immovableto. To see it in this way can be a barrier to understanding the nature of power. Sontag argues that the power of National Socialist ideology is the power of sexual repression. The reason I am arguing against a sexu- alised and eroticised reading of the mass ornament is because, as Michel Foucault has pointed out, power is weak when it is applied repressively:

> Power would be a fragile thing if its only function were to repress, if it worked only through the mode of censorship, exclusion, blockage and repression, in the manner of a great Superego, exer- cising itself only in a negative way. If, on the contrary, power is strong this is because, as we are beginning to realise, it produces effects at the level of desire – and also at the level of knowledge.
>
> (Foucault 1980: 59)

What images like those of the mass gymnastic display show are women happily internalising power over their bodies, power that has manipulated their desire to be part of a community. Through the pursuit of an elusive ideal, their bodies have become what Foucault has called docile bodies. A docile body is more useful to capitalist production than a robot or automaton. Whereas an automaton may do its task more efficiently than a human worker, it can only do what it is designed to do. A docile body, however, 'may be subjected, used, transformed, improved' (Foucault 1977: 136). The more disciplined a human worker becomes, the more useful she or he is within the production process because: 'Discipline increases the forces of the body (in economic terms of utility) and diminishes these same forces (in political terms of obedience)' (ibid.: 138).

It is in terms of movement in time and space that Kracauer described the shaping of modern subjectivity. Susan Bordo, following Foucault, describes a similar process through which bodies are made docile (although Foucault and Kracauer work with entirely different epistemologies). Thus Bordo proposes: 'Through the organisation and regulation of the time, space, and movement of our daily lives, our bodies are trained, shaped, and impressed with the stamp of prevailing historical forms of selfhood, masculinity, femininity, desire' (Bordo 1993: 165). In the 1920s and 1930s women were allowing their bodies to be habituated to just such external regulation, subjection and transformation when they took part in mass gymnastic displays and similar performances of mass ornamental movements during the Weimar period, as well as under the National Socialist regime or for that matter in Hollywood or in many other places around the world. The similarity is in the precision and abstractness of the patterns that can be created by these docile bodies. The difference lies not in the activity itself but in the nature of the ideals to which the participants were encouraged to aspire. It is only by examining complex historical, social and cultural circumstances of instances within which the mass ornament is produced and presented that any political ideologies can be identified. It is, however, because of the docility of the women's bodies engaged in producing mass ornamental movements that such practices can be so easily hijacked. Underlying the specific political ideologies that adhere to each of these examples of mass ornamental presentations, there is another level on which patriarchal ideologies are inscribed. The more healthy and fashionably thin the women's bodies become through the physical training that allows them to perform in their chosen field, the more obedient they are to forms of authority. The mass ornament should therefore be seen as one of a number of patriarchal practices through which women voluntarily impose on themselves regimes of discipline. Through the resulting docility, they therefore conform to patriarchal norms of femininity. It is surely no coincidence that attainment of what Levinson called a 'forme sportif' can for some lead to eating disorders like anorexia and bulimia. Susan Bordo, as was noted in a previous chapter, has identified ways in which this slender body has become a fashion norm in periods when women have challenged men within the public sphere of work, and political and cultural life. To call anorexically slender, well-exercised, female bodies generically fascist because of their association with Riefenstahl's *Olympia* is absurd. Such fuzzy thinking distracts us from understanding the ways in which dance and dance-like movement reveal the workings of power in the creation of modern subjectivities.

The embodiment of modernity

As I indicated earlier, underlying the discussion of the mass ornament are differing accounts of the social construction of embodiment in a modern, capitalist society. Kracauer held a materialist view of embodiment, arguing that any concern for the body other than attention to personal hygiene amounts to an attempt to recapture an organic connection with nature. He does, however, acknowledge that the individual as a rationally constituted subject is impoverished by modernity, and he discusses this impoverishment in terms of bodily experience. This leads him to argue that modernity, in its Taylorist mode, brings about the mechanisation of the individual – the Tiller Girls' movements are no longer those of a collection of individual bodies but an assembly of parts of bodies that constitute an automaton. Kracauer's most striking image of the effect of Taylorism on the modern subject is his use of spatial and temporal metaphors: modernity reduces subjectivity to minimal dimensions in terms of time and space. However, Kracauer does not pursue this insight in relation to the subjective experience of embodiment because he still clings to a Kantian notion of the subject. What Kracauer lacks is the kind of framework within which to theorise the psychological construction of identity that later theorists would develop from feminism and post-structuralism. Without such a framework Kracauer tends, despite a commitment to a materialist, anti-metaphysical philosophy, to prioritise the supposed rationality of the mind over the supposedly natural, organic connections of the body. Without an appreciation of the body's potential for agency, he recognises the significance of embodied responses to modernity but is unable to account for them.

Susan Sontag proposes that the leaders of the National Socialist party exercised power over the German people's bodies through a process of sexual domination and repression. She therefore theorises the psychological construction of embodiment in a superficially Freudian way in which all bodily experiences are reduced to sex. In such a view the body only exercises agency in a negative, subconscious manner. Sontag thus identifies signs of the exercise of fascist power over bodies in the way movements are confined, held tight, held in. While there may be examples of this in Riefenstahl's work and in the work of other fascist artists, Sontag's analysis seems inappropriate to the movement exercises which the women perform in the mass gymnastic display. In these, movements are not confined, held tight, or held in. Claudia Koonz's evidence about what many German women enjoyed about active participation in the communal activities and rituals of groups like Bünd Deutsches Mädel also contradicts Sontag's theory of fascist repression. The young women who took part in the mass gymnastic display did not do so because they were coerced but out of an active, positive enjoyment of such activities. Repression, as Foucault points out, is a weak form of control. Power is much stronger where it actively engages the subject through desire and knowledge.

'Fascinating fascism' is an attack on Riefenstahl and on those who would rehabilitate her work, that is carried out in terms of politics as ethics. Sontag argues that to allow oneself to take part in a Nazi propaganda performance, no matter how seductive, is a moral failure. To enjoy the aesthetic surface of Riefenstahl's films and photographs is also wrong: their fascist associations make them necessarily repugnant. In a move similar to Kracauer, Sontag seems to infer that a rational mind should override the sensual attachments of the body in order to make ethical judgements. For both Kracauer and Sontag a dualistic notion of mind and body supports a view of rational judgement that has its origins in the Enlightenment.[12]

To bring back the dancing bodies in the discussion of Kracauer's concept of the mass ornament is to focus on the non-verbal ways in which bodies communicate when performing in theatrical contexts. Anthropologist Mary Douglas (1966) has demonstrated that the body is an image of society and that rituals concerning the body's boundaries correspond to notions of the political, social, cultural or geographical boundaries of social groups. Foucault, in his discussion of Western ethics, argues that individuals work on themselves with self-forming activities so that they can relate reciprocally with others who have worked on themselves in similar ways. Notions of what constitutes being a good citizen are of course culturally and historically specific, and are propagated and policed by the institutions of society. It is in these ways that power is invested in individuals through stimulating them to work voluntarily on themselves, making themselves docile in particular ways. Kracauer, as has been noted, was dismissive of instructors of body culture who went beyond personal hygiene and added world views to their teaching; yet demonstrations of gymnastics (and other sports events) always signify more than just physical fitness. These events signify a range of meanings in relation to social categories such as class, 'race', nation, generation, and gender because such categories are produced through the investment of power in bodies. Social historians of sport have pointed out that events like the Olympic Games have never been politically value-free (see Hargreaves 1982), but for the wider public this is generally little appreciated. The only example where this begins to be recognised is the 1936 Olympic Games, and Riefenstahl's film has played an important part in bringing about such recognition.

The film extract of the gymnastic display undoubtedly reveals investments of power that the institutions of the National Socialist state applied to young German women's bodies. It is a mistake, however, to see this as the only example of such ideological investment. To condemn all instances of body culture and early German modern dance, including performances of mass ornamental movements, as fascist because of their association with Hitler's Germany, while declaring other forms of dance and sport ideologically value-free, is a dangerous delusion. To do so is to set up boundaries to protect a supposedly apolitical purity, yet such boundaries and exclusionary practices mirror those through which the institutions of the National Socialist state implemented its eugenic policies. The smiling young woman, featured in the film extract, invites the spectator to make a connection between her or his own subjective experiences of embodiment and her enjoyment of physical exercise. Such a connection is easily made: more difficult is to recognise that just as power has been invested in her body in socially and historically specific ways, so, in different ways, has it been invested in one's own.

6

DANCING ACROSS THE ATLANTIC

It is no longer true that American dance historians writing about early modern dance see American dance as entirely separate from and unconnected with early European modern dance. But it wasn't so long ago that they did. Writing in 1974 Selma Jeanne Cohen observed that 'Though American modern dance was a largely independent phenomenon, a similar – though distinct – form had risen in Central Europe' (1974: 122). The implication is that, although European dancers may have been doing something similar to their American contemporaries at about the same time, this was entirely coincidental, and each more or less developed in isolation from the other. Contrary to what Cohen suggests, the American and European modern dance worlds overlapped right from the start. The three earliest pioneers of modern dance were Americans – Fuller, Duncan and St Denis – but the first two were primarily based in Europe and St Denis achieved her first big success not in New York but in Munich. Deborah Jowitt, writing in 1988, may not mean to say that European and American modern dance developed simultaneously, but she gives that impression:

> Duncan's premature death, at fifty, happened in 1927, the year in which Martha Graham and Doris Humphrey presented their first certifiably 'modern' dances in America. Mary Wigman, the leading force in Germany's Ausdrucktanz, had founded a school and company two years earlier.
>
> (Jowitt 1988: 94)

The implication that Wigman is more or less contemporary with Graham and Humphrey is of course not true. Wigman was born in 1886 while Graham and Humphrey were born in 1894 and 1895 respectively. Wigman had made her choreographic debut with three pieces including her first *Witch Dance* in 1914 and established herself as a major artist with a series of concerts in Germany and Switzerland in the 1918/19 season, opening her school in Dresden in 1920 not 1925. She was therefore a mature and respected artist at a time when Graham and Humphrey were still newly arrived at Denishawn. The existence of a more mature modern dance culture in Europe was a fact that, in the late 1920s and early 1930s, American modern dancers had to deal with when establishing their own artistic identities.

While I have picked out here two instances where American dance writers have inaccurately represented the relationship between European and American modern dance, I do not wish to suggest that there is an American conspiracy to distort the facts. On the contrary, recent publications by dance scholars based in the United States have added much to our knowledge of the relationship between Europe and America at the time. Isa Partsch-Bergsohn has devoted a whole book to connections between modern dance in Germany and the United States (Partsch-Bergsohn 1994). It is central to my argument in this book that this relationship was significant. The first half of the book has therefore focused on dance and modernism in Europe during the 1920s while the rest of the book considers how the issues and experiences discussed in the first half found expression in dance in the United States during the 1930s. By way of effecting a transition between these two sections, the aim of this short chapter is to present an overview of the evidence of connections between early modern dance in New York and modern dance and ballet in Europe and introduce the areas of concern that are explored in the rest of the book.

The idea that modern dance in the United States was distinct and separate from European developments is contradicted by the way German modern dance was written about by Americans during the 1930s. Many dance critics of the period were cosmopolitan in their knowledge of European modernism. Merle Armitage and Virginia Stewart's 1935 collection *The Modern Dance* includes contributions by and about the work of modern dance artists in both Germany and the United States. In her introduction to it, Stewart states: 'Having appeared first in Germany, the modern dance sprang up about ten years later in America' (Armitage and Stewart 1970: xii). John Martin, although playing an important role as an advocate for modern dance in his reviews in the *New York Times* and in lectures and books, seemed to value some German modern dancers more highly than American ones. In his 1933 book *The Modern Dance* (1965a) there are a number of references to Mary Wigman, all extremely positive, while there are only two passing references to Graham and one to Humphrey. In his 1939 book *Introduction to the Dance* (Martin, 1965b: 55) Martin still reserves his highest praise for Wigman. Admittedly, Martin and Stewart are representative of a faction within the field of 1930s dance criticism in the United States that was favourable to European modernism. Edna Ocko, who wrote for the left-wing magazine *New Theatre* and held very different views from those of Martin and Stewart, often reviewed the work of European artists and companies when they visited New York. In 1936 she commented that Jooss' *The Green Table* was 'a brilliant and stirring dance drama exposing international diplomacy as the harbinger of war and destruction', adding that its influence on experimental dance groups (by which I presume she means in the United States) was immeasurable (Prickett 1994b: 97). Taken together, these books and reviews from the 1930s clearly contradict the contentions of later writers about the extent to which Americans were unaware of and uninterested in European dance.

Notions of the separateness and distinctness of American modern dance nevertheless did exist in the United States during the late 1920s and 1930s and these were in line with a strong isolationist tendency within the United States. To put this isolationism into a broader context, whereas German isolationism during the Nazi period was exclusive, isolationism in the United States was broadly informed by assimilationist ideologies, just as the French are in some ways also assimilationist. Many Americans during the period, including Martha Graham herself, saw theirs as a new country and as a land of opportunity for the stream of immigrants who were still arriving from across the Atlantic. These included George Balanchine and Hanya Holm. Balanchine has subsequently been claimed as an American choreographer and the origins of his work in Russian modernist choreography of the late 1910s and early 1920s are all too often either unknown or ignored. In a similar way Josephine Baker became assimilated as an honorary Parisian. Julia Kristeva – another foreigner who has been adopted by the French – wryly comments that if you are recognised as a great scientist or a great artist:

> The entire [French] nation will appropriate your performance, will assimilate it along with its own better accomplishments, and give you recognition better than elsewhere. This will not happen without a twinkling of the eye directed at your oddity, so un-French, but it will be carried out with great panache and splendour.
>
> (Kristeva 1991: 40)

In New York, the oddity would not even be noticed, as the United States is such a diverse mixture of comparatively recent immigrants, and New York is such a cosmopolitan city. Nevertheless, the assimilation of Hanya Holm as one of the four pioneers of American modern dance[1] has had the side effect of further obscuring the interconnectedness of modern dance in Europe and North America. Before starting the New York Wigman school in 1931, Holm had trained with Jaques-Dalcroze and then with Wigman and became one of the latter's most trusted assistants in Dresden.

While one of the so-called four pioneers of American modern dance was German and had trained with one of the leaders of German modern dance, the other three – Graham, Humphrey and Weidman – were American and were not directly in touch with European modernism; having said that, it is generally admitted that they cannot have been unaware of it. There was considerable interest among the New York theatrical avant-garde in European modernism. John Martin's initial background was in modernist theatre, which manifested itself for example in a fascinating account of the work of the avant-garde Russian theatre director Meyerhold that he wrote in 1930.[2] The young painters of the New York School who would become famous in the 1940s and 1950s were fascinated by the work of modernist European painters who were at the time based in Paris. Arshille Gorky, for example, on discovering that Picasso had changed his style and was using fluid paint, is famously supposed to have said 'If he drips, I'll drip'. Louis Horst, on his return from Vienna in 1926, is said to have introduced Martha Graham to modernist European painting and sculpture. Don McDonagh suggests that Horst showed Graham books and pictures of European modern dancers (1973: 54). Horst may also have spoken about these to Humphrey and other modern dancers with whom he was in touch and for whose rehearsals and concerts he frequently provided the musical accompaniment.

Graham, Humphrey and Weidman all met Wigman when the latter arrived in New York (Partsch-Bergsohn 1994: 64–5), and will probably also have seen Kreutzberg and Georgi when they performed in New York.[3] While Graham and Humphrey chose not to present their work outside the United States until after the Second World War, other dancers, including Pauline Koner, Ted Shawn, Anna Sokolow and Helen Tamiris travelled to Europe and performed there in the 1920s and 1930s. Shawn travelled to Germany to dance the leading role in Margarethe Wallmann's large-scale piece *Orpheus Dionysos*, performed at the Third Dancers' Congress in Munich in 1930 (Partsch-Bergsohn 1994: 62). At the same time several American dancers trained in Europe with either Wigman or Jaques-Dalcroze. for example, the African American modern dancer Alison Burroughs had studied Dalcroze eurythmics at the Hellerau-Laxenburg School near Vienna in 1931 (see Perpener 1992: 114). Until the New York Wigman School opened, there was nowhere in the United States where a student could undergo full time professional training in modern dance. Katherine Dunham took classes with Harald Kreutzberg when the latter was in Chicago.[4] Margarethe Wallmann taught 'Wigman' technique at the New York Denishawn studios in the late 1920s before the arrival of Hanya Holm. There were other immigrants from Europe who settled in the United States, such as Tina Flade, Fe Alf and Lucas Hoving, all of whom had a background in German modern dance. Valeska Gert performed in New York in 1936 and lived there and in Provincetown from 1939 until her return to Europe in 1947. She never made any impact as a dancer although her Beggars Bar in New York has gone down in the history of cabaret and experimental theatre.[5]

Another area in which American modern dancers came in touch with earlier European modernisms was ballet. In the 1920s and early 1930s Fokine and Massine were living and working in New York. Both Pauline

Koner and Helen Tamiris took classes with Fokine, and on one celebrated occasion in 1931 Fokine angrily encountered Graham at a lecture demonstration by the latter for John Martin's course at the New School for Social Research. Graham established a tense working relationship with Massine when she was cast as the Chosen One for the latter's 1931 staging of *The Rite of Spring* in Philadelphia, a project in which many New York modern dancers were involved, including members of Graham's company and of the Humphrey Weidman group. One consequence of this, an interest in 'primitive' ritual, is discussed in Chapter 8. The Ballets Russes de Monte Carlo performed Nijinska's *Les Noces* in New York in 1936. Marcia Siegel says this work made a significant impact at the time and suggests that Doris Humphrey may have seen this just before she started work on *With My Red Fires* (1993: 162–3).

As modern dance developed on either side of the Atlantic, European and American dancers were therefore more aware of each other's work than has sometimes been allowed. There were nevertheless significant differences between the way dancers on each continent were responding to their very different experiences of modernity. So far I have examined dance culture in Europe and argued that the most radical, avant-garde artistic ideas had more in common with libertarian social and political philosophies than with communist ones. Following Andreas Huyssen I have argued that this avant-gardism went into a decline when the financial collapses at the end of the 1920s did not bring about the hoped for collapse of capitalism and with it the start of a new life, but instead helped bring about the rise of fascism. In the last chapter I reviewed the way in which libertarian notions of the embodiment of German identity as expressed in body culture and early modern dance in Germany became absorbed during the early years of the National Socialist regime within the institutions and ideologies of the National Socialist party. Kurt Jooss stands out for his development of a modernist choreographic style in response to the threat of fascism, and in doing so reworking what had been a nationally focused modern dance into an internationally focused fusion of ballet and modern dance.

Jooss' trajectory is in line with Susan Manning's formulation of the relationship between modernism and nationalism. She has proposed that, after the First World War, modern dance became an arena for the forging of national identity while ballet became an arena for international competition (Manning 1988: 36). It was for an international competition that Jooss' *The Green Table* was choreographed. It was not just in Germany that modern dancers explored ideas of national identity. In *Frontier, American Document* and other pieces during the 1930s Martha Graham explored ideologies of American national identity. But whereas in Europe the financial collapses precipitated a shift to the right, in the United States they contributed to the election of President Roosevelt and a left-leaning Democratic government. The trajectory of modern dance in New York was from a radical, critical modernism in the late 1920s towards an increasingly left-wing modernism after 1936 through the influence of the communist-oriented Popular Front – a broadly based left-wing movement which opposed fascism. Internationalism had long been a key theme within communist and socialist rhetoric – the title of the most celebrated left-wing anthem is of course the 'Internationale'. The Popular Front proposed a class-conscious internationalism, stressing that there were ties between working-class people in different countries. Jean Renoir's 1937 film *La Grande Illusion* is frequently cited as an example of this type of Popular Front internationalism; the film follows the fortunes of an aristocratic and a working-class French airman captured by the Germans during the 1914–18 war, arguing that class ties are stronger than national ones.[6] It was the 'International Brigades' of mostly socialist and communist volunteers from Western Europe and North America who fought on the democratically elected republican side against the fascist Falangists in the Spanish Civil War. For some, like Graham, advocacy of the republican side in the Spanish Civil War may have been a liberal political stance; but for many others such internationalism was a communist or socialist position, as the American Communist Party made some accommodation with Roosevelt's administration and shifted away from criticism of capitalism to opposition to fascism.[7] Support for the Spanish republican cause among modern dancers in New York resulted in several dance pieces, including Martha Graham's *Chronicle* (1936) and *Deep Song* (1937), and José Limón's *Danza de la Muerte* (1937).

The other significant group of associations that internationalism carried in the 1930s were financial ones. The United States officially became isolationist in its foreign policy in 1919 when the American Congress refused to ratify the treaty to join the League of Nations. This isolationism ended in 1942 when the United States entered the war against Germany and Japan. In the 1920s and 1930s there was, however, a small group of capitalists who, for financial reasons, wished their country to adopt a more international approach. The possibilities for expansion for the very biggest American family business empires having been blocked by anti-trust legislation, these families turned their attention to the possibility of international markets. As Griselda Pollock and Fred Orton have shown, the Rockefeller family's strategy to bring about this change in American policy included their interventionist patronage of European modern art through the institution of the Museum of Modern Art in New York, which they founded and effectively controlled:

> The Rockefellers have always been internationalists and the foundation and growth of the Museum of Modern Art was a concrete representation of their class fraction's struggle to dominate not only in economic and governmental terms but also to shape an interna-

tionalist and modernising image of America both at home and abroad.[8]

It was through the writings and exhibitions of its first curator Alfred H. Barr that the idea of a historical development of modern art, first posited by the English critic Roger Fry, became popularly accepted.

The view of modernism in the visual arts that Clement Greenberg developed comes from both the Popular Front and Barr's putative history of modern art. As Greenberg himself subsequently commented: 'Some day it will have to be told how "Anti-Stalinism", which started out more or less as "Trotskyism", turned into art for art sake, and thereby cleared the way, heroically, for what was to come' (Greenberg 1961: 230). Greenberg is referring to the historical demise of the Popular Front at the end of the 1930s with the news of the Hitler–Stalin pact of 1939. This pact threw many artists and intellectuals into confusion by uniting the two figure heads that had up until then signified, on the one hand, what they supported and, on the other, that to which they were opposed.

Greenberg's article 'Avant-garde or kitsch?' published in the then Trotskyite periodical *Partisan Review* in the autumn of 1939, shortly after the announcement of the Hitler–Stalin pact, is a key essay in the development of a formalist high modernist account of the visual arts see (see Orton and Pollock 1985).[9] Pointing out the similarity between socialist realism under Stalin and National Socialist realism under Hitler, Greenberg argued that only the modernist tradition in painting represented freedom and progress. This view of the politics of progressive modern art was one with which the veteran Russian revolutionary Leon Trotsky was associated. During the 1930s the French Surrealist leader André Breton, the Mexican mural painter José Rivera and Trotsky, then in exile in Mexico, developed a view of modernist art that also aligned advanced modernist experimentation with international socialism. In an article published in *Partisan Review* in 1938, Trotsky wrote:

> Art, like science, not only does not seek orders, but by its very essence, cannot tolerate them. Artistic creation has its own laws – even when it consciously serves a social movement. Truly intellectual creation is incompatible with lies, hypocrisy and the spirit of conformity. Art can become a strong ally of the revolution only in so far as it remains faithful to itself.
>
> (Trotsky 1938: 10)[10]

At a time when Europe – up until then the heart of Western civilisation – seemed about to be submerged either by Stalinist communism or fascism under Hitler, Franco and Mussolini, Greenberg saw modernist artists as the only ones free from political restraints and thus able to keep the idea of civilisation alive. The choice for Greenberg thus appeared to be between a modernist avant-garde that was still at that moment oriented towards the left, and a politically manipulated realist kitsch. In the cold war period, however, this formulation took on a different significance and served a different political purpose as a now internationally-oriented United States exported American abstract expressionist painting (see Cockcroft 1985) and, to a lesser extent, American modern dance companies to Europe as cultural ambassadors. The argument then was that American modern art was free and progressive while communist-oriented realist art was old fashioned and politically dependent. What this amounted to was a shift away from a notion of art as a practice with a critical, deconstructive edge, that was in line with the critical modern consciousness identified by Zygmunt Bauman (1991), towards a notion of art as abstract, uncritical, and autonomous. Hence the post-war idea that dance which deals with social content of any political alignment is somehow of less aesthetic value than dance that is 'abstract' and supposedly independent of its social context. A recurrent theme of this book is that this idea gives a distorted view of the dance culture of the 1920s and 1930s.

The notion that dance is apolitical, abstract and autonomous led historians and commentators to discount and virtually exclude from the historical record the choreography of members of the New Dance League and others associated with the workers' dance movement in the United States. Recent research into the workers dance movement is therefore valuable for several reasons. It recovers an important component of the dance culture in New York during the period. As some dancers involved with the workers' dance movement also danced with Graham or with Humphrey and Weidman, it opens up questions about the relationship between the major choreographers of the period and the left. Writings about dance in left-wing magazines complement and balance the view of modern dance that was developed by Martin, Stewart and writers associated with the *Dance Observer*. As Mark Franko points out, the fact that left-wing commentators in the early 1930s criticised Graham for her abstract formalism is a necessary corrective to the later prejudice that Graham's work was expressionistic and emotivist (Franko 1995: 38–42). Similarly it is precisely through research into dance and politics in New York during the 1930s that much evidence of the relationship between American and German modern dance has recently been recovered. Susan Manning has written at length about the circumstances in which Graham turned down the invitation from the German government to take her company to the arts festival accompanying the 1936 Berlin Olympic Games (Manning 1993: 255–85). So strong was feeling against the German dancers who had collaborated with the Nazi regime that Hanya Holm subsequently decided to disassociate her school from any connection with Wigman. The irony in this was the fact that many of the left-wing dancers like Jane Dudley had initially trained with Holm, the *New Dance*

Group starting at her school.[11] In retrospect it is a little difficult to appreciate how in the 1930s dance could have become involved in left-wing politics because life styles have changed so much since then. Political culture in Western Europe and North America in the 1990s no longer operates on the large public scale it did in the 1920s and 1930s. An article in 1934 claimed that 34,000 people had seen performances by workers' dance groups (see Graff 1994: 5). Jane Dudley says that the audiences for whom the *New Dance Group* performed at union meetings and political meetings would come down town to see them when they were dancing with the Martha Graham company. In the 1990s people do not go out as much – either to live performances or political meetings – as they did in the 1920s and 1930s. Small, amateur theatres and pageants were popular during the first few decades of the twentieth century in Europe and the United States. Not much ideological distance separates the idea of a community expressing itself through theatre and pageants and the enactment and embodiment through performance of party political ideals.[12]

Susan Manning suggests that Wigman's large-scale 1929 work *Totenmal* pioneered many of the techniques used in the Nazi German genre of political 'festival' plays or pageants called Thingspiel (1993: 157–60). She cites as one example the incorporation of the audience within the action by placing actors, who read out letters, in amongst the audience. Barbara Stratyner points out that this device was used in one of the Communist Party pageants created in New York in 1937. *One Sixth of the Earth,* choreographed and produced by Bill Matons (a member of the Humphrey Weidman Group), included 'poignant speeches by anonymous witnesses in the crowd' (Stratyner 1994: 34). Stratyner observes that the source for this theatrical device was the tradition of theatrical agit-prop Living Newspapers which had their origins in the Soviet Union. That this was also the source for its use in *Totenmal* and various Thingspiel productions is backed up by Glen Gadberry's suggestion that suspicion of Thingspiel at a high level among the Nazi leadership was provoked by its similarities with communist agit-prop theatre (Gadberry 1980: 112). Not only was a particular theatrical device used both by the left – in the Soviet Union – and by the right – in Nazi Germany – but it was also used by modern dancers both in Germany – Wigman – and the United States – Matons.[13] While the political ideologies were poles apart, the sorts of politicised dance culture that Manning identifies in Nazi Germany were also present in the United States. These are not coincidences, as there were some similarities (but also significant differences) of social experience on each side of the Atlantic, together with a flow and exchange of artistic ideas.

Nevertheless, Martha Graham and Doris Humphrey were both committed to creating dance relevant to modern American experience which they saw as distinct from modern European experience. Writing about her teaching with Charles Weidman in New York in 1928, Humphrey states:

> The students were stimulated by our enthusiasm for some discoveries about movement, which had to do with ourselves as Americans – not Europeans or American Indians or East Indians, which most of the Denishawn work consisted of, but as young people of the twentieth century living in the United States.
>
> (Cohen 1972: 61)

Although Humphrey is primarily referring to Denishawn, it is surely significant that she also mentions Europe and thus by implication German modern dance. Virginia Stewart wrote in 1935 that modern dance appeared first in Germany, and sprang up about ten years later in America (Armitage and Stewart 1970: xii). It was around this time that José Limón joined the Humphrey Weidman group, having been inspired by seeing a performance by Harald Kreutzberg who Limón nevertheless felt was 'too Gothic' (see Pollack and Woodford 1993: 13).

In seeking to develop a distinctively American modern dance Humphrey, Graham and their contemporaries in New York were responding to perceived needs which nevertheless corresponded to more general isolationist, nationalist ideologies within American society. Additionally, as Susan Manning (1996) has pointed out, for Graham and other female American modern dancers, American subjects allowed an escape from stereotypical notions of feminine dance. The female dancing body in Graham's work, she points out, was capable of representing the diversity of human experience. A key example of this is Graham's *American Document* in which her dancers represent in succession the Founding American Fathers, the American Indians, the freed African American slaves and contemporary American people. It was, however, only white dancers who were allowed multiple roles and fluid identities and this, Manning points out, 'reasserted the binary of racial difference through its one-way representation: only the white body could take on alternative racial and ethnic meanings' (Manning 1996: 192). Whereas, as was seen in Chapter 3, Josephine Baker's 'savage' dances were seen by Europeans as representing the true spirit of the Negro race, in the United States it was not African American concert dancers but white dancers like Helen Tamiris, and Ted Shawn's male dancers performing choreography that used Negro spirituals who were acclaimed by critics for mirroring the Negro spirit and rhythm in the modern idiom.[14]

It is the question of how the modern idiom was exemplified in modern choreography in the United States during the 1930s that the rest of this book addresses. I have discussed the extent to which jazz music for Europeans was both jungle music and the song of the machine, a seemingly contradictory combination. The 'savage' dance of Josephine Baker and the street walker in Gert's *Canaille* exemplified the 'primitive' while the precise and, for Kracauer, almost Tayloristic movement of the Tiller Girls and of the de-individuated, modernist skaters in *Skating Rink* exemplified the social impact of mechanisation and industrial restructuring. It is American versions of these two aspects of modernity that underlie the discussion of the next two chapters. Chapter 7 examines how key examples of modern choreography in the United States made use of discoveries about movement, which, as Humphrey put it 'had to do with ourselves as Americans' (Cohen 1972: 61). Chapter 8 revisits the ways in which ideologies of the 'primitive' were used on both sides of the Atlantic to explore the tension between modern social existence and modernist culture. What is examined in both chapters are the ways in which modern dance produced alien dancing bodies which exemplified the social and psychological construction of 'prevailing historical forms of selfhood, masculinity, femininity, desire' (Bordo 1993: 165).

7

AMERICAN MODERNS

To the American dancer I say 'Know your country'. When its
vitality, its freshness, its exuberance of youth and vigour, its
contrasts of plenitude and barrenness are made manifest in movement on the stage, we begin to see the American dance.

When we speak of this country, we speak of a vast concept whose
infinite facets cannot all be seen. But in spite of this immensity let
us find fundamentals of which we are all a part. Let us consider for a
moment the striking difference in the Continent's and our own
reaction to an important factor in modern times – the machine.
Talk to the Continental, talk to the American of the machines' part
in the tempo of modern life. The reactions are unmistakably characteristic.

To the European the machine is still a matter of wonder and excessive sentimentality. Some sort of machine dance is a staple of every
European dance repertory. But to the American sentimentality for
the machine is alien. The machine is a natural phenomenon of life.

An American dance is not a series of steps. It is infinitely more.
The characteristic time beat, a different speed, an accent, sharp,
clear, staccato.

(Armitage 1966: 105)

This is Martha Graham writing in 1936. Her assertions of the American-
ness of American modern dance come in a decade when she was making a
series of dances on American themes – some represented pioneering white
Americans while others were inspired by the example of American Indian
religious rituals. Graham, like many modern American artists of her period,
was isolationist in her attitudes towards her art, paralleling the isolationist
foreign policy which the United States pursued throughout the 1920s and
1930s. For her as for Doris Humphrey and Charles Weidman an assertion of
the validity of modern American experience as a subject for choreography
was a necessary counter to the superficially oriental, tribal, folk and other

borrowed dance styles that typified the productions of Ted Shawn and Ruth St Denis. Furthermore, as I pointed out in the last chapter, by the early to mid-1930s claims about the American-ness of American modern dance were also, for Graham and her contemporaries, a rejection of the idea then current that their modern dance styles were merely derivative of the then more developed and more mature work of visiting German artists like Wigman and Kreutzberg.

As a European I find Graham's broad generalisations about 'Continentals' grating. They are certainly chauvinist, somewhat arrogant and ill informed. Where did Graham get the idea that machine dances were 'a staple of every European dance repertory'?[1] How could anyone think that European intellectuals like Siegfried Kracauer could look upon the machine as a matter of wonder and excessive sentimentality? At the time, Graham had never been to Europe (except for a brief tour with Denishawn, performing in England in 1922). Nor did she want to go to Europe. In 1935 she wrote:

> It has been the common practice [for Americans] to seek instruction in lands alien to us, fettered as we are to things European. What does this mean? It means to me losing all that we should hold most dear in the development of American dance.
>
> (Armitage and Stewart 1970: 54)

In March 1932 she had been awarded a Guggenheim fellowship which offered her the opportunity to travel to Europe and study with Mary Wigman, but, she later wrote: 'I said no. I didn't want to go to Europe without something American so I chose Mexico as a compromise. Some people still think that I studied with Wigman' (Graham 1991: 143).

All of Graham's comments tell us little of interest about European dance but a lot about Graham's idea of America. When she says 'let us find fundamentals of which we are all a part' Graham is expressing the classic, liberal American, assimilationist position. Having appealed to these American fundamentals, it is telling that she uses a supposed difference between European and American sensibilities to consolidate what 'we Americans' all have in common, and that she should choose modernity as the site of that supposed difference. This indicates that she thought about her modern dance in nationalistic terms which are romantic and essentialist, and that she considered the ways in which modern life was being changed by modernisation and mechanisation were significant subjects for dance. Clearly Graham is discussing here the same types of issues which in previous chapters I have identified in European work. Ideologies of nationalism and internationalism affected dance in the United States just as they affected dance in Europe; and just as in Europe, American dance and critical discourses about dance were areas in which the experiences of modernity were articulated and contested.

This is not to deny that the United States was, by the 1930s, much further advanced in the process of modernisation than any European country; or that the choreographic work of Graham and Humphrey was different from the work of Wigman or Kreutzberg. This chapter looks at the ways in which American modern dance of the 1930s mediated American experiences of modernity, and of what it meant to be an American in the 1930s. Graham, in the quotation with which this chapter began, spoke of the American dance as moving to a rhythm which she characterised as fast, sharply accented, clear and staccato. The implication is that the pace of American dance expressed the pace of life in the modern American city – a pace whose tempo was affected by the processes of modernisation and mechanisation. The dance pieces discussed in this chapter all drew on this experience, most celebrating the dream of a positive future which modernity seemed to offer. The analysis of these pieces that I make in this chapter proposes that these American choreographers found new ways of expressing the individual's experience of the dynamism and scale of modern society, and explored the modern ways in which individuals related to one another and to the larger group that represents society as a whole.

The idea which Graham so clearly articulates that American experience was newer, more vibrant and above all different from European experience needs to be placed in the context of debates in the United States during the 1930s about nationalism and internationalism and about the social role of the artist in modern society. If much of the American critical discussion about dance generated by left-wing writers was concerned with realism and social relevance, this was because the Communist Party had, at the Congress of Soviet Writers in 1934, officially chosen to favour socialist realism over modernist, formalist abstraction (and the Russian avant-garde) which the John Reed Club of New York accepted (see Harrison and Wood 1992: 401–4 and 409–12). Meanwhile little intellectual support for modernist abstraction was offered from those writers not on the left. Franko has rightly observed that what modern dancers needed but lacked in the mid-1930s was 'a formalist witness to articulate its modernism in words' (Franko 1995: 39). Theoretical frameworks for conceptualising and interpreting formal aesthetic qualities were being developed during the 1920s and 1930s by German marxist intellectuals and philosophers. The ideas of theorists like Adorno, Benjamin, Bloch and Kracauer were not at that time widely known outside Germany nor acceptable to the Communist Party itself. Some of this body of theory has already been used in early chapters of his book to interrogate the modernism of early European modern dance and ballet.

The same or similar concerns can be identified within the work of modern dance artists in the United States during the period, with significant differences. The European avant-garde saw in modernity a utopian ideal that would follow the collapse of capitalism, and this led to a fascination with America. For Americans, on the other hand, modernity was the area in which they were in advance of Europe. Understandably, therefore, they

perceived it in isolationist, nationalist terms and saw it as the means to real-
ising the American dream. Whereas the European avant-garde were largely
libertarian, the American left were mostly marxists and those who wrote
about dance and theatre consequently held fairly conservative views about
aesthetic modernism. American choreography, which took American modernity as its inspiration, therefore conformed to isolationist notions of national
identity.

What is interesting and significant about the essay 'The mass ornament'
(discussed in Chapters 4 and 5) is not just the fact that Kracauer was
prepared to look seriously at mass culture, but also that he was interested in
locating the formal qualities that characterised the dancing and movement
of mass ornament performances in relation to social changes brought about
as a consequence of industrial modernisation. Despite his pessimism,
Kracauer was initially just about able to see the modernist abstraction of
chorus line dancing as a utopian ideal suggestive of a better future that the
process of rationalisation might be able to bring about. However, as we have
seen, by the time he wrote 'Girls and crisis' in 1931 Kracauer had come to
believe that the mass ornament no longer offered a credible ideal but was a
delusion and a distraction. Kracauer's pessimism was not unique within
Germany or indeed Europe as a whole at that time but it was largely alien to
Americans. Dance artists like Graham and Humphrey, together with some
who wrote about their work, subscribed to a positive view of the potential of
American industrial knowledge and experience to create the conditions that
would fulfil the American dream. What is generally argued is that American
modernist works like Balanchine's *Serenade* (1934) and Humphrey's *New
Dance* (1935) present an ideal because they achieve some timeless aesthetic
goal. In this chapter I propose that some of the more celebratory American
works of the mid-1930s present, in formal terms, levels of order and energy
that could be seen as ideal and utopian precisely because these levels were
the opposite of current conditions; in other words what real life lacked and
thus needed, these works exemplified in abundance.[2] Whereas an orthodox
modernist view would evaluate the timeless truths of great masterpieces –
asserting that a thing of beauty is a joy for ever – I want to insist that
cultural productions like ballets and dance pieces are historically specific.
This means therefore that, although the utopian ideals exemplified in these
works are necessarily apart from present reality, the parameters governing
what might or might not have an effect upon these works were ideologically
determined and socially and historically specific. One should therefore be
alert to the possibility of contradictions, absences and exclusions within the
sorts of ideals they suggest.

This chapter therefore proceeds as follows. As modernity and mechanisation were significant issues around which the American-ness of American
modern dance differed from similar developments in Europe, I look at the
ways in which modernity as a theme was dealt with in American modern

dance. This leads on to a more detailed discussion of the relationship between modernity and utopian ideals in Balanchine's *Serenade*, Humphrey's *New Dance* and the dream ballet choreographed and performed by Katherine Dunham with her dance company in the 1943 film *Stormy Weather*.

Choreography and modern American life

What is at issue in the various accounts of dance modernism that were expounded in the United States during the 1930s was not whether modernist dance bore any relation to contemporary life, but what the relationship between dance and life ought to be. For John Martin, subject matter on its own was no guarantee of modernity. 'In the early days of the modern dance', he wrote in 1936, 'there was a veritable deluge of machinery dances presumably created in the belief that nothing could be more modern than machinery and no way easier, therefore, to the field of modern dancing' (1968: 72). It is not the subject, Martin asserts, that makes a piece modern, but its content: 'A dance entitled "Opus 24" with no more program than its title would indicate might contain more deeply grounded social significance and vastly more immediacy, provided it were born of that inner illumination by which alone the artist conceives' (ibid.). Martin further explains this artist-centred view of modernity by referring to Isadora Duncan. Duncan, he says, 'was "driven as a leaf is driven before the wind" faced by her responsiveness to the unformulated will of her epoch to do what the time required' (ibid.: 83). Martin seems to have thought that in the 1930s 'what the time required' was abstract dance which, following Mary Wigman, he called the 'absolute' dance: 'dance alone, an autonomous art exemplifying fully the ideals of modernism in its attainment of abstraction and in its utilisation of the resources of its materials efficiently and with authority' (Martin 1965b: 235). Graham herself seems to have thought in similar terms:

> One has to become what one is. Since the dance form is governed by social conditions, so the American rhythm is sharp and angular, stripped of unessentials. It is something related only to itself, not laid on, but as a piece with that spirit which was willing to face a pioneer country.
>
> (Armitage 1966: 101)

Clearly both Martin and Graham articulated their understanding of modernist abstraction in similar terms and both saw it as a direct response to American experiences of modernity. Both also saw American modern dance in terms of positive affirmation. While dance for Graham expressed the pioneering American spirit, Martin proposed in 1939 that the American dancer does not meekly accept life 'but undertakes to shape it to his [sic] own ends. He is not content with experiencing and revealing states of being, but insists on dealing in states of action' (Martin 1965b: 238). Graham's *Celebration* (1934) is not only a clear example of a dance piece that exemplifies this positive affirmation, but also a piece whose critical reception indicates the range of political stances held by critics at the time.

What immediately strikes the viewer of *Celebration* is its dynamism and energy. It starts with twelve dancers (originally all women) in a close formation jumping together into the air, seemingly propelled by the 4/4 march tempo of a trumpet tune in Louis Horst's music. As they bounce on the beat, they start to stretch up their arms, making striking images – sometimes symmetrical, sometimes not – that change with each jump. After this first section the music changes to a more winsome melody played on the oboe to which the dancers, breaking out of the solidly massed group to spread across the stage, stretch out their arms and turn their torsos so that their arms sweep around them through space. Then the trumpet tune recurs and with it the jumps (and in the 1996 version I saw big balletic lifts which surely couldn't have been part of the original dance).[3] The piece returns once more to the oboe melody and ends as it began with the trumpets and a reprise of the opening jumps.

Marie Marchowsky, who was one of the dancers with whom Graham originally made the piece, told Alice Helpern that Graham used images of upward thrusting skyscrapers and percussive rhythms of the modern city. Helpern suggests that 'the pulsating power of *Celebration* echoed the throbbing energy of America, a strong industrial nation' (Helpern 1991: 13). America in the early 1930s was of course recovering from the effects of the Wall Street Crash and there was widespread unemployment and economic hardship. President F. D. Roosevelt was voted in in 1932 on the strength of his vision of economic regeneration and with it a new deal for 'the forgotten man at the bottom of the economic pyramid'. It is inconceivable that *Celebration* could have celebrated the reality of life on the streets of depression-hit American cities; what it expressed was the hope that the American dream must be valid if it could produce such modern marvels.

John Martin in 1936 saw *Celebration* as one of the pieces in which Graham moved on from her Indian ritual phase (with pieces like *Primitive Mysteries* and *Primitive Canticle*) towards 'the equally exigent rituals which underlie contemporary life' (1968: 199). *Transitions, Celebration* and *Course* were all in his opinion touched with a 'strong social awareness' (ibid.). *Celebration*, he wrote, is 'filled with vitality and the consciousness of victory. It is, from a compositional standpoint, one of the fullest and most finished of all [Graham's] group dances' (ibid.: 200). Paul Love, reviewing the premiere in the *Dance Observer* praised its opposition of fast and slow sections 'of vigorous excitement and almost ritualistic gravity' which 'is brilliantly worked out and brings immediate response from the audience' (1934: 17). Love complains however that sometimes there is too much going on on stage for the viewer to take in the whole, leaving, he says, 'my remembrance of the form shot through with occasional small holes' (ibid.). But how like the pace and scale of metropolitan experience not to be able to take in everything in one glance. Edna Ocko made an – at the time – uncharacteristically positive judgement of *Celebration* in the December 1934 issue of *New Theatre*. The piece, she suggested, might have been called *Demonstration* because it evoked images of May Day parades and union organising. Another left-wing critic, Paul Douglas, took a sterner view. Graham, he thought, would be remembered as 'the greatest dance exponent of the last stages of capitalism struggling in its final agonies to salvage something out of its chaotic and decaying torment' (Douglas 1995: 140–1). This in his view caused her to be unable to apply herself successfully to 'vital subject matter' (ibid.). Yet clearly Douglas too was impressed by *Celebration*: having written Graham off, however, he seems to have had to make a special case for it:

> There is discernible in Graham's recent group dances, however, a noticeable change. In *Celebration*, for instance, a greater use of space and more elevation is attained than ever before. This, I believe, indicates the influence of some of her students, who from an ideological viewpoint are more advanced than Graham herself. The change is encouraging. The group has superb technical ability. But it will be wasted unless they continue to depart even more radically from the fundamental features of Graham's dance forms.
>
> (ibid.: 141)

The dynamic energy of *Celebration* – its speed, accent and characteristic time beat – was therefore acknowledged as a response to modernity at a significant moment in the establishment of the New Deal. This energy was, however, interpreted in different ways from different political positions. If its characteristically American energy seems to have been appreciated by both Ocko and Martin from differing political stances, Mark Roth has argued that the Warner Brothers musicals which Busby Berkeley made in 1932 and 1933 used modernist imagery in ways that were more explicitly supportive of Roosevelt's New Deal. The final number from *Gold Diggers of 1933* 'Remember My Forgotten Man' echoes Roosevelt's words directly. Roth suggests that in *42nd Street* and *Footlight Parade* the strong director who forces his cast to work hard and succeed embodies the spirit of the New Deal (1981: 47–8). Berkeley's extraordinary, mass ornamental production numbers represent the fruits of this successful labour. As Roth (1981) and Hoberman (1993) both suggest, in the context of the New Deal these mass ornaments signify putting Americans back to work. Berkeley's choreography offered precisely the hope that Kracauer had dismissed as illusory in his 1931 article 'Girls and crisis' (see Chapter 4). The mechanical efficiency and clarity of the geometric patterns in these numbers celebrate the power of modern industrial production just as Graham's *Celebration* celebrated the modern metropolis.

While Graham's *Celebration* and Berkeley's film numbers used the dynamic energy of dance to present a utopian image of modernity, Jane Dudley's *Time is Money*, which she made in 1934, attempts to show what it was like to be one of Roosevelt's forgotten men at the bottom of the economic pyramid; and while Graham may not have known about Taylorism, this piece indicates that it was a topic of discussion for Dudley and other dancers on the left in New York. Dudley was a member of the New Dance Group who used to perform at union meetings and the group developed a close relationship with the Needlework and Allied Trades Federation (Prickett 1990: 52). In *Time is Money*, which Dudley recently reconstructed for performances in London and New York, she used a poem of the same name by Sol Funaroff which includes the lines:

> Time is money and the tailors' shears
> become the whirring cutters'
> gears of efficiency engineers.
>
> (quoted Prickett 1989: 53)

A left-wing poem about tailors would have been apposite for a dance performed for members of the needlework union. The term 'efficiency engineers' was used at the time to refer to specialists in the type of industrial restructuring that Taylor had pioneered, and this is perhaps behind Funaroff's reference to tailors.[4] At this point in *Time is Money* the dancers' movements mime those of a machine turning mechanically at right angles between two operations.

These three examples all come from the early 1930s. *Time is Money* was reviewed in the December 1934 *Dance Observer* by Henry Gilfond on a page facing a review by Ralph Taylor of *Celebration*.[5] All three pieces were produced for different contexts and each articulated different ideological positions. From a political point of view, Berkeley's choreography is the most conservative in that it lacked any kind of critical edge, while Dudley's piece is the most radical of the three. Like Kracauer's essay, *Time is Money* suggests that it is the individual's body that most clearly reveals the negative, dehumanising effects of contemporary industrial reforms aimed at greater efficiency; and Dudley's piece also evokes the extent to which the individual yearns to be able to free her or himself from such dehumanisation. Mark Franko has shown that what those on the left in New York admired in Graham's choreography was the way it showed how dance could present images of the individual's desire for freedom and of a possible utopia. What these three pieces have in common is the embodiment in movement of the lived experience of metropolitan modernity.

Choreographing the new communities of consumption

The relationship between modern dance and the pace of modern, mechanised life, which these three pieces each exemplify in different ways, is only part of the experience of modernity. Taylorism and Fordism were strategies for changing industrial work practices in the interests of greater production. Increasing production requires ever bigger and more standardised and homogenised markets. If for most of the twentieth century the United States was the leading industrial nation, this was not only because of its industrial efficiency but more importantly because of the ways in which American society was changed by the dynamics of consumption. As Victoria de Grazia points out, the key issue in understanding the social experience of modernity is:

> how conceptions of market, merchandising techniques, and adver-
> tising design of American provenance forced the development of
> new patterns of consumer culture and thus came to define what it
> meant to be modern. . . . Increasingly, the contractual relations of
> market shaped notions of community, pressures for entitlement, and
> the modalities of political consensus. This change was accompanied
> by the construction of new social subjects such as consumers.
>
> (de Grazia 1989: 223)

One difference between European and American modern dance of the 1930s is the extent to which American dance explores the embodiment of these new subjectivities and considers how they combined together into new conceptions of community in ways which were not yet significantly present in Europe. De Grazia calls these 'communities of consumption'. The new dynamic principle of consumption depended upon and effected a levelling of social hierarchies and regional differences in the interests of a greater and more homogenous pool of consumers each buying the same product and responding to the same merchandising techniques. Theoretically this suggests a society of equals. So when Doris Humphrey wrote of her enthu-siasm for some discoveries about movement, which had to do with the experience of young people of the twentieth century living in the United States (see p. 130 above), that experience was from the point of view of the new subject positions and within new forms of collectivity brought about by the needs of modern industry.

Two of the key themes which underlie some of the most interesting modern dance created in the United States during the period covered in this book is the relationship between subjectivities and collectivity as expressed in the dynamics of the group and the relationship between the individual and the group. From Graham and Humphrey's writings and statements it is evident that each in different ways was concerned with the group as a theme in their choreography: this manifested itself in the precarious balance between the need for social conformity and the freedom to explore individual aspirations. Jowitt (1988), Graff (1994) and others have discussed the differences between Humphrey and Graham's approach to the group. In pieces like *Heretic* and *Primitive Mysteries*, it is argued, Graham casts herself as the individual who is separated from or at odds with the group; Humphrey's works like *Passacaglia* and *New Dance*, however, show a group of individuals who each have their own solos but come out of and return to the larger group which ultimately seems to represent something more important than anything that individuals can achieve on their own. Since I have already devoted some space in this chapter to discussing Graham's work and ideas and shall be looking at her *Primitive Mysteries* in the next chapter, I shall not discuss her work further here. Instead I shall look at the ways in which group choreography in the work of George Balanchine, Katherine Dunham and Doris Humphrey expresses American hopes and fears about the new subject positions and new forms of collectivity that were being brought about by the needs of modern industry. I am therefore looking at Balanchine's innovative and unusual use of the interplay between soloists and corps de ballet in *Serenade* (1934), which was made soon after his arrival in the United States and which, I shall argue, is informed by his perception of the difference between European and American society; Humphrey's concern with modern social ethics and the group which informed her pieces *New Dance* (1935) and *With My Red Fires* (1936); and the dream ballet from the motion picture musical *Stormy Weather* (Twentieth Century Fox 1943) choreographed by Katherine Dunham, which is clearly situated in a modern, urban environment and informed by African American experience of modernity.

Balanchine's *Serenade* and Humphrey's *New Dance* were choreographed within about a year of one another. There are similarities between the modernist structure of the way each piece presents the group but there are also large differences both in movement style and in the way each represents gender. Dunham's dream ballet in *Stormy Weather* can also be seen as a modernist work; the technical basis of its movement material exemplifies much of the discipline found in *Serenade* but is at the same time informed by ideologies of individual freedom that bring it closer to Humphrey's work. I shall therefore contrast and compare *Serenade* (focusing on the opening 'Sonatina' section) and *New Dance* and then use the conclusions drawn from this discussion as a basis for looking at *Stormy Weather*.

The idea of finding points of comparison between George Balanchine and Doris Humphrey might seem slightly bizarre. On the face of it each belonged to entirely different constituencies within the dance world. Balanchine, born in Tsarist Russia, gave new life to the traditional vocabulary of classical ballet but was also attracted to jazz dance and, at the time of his arrival in the United States, was keen to work with African American dancers. In New York during the 1930s, as well as making ballets and

producing choreography for opera productions, Balanchine also choreographed successfully for musicals and revues. Although Humphrey also
choreographed for operas and had work shown on Broadway, she felt deeply
uneasy about these activities, and she decisively rejected 'European' ballet in
order to develop new ways of moving through which to express the experience, as she put it, of young people of the twentieth century living in the
United States.[6] While Balanchine felt secure enough about his status as a
ballet choreographer to make a piece for performing elephants, Humphrey
felt strongly enough about contemporary social conditions to become deeply
involved with the dance section of the Federal Theater Project. Balanchine
would never have become involved with anything as socialist as the Federal
Theater Project, and Humphrey would never have got involved with circus
animals.

Having established the contextual and temperamental differences
between Balanchine and Humphrey as individuals, the fact remains that
Balanchine's *Serenade* and Humphrey's *New Dance* were made within a year of
one another.[7] Both are extended pieces of modernist choreography which
present not dissimilar views of the relationship between the individual and
the group. And both Balanchine and Humphrey, as Eleni Bookis Hofmeister
(1993) has observed, were highly musical and used their intellectual understanding of musical forms to create the complex and sophisticated structures
found in their finest choreography. My proposition is that the formal configurations Balanchine created in his stripped down modernist ballets had the
particular appeal they undoubtedly had because of a relationship between
the ideals of order they suggested and the particular sorts of chaos and
disorder that were the everyday experience of Balanchine, his dancers and
the ballets' original viewers. Where Doris Humphrey is concerned, it is clear
that she was particularly interested in creating group choreography that
represented the ideal of a 'modern brotherhood of mankind'. Whereas both
Serenade and *New Dance* are pieces of the sort of modernist dance that is often
called 'pure dance', my argument is that both are works whose formal qualities signify the possibility of utopian alternatives that satisfied needs which
had their roots in the mundane and imperfect nature of everyday life as
experienced from the new subject positions of developing consumer society
in the United States.

Serenade

It is often stated that Balanchine consistently undermined the hierarchy of
the traditional classical ballet company in the oeuvre he developed in the
United States. This was done by levelling the distinctions between soloists
and other dancers so that the personnel required for many of his ballets is
not the traditional large corps with a few soloists, but often a smaller overall
number of dancers who form an ensemble and share the limelight more

equally. Balanchine's *Serenade* stands out among this oeuvre as a piece with a large number of dancers in which the distinction between corps de ballet and soloists is consistently deconstructed and intentionally confused. This, I shall argue, is a consequence of Balanchine's experience as a newly arrived immigrant to the United States of the pace and quality of modernity American-style.

Balanchine's master plan (as one might call it) to create an American ballet was to start a school in New York which would train dancers, the best of whom would then be used to create and perform his American ballets. *Serenade* was made with dancers from the first intake at this school who attended an evening class Balanchine offered in stage technique. Instead of teaching them an existing piece of repertory, as is usual in such classes, Balanchine decided to make something new for them. He presumably wanted to make his students into useful dancers as quickly as possible. The most effective way of letting them know how the steps they were learning in class could be used on stage would be with a piece that was within their technical range; but the young dancers would undoubtedly have responded more favourably if the ballet also related to their experience, and a European ballet might not do this so well. If one considers the first section – the Sonatina – the appropriateness of the format Balanchine devised in *Serenade* becomes evident. In the original version the leading role in the ballet was shared among various dancers who each emerge from the corps de ballet to dance a solo and are then absorbed back into it.[8] From the point of view of the original evening class, this meant a number of students got to dance solo material without the parts being too overwhelming or beyond their capabilities. Similarly, as is often observed, a significant amount of the movement material in *Serenade* consists of exercises lifted with little alteration from the ballet class. And if Balanchine did not therefore have the possibility of dazzling his audience with displays of technical virtuosity (the piece must have aimed at introducing audiences as well as dancers to modern ballet), he made up for this through the extraordinary way in which dancers group and regroup in series of fascinating spatial transformations.

A certain mythology has developed about the circumstances of the ballet's composition. On the night of the first class, Balanchine tells us, seventeen women enrolled for the class but no men (1968: 365). So Balanchine created the 'necktie' formation with which the ballet opens.

```
        F                 F
    F       F       F       F
F       F       F       F       F
    F       F       F       F
        F                 F
```

Figure 6 Balanchine's 'necktie' formation

Balanchine implies that seventeen is an awkward number to work with and that he would never have come up with this configuration had it not been for these fortuitous circumstances. This may be true but, as Roberta Hellman and Marvin Hoshino (1995) have pointed out, if one were going to create a ballet with solo material shared by various members of a corps de ballet, seventeen is actually a very useful number to work with: when a soloist comes out from the mass, she leaves behind sixteen dancers, and sixteen can be divided into a useful variety of different sub-groups as Balanchine shows throughout *Serenade*. The dancers are of course not all on stage throughout the piece and Balanchine says he worked through the music (Tchaikovsky's *Serenade for Strings in C*) choreographing with however many dancers were present that evening. As men started to attend the evening class, they too were given roles. Other incidents were incorporated. At one moment when Balanchine told the women to rush off the stage, one of them slipped to the floor and started to cry. 'I told the pianist to keep on playing and kept this bit in the dance' (1968: 364). One dancer, arriving late at a class when the others were already working, calmly picked her way across the floor through the dancers to take her place. This moment too is preserved in the choreography. As a result of Balanchine allowing himself to respond to these fortuitous accidents, *Serenade* has a very free structure – it has even been likened to a Joycean stream of consciousness. Another factor that adds to this looseness is the fact that Balanchine chose to reverse the order of the last two movements of the music so that what Tchaikovsky intended to be the climactic musical ending is followed by the mysterious 'dark angel' section. And it is out of this loose framework that there emerge, often quite unexpectedly, the piece's dazzling, ever shifting spatial and rhythmic patterns. Francia Russell, who has staged Balanchine's ballets with a number of companies, says that *Serenade* is one of the most difficult for her because everybody's part is slightly different 'and the patterns – It's like sand' (Dunleavy et al. 1983: 87).

Marcia Siegel has commented that, as a result of incorporating accidental events and giving the piece a very free form, *Serenade* turned out to be an odd-looking ballet. In the way soloists merge in and out of the group Siegel sees 'an assertion about the theoretical equality of all dancers, about the right each of them has to belong – to fit in and to stand out' (1979: 72). She goes on to suggest that:

> Balanchine could almost be declaring his own independence from the undemocratic ranking systems of the old Russian companies, where this one is the Ballerina, another is the Cavalier, and others are the corps or the second lead, and they never do anything more or less than their assignments.

> (ibid.)

144

Declaring this independence from the old world ballet companies could also be read as claiming allegiance with the new world, with a state that was founded upon ideals of liberty, equality and fraternity. The levelling of the distinction between soloists and corps in *Serenade* can be read in relation to the comparative lack of social hierarchy in the United States compared with most European countries at that time. *Serenade*'s free form can thus be seen in relation to American modernity, to the homogenisation and levelling of social and regional distinctiveness in order to produce large new communities of consumption within which to market ever increasing quantities of standardised, mass produced consumer goods. Consider the very beginning of the ballet: the dancers start in the 'necktie' formation and each raises a hand as if to shade her eyes from the light. If one dancer performs this gesture on its own it seems to signify some sort of emotional or dramatic content: it is the sort of movement a principal might make in a narrative ballet. Marcia Siegel has commented that:

> There is something strained about this tableau – the pose is too angular and eccentric to match the formal way the women are distributed, and yet the way they all do it alike denies any realistic or dramatic ideas we may have about it.
>
> (ibid.: 73)

Siegel also points out that towards the end of the 'Sonatina' section all the dancers execute piqué turns in unison, and such showy steps are usually only used for solos by ballerinas. Whereas Kracauer saw in the Tiller Girls a work force that has been standardised and turned into deindividuated robots, *Serenade* might be said to exemplify the point of view of the new communities of consumption in which delicate sensibilities are not the privilege and prerogative of an hereditary elite but everyone (who can afford it) has access to the same experiences.

New dance

Doris Humphrey once wrote in a letter: 'I want to visualise with [the group] the visions and dreams that make up the entire impetus and desire of my life. The group is my medium, just as marble is the sculptor's medium' (quoted in Jowitt 1988: 184) But she also wrote

> With one hand I try to encourage [the dancers] to be individuals – to move regardless of me or anyone else – and in rehearsals it is necessary to contradict all that and make them acutely aware of each other, so that they may move in a common rhythm.
>
> (ibid.)

This is how she makes them move in *New Dance*, *Passacaglia* and in parts of *With My Red Fires*. In these pieces Humphrey aimed to show that there is, in her words, a 'modern brotherhood of mankind'. Of the three works, she preferred *New Dance*, which showed 'the world as it could be and should be where each person has a clear and harmonious relationship to his fellow beings' (Cohen 1972: 238), and *Passacaglia*, which showed 'that there is still happiness, a measure of harmony, to be found while working towards that goal', to *With My Red Fires* which, by comparison, she thought 'obvious and crude . . . but easy to understand – dramatic, with a plot and characters – much more what people have learned to expect from the dance' (Kriegsman 1981: 181). What in her view was wrong with modern dance was that 'anyone could tell you what was wrong but no one seemed to say what was right' (ibid.: 284).

In her drafts for a lecture on *New Dance*, Humphrey states that 'comment on our times through group action has always been my sole aim' (Kriegsman 1981: 284) and continues:

> Even my earliest dances stressed the group and used the individual entirely in relationship to that group. This was really a difference between a democracy and an empire and obviously required a complete reorientation. New forms had to be discovered which could express concerted action and replace the solo system of the ballet.
>
> (ibid.)

Serenade, I have argued, also attempted to create forms that expressed the difference between a democracy and an empire. But whereas Balanchine modified and to a certain extent deconstructed the solo system, he did not reject the academic vocabulary of ballet itself in order to create those forms. While in both *Serenade* and *New Dance* individuals relate to a larger group from which they emerge to dance solo material and into which they then become reassimilated, the two pieces differ radically in the technical basis of the movement vocabularies each employs. Balanchine was happy to initiate new dancers and audiences into the existing, canonical vocabulary of ballet movement. Humphrey felt that ballet movement itself could not be used to represent her experience and that of her fellow Americans. In order to express the specificity of her experience, Humphrey invents a new movement vocabulary for *New Dance* which gradually develops and establishes itself as the piece evolves.

New Dance lasts forty minutes and was the most ambitious piece Humphrey (or indeed any of the American modern dancers) had up until then attempted. John Martin reviewing it in the *New York Times* (11 August 1935) wrote:

Certainly a more authoritative piece of creation in the dance has not been seen for many a long day. It is especially significant in this time when it has become habitual to question the validity of 'absolute' dance that here is a work which has the same power to stir the emotions, to kindle aesthetic excitement, as is to be found in symphonic music.

(Kriegsman 1981: 130)

When Martin refers to a tendency to question the validity of 'absolute' dance, he is surely referring to the critical positions being developed by Edna Ocko and others on the left. A good example of this is Norma Roland's criticism of *New Dance* published in the left-wing magazine *New Theatre*: 'The work exists on the sheer excitement of its movement. We regret to see such tremendous possibilities used for form and technique alone – with little attempt made to integrate content and idea into the form' (ibid.). Roland is following the party line which seems to have been to dismiss formalism merely because it was not social realism. Although she recognises that the work is exciting, she seems to inhibit herself, and not allow herself to relax and enjoy the piece. (Or perhaps she cannot accept that the type of utopian meanings Humphrey intended the piece to signify could be produced by a bourgeois artist in a capitalist society.) Without a theoretical structure with which to interrogate *New Dance* in ideological terms, Roland cannot respond to the piece on the sort of level that Marcia Siegel later did when she wrote: 'When it's over I feel radiant, optimistic. *New Dance* confirms my failing hopes for action and change in the world. That is undoubtedly what Doris Humphrey intended it to do' (Siegel 1979: 89).

Siegel can state Humphrey's intentions categorically because we have two fascinating but very different drafts by Humphrey of a lecture or lectures on *New Dance* (Cohen 1972: 238–41; Kriegsman 1981: 284–5) from which I have already quoted. In these Humphrey explains that the piece starts with the two leaders (herself and Weidman) dancing a duet while the rest of the dancers are grouped on stage boxes piled at each side of the space. These are for the 'audience' of other dancers who the leaders gradually encourage to take to the floor and to dance with them. So after the opening solo the female leader brings the women onto the floor, then as the women watch from the sides, the male leader brings the men onto the floor. The female leader then initiates a procession that brings all the dancers together 'bringing the whole group into an integrated whole' (Cohen 1972: 240). Together they dance a celebration and what Humphrey calls a square dance. However, Humphrey carefully ensured that all through the development from the initial duet to this statement of group values, she kept back and only developed little by little the full resources of her movement and choreographic vocabularies. The duet material primarily used leg and foot movement and the men's and women's dances only used a limited range of ways of crossing space. Therefore, when the group had been united in celebration, she still had something left to show. She explains:

> Having unified the men's group and the women's group, one more section was necessary in order to express the individual in relation to the group. Too many people seem content to achieve a mass-movement and then stop. I wished to insist that there is an individual life within that group life.
>
> (ibid.)

This she set out to exemplify in the last, best known part of *New Dance*, the 'Variations and Conclusion'. Using the now familiar vocabulary of dynamic and exuberant movement – with its sweeping, off centre turns that use the body's momentum – and creating complex centrifugal series of floor patterns for the group, all the dancers take it in turns to perform some solo material before gradually taking their place on the cubes that have been moved from the wings to a stepped tower centre stage. It is this high energy finale that has left so many viewers with a feeling of radiance and optimism.

Humphrey states that *New Dance* shows a development from the 'primitive' to the civilised:

> My main theme was to move from the simple to the complex, from an individual integration to a group integration, and therefore I thought it best to confine myself to movement which was in a way primitive. The primitive urge for movement – in fact, all early dancing made use of steps and leg gestures but scarcely ever used the rest of the body with emphasis. Therefore until the group integration had been achieved, the feet and leg themes seemed more expressive.
>
> (Cohen 1972: 239)

Marcia Siegel has suggested that in *New Dance* Humphrey searched out ways of reconciling 'the conflicting demands of the frontally focused proscenium stage and the inward-facing communality of folk dance' (1993: 156). Although Humphrey called a section 'square dance', *New Dance* doesn't look like a folk dance: it does however have a folk dance type of energy with, at times during the final variations, as Siegel observes, some members of the group beating time as if urging on the featured dancers. Here yet again in this book (although for the first time in an American context) is modernist dance drawing on imagery or expressive qualities from 'primitive' dance in order to express modernity, although in this instance Humphrey's 'primitive' dance seems to be of European origin. Nevertheless, Humphrey clearly sees group integration as a move from the 'pre-urban' to a modernist utopia. If *New Dance* showed the world as it could be and should be, it avoided showing how it is, leaving that to the other two pieces in the New Dance

Figure 7 Doris Humphrey and Charles Weidman as leaders with the group on plinths behind them at the beginning of 'Variations and Conclusion' from Doris Humphrey's *New Dance*, photo by Thomas Bouchard

Source: © New York Public Library Dance Collection

Trilogy – *Theatre Piece* and *With My Red Fires*. Yet the implication is that within what was wrong with Humphrey's metropolitan, modernist world was a loss of something that could only be brought back through reference to 'primitive' and folk communities.

The relationship between urban and 'pre-urban',[9] between city and folk or peasant communities was a subject to which the sociologist and anthropologist Robert Redfield, at the University of Chicago, devoted himself during the 1920s and 1930s. Redfield was one of Katherine Dunham's professors, but his ideas are useful here for contextualising Humphrey's ideas on modernity and morality which underpin the New Dance Trilogy. Humphrey, like Dunham, was born in Chicago, and urbanism was a central concern of the so-called Chicago School of sociology during the 1920s and 1930s. From his field research in Mexican town and village communities, Redfield proposed a dialectical process through which local, 'pre-urban' moral orders tend to disintegrate when peasant communities come in touch with urban civilisation. Thus he observed that one band or tribe 'regard their own way of life as better than other people' (1968b: 64). But as people developed civilised values, Redfield proposed, there arose new, more inclusive moral orders. It is surely the process of developing this new, more inclusive moral order that Humphrey wanted to demonstrate in *New Dance*.

Humphrey's other great but puzzling work of the mid-1930s, *With My Red Fires*, can be looked at from the point of view of morality and community. I call it puzzling because people who have written about the trilogy have often found it difficult to explain how what appears to be a love story fits into Humphrey's grand overall scheme. Also Humphrey herself, although so clear at describing the reasons why she had devised certain formal qualities and devices in her choreography, was surprisingly obtuse in explaining what *With My Red Fires* is about. This may account for the mixed critical response the piece initially received. Its title, which comes from *Jerusalem II* – one of William Blake's long prophetic poems, caused Edna Ocko to blame Humphrey's dependence on an obscure mystical poem for the piece's artistic failure. 'Miss Humphrey is too fine and too modern a talent' Ocko protested, 'to dissipate her important energies among mystics and cultists' (quoted in Kriegsman 1981: 144). None of the other critics in 1936 went quite so far, yet many clearly felt that romantic love was a disappointing and inappropriate theme for modern dance.

The plot of *With My Red Fires* is as follows. The first half shows a Young Man (initially Weidman) and a Young Woman (initially Katherine Linz, and note the impersonal, modernist names of the roles) find and fall in love with one another as part of a group of dancers who have processed together onto the stage. In the second half, the Young Woman's mother, the Matriarch (initially Humphrey), objects to the relationship. Initially she calls her daughter home but when the latter goes out again to see the Young Man she raises the alarm and sends the community out to find and punish the lovers.

Finally the couple are left alone on stage, despised and rejected, and they end together in a noble, symmetrical pose that suggests that it is their love that is to be respected while the Matriarch's jealousy and the community's intolerance are at fault.

I have written elsewhere about *With My Red Fires* (Burt 1995b). What I want to discuss in the present context is the way it is informed by the same ideas about morality that I have identified in *New Dance*. While the title *With My Red Fires*, together with quotations in the programme, came from Blake, apparently Humphrey only came across these lines after finishing the piece.[10] Paul Love, writing in 1937, said that initial inspiration came from reading Edward Carpenter's book *Love Comes of Age*. Edward Carpenter (1844–1928) was an Englishman who was prominent in the late nineteenth-century socialist revival. He was homosexual and an eloquent advocate of the liberation of homosexual love. It is curious that Humphrey should at this time have been reading his writings. By the 1930s his ideas on sexuality would have appeared rather dated in the light of psychoanalytic theory (which many artists including Graham and Wigman were interested in), although his views on the ethics of sexual politics were subsequently redis-covered in the 1970s by the women's and gay liberation movements. In the 1890s and early 1900s Carpenter knew many early feminists involved in the Independent Labour Party and ardently supported feminist aspirations. *Love Comes of Age: a Series of Papers on the Relation of the Sexes* was published in 1896. In it, as Sheila Rowbotham has observed, Carpenter does not deny the complexity of sexual desire but tries 'to probe the irrational and come to terms with deep sexual passion' (Rowbotham and Weeks 1977: 109). Writing about jealousy, Carpenter identifies a nice distinction between love as an 'initial preoccupation with a lover's uniqueness' (ibid.) and the jealous, possessive feeling that (generally male) lovers sometimes have that comes from a feeling of owning their beloved and having proprietary rights over them. Carpenter saw this possessive love as a product of capitalist society (women as chattels) and proposed that socialists should strive, therefore, not to give in to it. Carpenter's notion of non-possessive love is surely consonant with Redfield's notion of new, more inclusive moral orders. *With My Red Fires*, by contrasting the possessive, destructive love of the mother with the romantic love of her daughter for the Young Man, is surely exploring the romantic problems that Carpenter discussed but looking at them from the point of view of feminine experience.

Two moments in *With My Red Fires* recall choreographic images in *New Dance*. In an unforgettable sequence, the Matriarch whips herself into a frenzy in order to infect the group with a fanatical hatred of the lovers, compelling them to find them and treat them inhumanely. She makes the group rotate slowly like spokes of a mechanical wheel with herself at the centre, every now and then stopping them dead in a frozen, silent tableau. The choreographic image of a rotating, spoked wheel is very similar to that at the end of the celebration in *New Dance* and repeated at the beginning of the Variations; but whereas in *New Dance* the circular motion around the centre of the stage signifies social integration and harmony, here, with the Matriarch centre stage, it represents blind hatred and intolerance. Just as earlier the young couple found themselves within and because of the group, so it is the group, not the Matriarch, who actually punish the couple, and it is the community who expel them from their midst. As Humphrey described this at the time in a letter to her husband:

> people are running, shouting, they're on the morbid scent, they gleam with virtuous hate. She's run off with a nobody? Which way? To the town, to the inn? No, here by the wall. Tear them apart, the dirty things. What shall we do, old one, marry them with a gun and a giggle or run them out?
>
> (quoted in Kriegsman 1981: 140)

Marcia Siegel (1993) has pointed out the similarity on the level of theme between *With My Red Fires* and Charles Weidman's *Lynchtown*, also choreographed in 1936. In terms of Redfield's ethnographic view of morality, Humphrey shows a community in transition, which, through contact with modernity, has lost its balanced 'primitive' or folk morality and now expresses its fears through hatred and intolerance. They have yet to develop the new more inclusive moral order that I have argued *New Dance* exemplifies.

The other moment that recalls *New Dance* comes at the end. The Young Man and the Young Woman, alone on stage, circle round one another holding hands as they mount tiers to stop centrally upstage. They stand opposite one another in profile, one straight leg planted forward, the other behind (like Greek athletes or the heroes in David's painting *Oath of the Horatii*). Their upper backs arch and their heads fall back to gaze upwards as they stretch out their arms to rest their hands on each other's shoulders. Each is making equal claims on the other and expecting equal respect. The symmetry of this striking tableau is unashamedly pure and clear, and recalls an identical pose in the opening duet of *New Dance*. The inference is that love (come of age, and with equality between the sexes) is the starting point that can transform the negative energy with which the Matriarch whips up the community to fanatical hatred, into the ideality exemplified in the 'Variations and Conclusion' of *New Dance*. What is clear from this discussion of the two pieces is the extent to which the ideal presented in *New Dance* is a transformation of what is shown to be morally and ethically wrong and at fault in *With My Red Fires*.

Both *Serenade* and Humphrey's New Dance Trilogy present danced representations of ideals that are responses to the disruption and disorientation brought about by the formation of what de Grazia calls new communities of consumption. Balanchine's *Serenade* attempted to rework the aesthetic ideals of classical ballet in ways appropriate to American experience, while *New Dance* presented ideals that were rooted in similar social experience and in the intellectual climate of its time and place. The ideals which these pieces present had a particular resonance in their time because each grew out of a response to needs that were real. But, as Richard Dyer has pointed out, the exemplification of such timely ideals also amounts to a definition and delimitation of what constitutes the legitimate needs of people in society (1981: 184). Dyer identifies a problem in the ways in which a process of definition and delimitation of certain kinds of needs and inadequacies can exclude and delegitimise other needs and inadequacies, often in relation to class, patriarchal, sexual and racial struggles. The ideal which Balanchine presents in *Serenade* is obtained through a fetishised display of women dancing on pointe: Balanchine may initially have had only seventeen women and no male dancers when he started to make *Serenade* but that undoubtedly suited his aesthetic: he famously defined ballet as woman, thus reinforcing limiting stereotypes of femininity (see Daly 1987). The ideal that Humphrey evokes in *New Dance* reacts against the sorts of normative gender roles presented in *Serenade*. While male and female roles in *New Dance* are different from one another, it conveys a greater sense of equality between the sexes than *Serenade*, and both male and female dancers assume universal significance rather than being limited to meanings that are gender specific. Nevertheless, this is circumscribed by Humphrey's adherence to a positivist view of human development as the assimilation of 'primitiveness'. The underlying assumption within her argument about 'the primitive urge for movement' (Cohen 1972: 238) is that superior modern civilisation has the right to appropriate this 'primitive urge' for its own ends without considering the consequences of this appropriation for those deemed to be not yet wholly part of civilisation.

What is excluded from the universalising ideals of both *New Dance* and *Serenade* are the particularities of African American experience. If Balanchine's *Serenade* and Humphrey's *New Dance* explore the embodiment of new subjectivities and new conceptions of community brought about by the needs of modern industry, then Katherine Dunham explores African American experiences of these in her dream ballet in *Stormy Weather*. This film was made in 1943, eight years later than *Serenade* and *New Dance* and after the United States had entered the war against Germany and Japan. It is one of a small handful of big budget films which the Hollywood studios made at that time with all black casts. It constituted part of Hollywood's contribution to the war effort, given that many African Americans were joining the armed forces and being killed for their country and for ideals of freedom and democracy which they did not yet fully enjoy themselves. The dream ballet nevertheless has much in common with *Serenade* and *New Dance* in the optimism of the utopian ideal it presents.

Stormy weather

Katherine Dunham's dream ballet is shown as part of a night club performance at the end of *Stormy Weather*. Lena Horne[11] sings the title song, while behind her on stage is a window through which can be seen a rainy city street. As she reaches the musical 'break' in the song the camera goes through the window to enter a city street. Sheltering from a thundery shower of rain under the bridge of an elevated urban railway gather a number of African Americans who are in fact Katherine Dunham and members of her dance company. All the men are dressed in slightly exaggerated versions of zoot suits made from material with a distinctive, asymmetrical, chequered pattern. There is a similarly exaggerated quality about the way everyone is moving, that suggests the way 'real' people might hurry under cover in the rain. Movements are larger than life – almost operatically so – and imperceptibly become synchronised with the beat of the music. The spectator is being subtly prepared for the dancing to come. Under the bridge, always at the centre of the frame, is Dunham herself with two big tropical flowers in her hair and a satin dress with fur trim which contrasts with the plainer dresses of the other women. One man looks at her in what could be a request to dance or a sexual advance, but he is claimed by his female partner who shoos him respectfully away; another touches her on the shoulder but she rejects him with a slight shake of the head. Everyone under the bridge except Dunham has begun to slowly dance in heterosexual couples but their energy level is low; they look tired and more than one couple prop one another up with their shoulders while their torsos and pelvises jut away from one another like exhausted competitors in a dance marathon. This present 'reality', that frames the dream of ideality which follows it, is a city that is cold, wet and full of exaggeratedly extrovert but tired characters.

A thunder clap causes Dunham to look reproachfully up at the cloudy sky, and these clouds turn into the stage smoke which along with gauze curtains and a wind machine are the sine qua non of filmed dream ballets. Like peeling skins off an onion, the camera, having gone from the night club set into a street set, now goes through the clouds into a glamorously exotic dream set. Dunham enters this new stage alone down a ramp performing a series of slow, high leg extensions. At the bottom she is joined by a group of male dancers while the other women in the company follow behind her. In comparison with the flashy but heavy street clothes of the previous scene, the women dancers now have bare legs, tight fitting tops with a gauzy, trailing skirt. Both male and female costumes are trimmed with patterned material that recalls the checks of the street clothes. But whereas the city was cold and inhospitable, the dream is clearly warm, and on many levels presents an excess of what was marked as lacking in the city. The shambling, tired and awkward couple dancing is replaced by faster, more energetic and more unified movement. Gone also is the awkwardness of the men's earlier requests to dance with Dunham. If she was in control earlier by saying no, she is in control now as she unhesitatingly chooses to dance for a moment with one and then another and another man, briefly leaning back to stretch over and rest her weight against their bowed backs.

Central to the utopian scene that the dream ballet evokes is the style of the movement itself. This combines ballet vocabulary with movement of African origin that Dunham had studied during her anthropological field trips in the Caribbean. The ballet style is established first, disciplined but also powerful and exciting: the male dancers all together spring into the air and spin round, the women sail forwards with a beautiful balletic porte de bras. Towards the end of the 'break' a new, more syncopated rhythm comes into the music and the dance material becomes more polycentric and polyrhythmic – qualities Gottschild (1996) identifies as particularly Africanist. Isolated ripples of stomach and lower back pick up a cross rhythm in the music, which is then emphasised with characteristic flexion at the tips of the shoulders. Looking back from the 1990s, dance historians recognise this as a key document in the development of the Dunham technique, but seeing it in these terms can obscure what it meant at the time.

Dunham herself remembers an unidentified Chicago critic complaining about her use of ballet vocabulary,[12] It is important to recognise both on a practical and an ideological level the significance of Dunham's use of the ballet tradition. From the early 1930s Dunham had trained in ballet with Mark Turfybill and Ludmilla Speranzeva: at the time there was no significant modern dance teacher in Chicago. When in 1937 she returned to Chicago from her field work in the Caribbean, she put on a concert with Ludmilla Speranzeva of what she then called The Negro Ballet. As far as the older established black middle class in Chicago were concerned,[13] this was the right name to call the company, but from a white point of view it was not; they became the Katherine Dunham Dance Company instead. John Martin, reviewing a company performance in 1940, complained about their use of ballet:

> The group as a whole is handsome and competent, though there is among certain of the male dancers, including Talley Beatty, a distressing tendency to introduce the technique of the academic ballet. What is there in the human mind that is so eager to reduce the rare and genuine to the standard and foreign?
>
> (Martin 1978: 64)

The key words here are standard and foreign. Martin thinks that African American dancers possess innate abilities which are inimical to 'standard' dance techniques like ballet. Dunham, however, eloquently made the case against essentialism in a 1938 interview. While recognising that a sensibility for dance and rhythm may be a sociologically conditioned aspect of peoples of African descent, Dunham nevertheless argued that African American dancers still need professional training:

> We are sociologically conditioned by our constant contact with [African musical rhythms]. In the West Indies, women dance to the drums almost until the hour the child is born – and they nurse it, still dancing. But that doesn't mean there is no technique. There is. And it is every bit as essential that we train as rigorously as any other group, even in presenting ordinary folk material.
>
> (Orme 1978: 60)

Later in the same interview, Dunham says she aims:

> To establish a well-trained ballet group. To develop a technique that will be as important to the white man as to the Negro. To attain a status in the dance world that will give the Negro dance-student the courage really to study, and a reason to do so. And to take *our* dance out of the burlesque to make it a more dignified art. We lack a tradition in the dance as we present it now, and the young Negro has no aesthetic creative background.
>
> (ibid.: 61–2, emphasis in the original)

From a practical point of view it made sense to use the ballet tradition, which Dunham knew well, as a basis for developing this new technique and this new aesthetic. Marcia Siegel suggested that Humphrey sought to reconcile 'the conflicting demands of the frontally focused proscenium stage and the inward-facing communality of folk dance' (Siegel 1993: 156). The same is true of Dunham. Folk or 'primitive' dance won't work if put on a modern theatre stage in an unmodified state. Ballet, with its tradition of turning folk dance into character dance, offered Dunham a useful means for theatrically representing the dances she had observed in the Caribbean.

Martin objected to her company's use of ballet because he said it was foreign. Admittedly Martin at the time was no balletomane. But underlying his idea of the 'foreign-ness' of ballet is a notion that African Americans should keep to their indigenous, 'natural' dance and musical traditions. From the point of view of white hegemony, the exoticism of African or Caribbean dance and music is acceptable because it reinforces the separateness between black and white. Dunham however suggests that her technique could be as important 'to the white man as to the Negro'. But this, and the idea of black ballet dancers, suggested a commonality between black and white that evidently disturbed Martin as much as it had disturbed Levinson and Haskell (see Chapter 3). Dunham, however, didn't want to represent the sort of 'rare', 'genuine', 'primitive' spectacle Martin clearly wanted to see.

What she shows in *Stormy Weather* are disciplined, modern, African American dancers.[14]

In her autobiography, *A Touch of Innocence*, Dunham recalls in the third person a time when she was very young and made a daily journey home in the elevated train from the centre of Chicago to her Aunt's flat in the South Side:

> At the bottom of the stairs [linking station and sidewalk] there was a whole new world. The train rumbled away overhead to lose itself in the far South Side, and the impact of Negro sounds and smells hit the child with such force that she nearly melted with fear, clinging close to her Aunt Lulu and drawing as far away as she could from the dark stares and sullen laughter and bold flaunting, the dust and litter on the pavement, the weariness and sickness.
>
> (Dunham 1994a: 41–2)

Written in the late 1950s, this is very similar to the setting that Dunham chose for the rainy opening of the *Stormy Weather* ballet. Elsewhere in *A Touch of Innocence* she writes about the flashy African American city dwellers of Chouteau Street, East St Louis:

> Chouteau Street's own kind, who had made good and who showed it in a way Chouteau Street understood, with a lot of gold teeth and hair made slick with straightening combs and pulling irons and gleaming with Madame Walker's pomade; and with diamond stick-pins and pointed yellow shoes with mirrors in the toes and broad-striped suits and shirts . . .
>
> (ibid.: 178)

Here she reveals an ethnographic understanding of detail that is not dissimilar to that developed by sociologists of the Chicago School with whom Dunham studied for her undergraduate degree. Dunham's appreciation of the over-exaggerated, extroverted mentality of the city dweller recalls George Simmel's notion of the blasé, neurasthenic city dweller discussed in Chapter 2; Robert Park, one of the founders of the Chicago School, had studied with Simmel.[15] In showing the characteristically loud-dressing inhabitants of modern Chicago in the street scene of the *Stormy Weather* ballet, Dunham drew on what she had learned at the University of Chicago.

While her academic training may have taught her how to distance herself, observe and judge, Dunham used ethnography to make sense of her own position as a modern African American and to clarify what she had in common with other African Americans. Dunham wrote of the night when as an adolescent she first saw Chouteau Street as the beginning of a 'possession by the blues, a total immersion in the baptismal font of race' (ibid.: 179). The blues turned people 'way, way inwards, deep into something people are supposed to know about and don't look at, or knew a long time ago and lost touch with. Single road to freedom' (ibid.). The song 'Stormy Weather' may not actually be a blues number but the dream ballet shows a process of going inwards and getting back in touch with something of Africa that Dunham and her fellow African Americans as a diasporic people knew and kept alive.

Conclusion

It is clear that *Stormy Weather* is situated in a modern urban environment. Like Balanchine's *Serenade* and Humphrey's *New Dance*, it is informed by American experiences of the new subjectivities and new conceptions of community brought about by the needs of modern industry – with the important proviso that Dunham's *Stormy Weather* ballet was only filmed eight years later. Nevertheless Dunham's role in *Stormy Weather* is similar to that played by Humphrey and Weidman in *New Dance*, in that all three were leaders. It is they who in each piece direct the community towards a utopian ideal of harmonious and celebratory dancing. And, as I have shown, the ideals in all three pieces directly or indirectly addressed needs experienced in everyday metropolitan life.

Balanchine, in order to create an ideal movement style in *Serenade* and other ballets, appropriated some characteristic movements from the vernacular African American dance and music tradition (see Banes 1993; Gottschild 1996; Hill 1996), in order to give the academic ballet vocabulary an 'American' style. Humphrey, for her part, based the development of *New Dance* on a progression from 'primitive' to civilised: from what she considered to be the limited bodily movements inherent in the 'primitive urge for movement' to the engagement of a larger degree of bodily involvement in dancing. This for her represented the summit of contemporary potential while retaining the high energy level and sense of community found in a barn dance. The ideal modern society, in Humphrey's view, is one that assimilates 'primitive' communality just as the ideal movement vocabulary for Balanchine is one that assimilates what Gottschild calls an Africanist aesthetic. Dunham, however, recognised that African American needs could neither be satisfied through assimilation nor through an isolationist return to a mythically utopian 'Africa'. What *Stormy Weather* presents is an ideal vision of modern African Americans who have both the strength and discipline implicit in ballet and a pride that comes from the rediscovery and maintenance of links with deeply hidden African roots.

Dunham's view of what is wrong with city life is closest to that of European choreographers like Jooss and Börlin, just as her understanding of urbanism is not dissimilar to that of Simmel, Kracauer and Benjamin. Doris Humphrey complained that too many modern dances represented what was wrong with modern life but no one seemed to say what was right

(Kriegsman 1981: 284). Yet what seems to characterise her own *New Dance* and *Passacaglia*, Graham's *Celebration*, Dunham's *Stormy Weather*, Busby Berkeley's filming of mass ornamental dance numbers and other American dances of the 1930s and early 1940s is their positivist celebration of the potential of modernity to create a better society. If they didn't say what was actually right with modern life they showed what could be right about it. Yet in doing so there were nevertheless absences in these works and exclusions. Until the United States changed its isolationist foreign policy and joined the war against Germany and Japan, African American dancing bodies were absent from the pieces which presented these ideals. The ways in which modern white American and European dancing bodies came to signify universal meanings through the appropriation of 'primitive' ritual is considered in the next chapter. What *Stormy Weather* demonstrates is that African American dancing bodies were only allowed to express universal meanings after 1942 and at a time when most white modern dance artists no longer held those ideals.

8

PRIMITIVISM, MODERNISM AND RITUAL IN THE WORK OF MARY WIGMAN, KATHERINE DUNHAM AND MARTHA GRAHAM

In 1931 Martha Graham gave the title *Primitive Mysteries* to a new group dance that became one of her most acclaimed works. The term primitive at the time referred to what seemed a common sense distinction between the social and cultural achievements of modern (Western) society and those of so-called primitive societies. What may have seemed common sense to Graham and her contemporaries has subsequently been substantially challenged by work on post-coloniality so that the adjective primitive generally now appears in academic discourse between inverted commas. These common-sense notions of the primitive, it is now argued, have concealed an underlying blindness about the nature of the power relations between the dominant, Western nations and subordinate colonised or otherwise substantially dependent nations and societies. In the inter-war years, 'primitive' societies were objects of widespread interest: they were increasingly the subject of anthropological investigation, while ethnographic artefacts were valued by Western collectors, artists and intellectuals as 'primitive' art. In Chapter 3 this widespread interest in 'primitive' art was cited as a factor in Josephine Baker's initial success in 1925. In the inter-war years, modernist artists, writers, composers and choreographers, when searching for forms and imagery with which to express the lived experience of modernity, frequently borrowed from the cultural traditions of 'primitive' societies. My aim in this chapter is to interrogate the use of 'primitive' ritual in modernist choreography by comparing and contrasting the work of Katherine Dunham, Martha Graham and Mary Wigman. The three specific examples on which I focus are: Wigman's description of her experience dancing *Monotony: Whirl Dance* (1928), the movement for this piece being

160

abstracted from Sufi 'whirling' ceremonies; Graham's *Primitive Mysteries* which was inspired by the religious practices of the Penitente Indians of New Mexico; Dunham's description of a vaudun[1] ritual she took part in as part of her anthropological field work in Haiti in 1936 and her subsequent piece *Shango*, initially created as part of the 1945 musical *Carib Song* which was based on Haitian ceremonies, together with others she observed in Trinidad and Cuba.

When Martha Graham drew on her responses to the dances and ritual practices of the Penitente Indians to make *Primitive Mysteries* she was working within a clearly defined modernist tradition. Not everyone would agree that works by Graham such as *Primitive Mysteries* or works by European choreographers of the period like Mary Wigman should properly be considered modernist. Marshall Cohen (1981) and Roger Copeland (1996) have argued that Graham and Wigman's work is primitivist – where primitivism is seen as the polar opposite of a modernist tendency towards increasing abstraction. The primitive impulse, according to them, is a desire for a return to primitive one-ness with nature and for a 'fusion of image and reality which characterises primitive art' (Cohen 1981: 139). Cohen and Copeland's target is an adherence to ideologies of expressive dance which many early modern dance artists, including Isadora Duncan, Rudolf Laban, Mary Wigman, Martha Graham and Doris Humphrey, absorbed from their reading of Nietzsche. But Cohen and Copeland's theory of primitivist expressionism breaks down when it comes to interpreting actual choreography. The work which Graham produced during her 'long woollens' period, of which *Primitive Mysteries* is probably the most important example, were not the overwhelmingly emotivist dances that a primitivist account of early modern dance might lead one to expect. As Mark Franko has pointed out, Graham's early group pieces and solos were criticised by left-wing journalists for their austere formalism and lack of emotional engagement (Franko 1995: 38–74).

The artistic ideologies of primitivism and modernism should not be seen as polar opposites, and were in fact often linked together in writings from the period. Martha Graham, for example, writing about indigenous dance traditions found in America, proposed:

> These [Native American and African American dances] are primitive sources which, though they may be basically foreign to us, are nevertheless akin to the forces which are at work in our life. For we as a nation are primitive also – primitive in the sense that we are forming a new culture. We are weaving a new fabric, and while it is true that we are weaving it from the threads of many old cultures the whole cloth will be entirely indigenous.
>
> (Graham in Armitage 1966: 100)

What Graham feels Americans need is a new culture that has been stripped of a decadent decorativeness that she encountered at Denishawn and which elsewhere she implicitly associates with European culture. In other words she does not value 'primitive' Native American dance out of a desire for a return to primitive one-ness with nature but for its potential to deconstruct outmoded cultural traditions, just as Cubist, Expressionist and Dadaist artists in Europe had used 'primitive' art to break away from and destroy the aesthetic forms and conventions of nineteenth-century bourgeois culture.

During the 1930s and 1940s, while Graham was drawing on Native American dances and ritual practices, painters of the New York School like Jackson Pollock, William Baziotes and Wolfgang Paalen[2] were drawing on Native American artefacts for similar purposes. These visual artists were attracted to these artefacts not out of a desire for a return to primitive oneness with nature but due to an interest in the connections between art and the unconscious that was informed by Jungian psychoanalysis. The stark modernism that Graham and Wigman developed in the 1920s and 1930s was also informed by a general awareness of modern psychoanalytic ideas about the unconscious. What they experienced while performing work derived from primitive ritual was not a primitive fusion of image and reality but an encounter with the Other – not regression to the primitive as premodern but an experience informed by modern psychoanalytic ideas. When Graham titled her autobiography *Blood Memory* (1991) she was referring to Jung's notion of the collective unconscious, describing herself as someone who brings back things from the past, retrieving them 'from our common blood memory' (1991: 16). For her, choreography was a means of retrieval: 'There are always ancestral footsteps behind me, pushing me, when I am creating a new dance, and gestures are flowing through me. You get to the point where your body is something else and it takes on a world of cultures from the past' (ibid.: 13). This was undoubtedly what she felt she was doing when she used 'primitive' and mythic material in many other works during the 1930s and 1940s including *Primitive Mysteries*.

The most influential theorisations of the unconscious linked it with notions of the primitive. Writing about the 'id' in 1915 Freud called it 'the primitive mind' and identified it with 'savages', while consigning 'primitive' people to the same innocent, unsophisticated state as children and the mentally ill. On one level, 'primitive' dances were thought to reveal the backward, childlike, simple nature of the 'savage'. John Martin, for example, reviewing *Primitive Mysteries* in 1931 wrote: 'Its simplicity of form and its evocation of the childlike religious elevation of a primitive people never falters for a moment' (Armitage 1966: 12). Leaving aside for the moment whether this was a fair comment on the piece, Martin's comments might have seemed merely common sense to many people at the time; but in the light of more recent debates about colonialism, the ideological nature of

Martin's judgement becomes apparent. Susan Hiller sums up the recently revised view of primitivism:

> In borrowing or appropriating visual ideas which they found in the class of foreign objects that came to be labelled 'primitive art', and by articulating their own fantasies about the meaning of the objects and about the peoples who created them, artists have been party to the erasure of the self-representation of colonised peoples in favour of a western representation of their realities. While anthropology tries to turn the peoples who are its subject matter into objects, and these 'objects' into 'theory', art tries to turn the objects made by the peoples into subject-matter, and, eventually, into 'style'. Both practices maintain, intact, the basic European picture of the world as a hierarchy with 'ourselves' at the top.
>
> (Hiller 1991: 2–3)

While Hiller is concerned with appropriations by Western visual artists, the same is also true of appropriations by those working in other art forms, including choreography. Following Hiller one could argue that modernist choreographers who borrowed 'primitive' ritual practices were articulating their own fantasies about the meanings of these practices and about the peoples who created them.

Very few choreographers had the insight that Doris Humphrey showed when she commented retrospectively on her use of Shaker rituals in her piece *The Shakers* (1931):

> One thing I vow I will not do again: imitate in an art form the rituals of the faithful. No more Shakers. I am ashamed of the poverty of my age that it sent me sniffing around people and things that are none of my business.
>
> (quoted Siegel 1993: 101)

There are nevertheless some legitimate reasons for looking at cultures other than one's own. Dunham, for example, sought to demonstrate in *Shango* the richness of African retentions among the Negro peoples of the New World. However, one significant insight she gained from her membership of a Haitian vaudun cult was just how different her experience as an educated modern American was from that of rural Haitian peasants. Graham, by contrast, had far less exposure to the Penitente Indians when she made *Primitive Mysteries* and far less insight into the consequences of reproducing, albeit in an abstracted way, their ceremonial rituals. At the end of her life she wrote:

Although I have been greatly exposed to the Native American
Indian tribes, I have never done an Indian dance. I've never done
any ethnic dance. I've received an excitement and a blessing and a
wonderment from the Indians.

(1991: 176)

When she said she had never done an Native American or an ethnic dance
she presumably meant she never choreographed one; but she certainly
danced in them as a member of the Denishawn company. Her abstracted,
modernist pieces on Native American themes were based on her own subjective response to her exposure to Native American culture. Graham
nevertheless believed that she as a modern American was a primitive and
could get in touch, through dancing, with fundamentals that both modern
Americans and 'primitive' people had in common. By explicitly associating
Primitive Mysteries with the Penitente Indians she was implicitly speaking for
them. Even though the representation she made was abstracted, she must
surely bear some responsibility for giving observers like Martin an opportunity to talk about the childlike nature of 'primitive' people.

Pieces by Dunham that were based on Caribbean religious rituals – such
as *Shango* – and pieces by Graham that were based on Spanish-American and
Amerindian religious rituals – such as *Primitive Mysteries* – all refer to beliefs
that are examples of the fusion of white Western and indigenous religious
and cultural forms; the 'borrowing' of these rituals allowed each choreographer to present dance material of a physically and psychologically expressive
nature. Despite these similarities, Dunham's pieces are nevertheless different
from Graham's; the problem is how to identify and analyse this difference.
Recent interrogations of the social and political context of modernist choreography that drew on cultures that were radically different from that of the
choreographer have not always been well received. Jane Desmond's 'Dancing
out the difference: cultural imperialism and Ruth St Denis' *Radha* of 1906'
pointed out the ways in which St Denis presented a fetishised spectacle that
reinforced orientalist notions of the 'natural', sexualised, mute colonised
oriental female body (Desmond 1991: 41–2). It provoked Roger Copeland
to remark: 'If you're looking for an article that merely berates Western dance
artists for their imperialist/colonial/sexist/racist/you-name-it attitudes towards
the Eastern "Other", then see Jane Desmond's moronic "reading" of Ruth St
Denis' *Radha*' (Copeland 1996: 14). Yet from the rest of the article within
which this comment comes as a footnote, Copeland is not entirely unsympa-
thetic to feminist and post-colonial critiques of first world cultural
production. It seems to be a case of 'not in my back yard' where questions of
aesthetic judgement seem to be at stake. Too much is invested in the idea of
a canon of landmark twentieth-century choreographic innovation: those
within the approved canon, must, like Caesar's wife, be above reproach.
Despite Copeland's pronouncement, there is surely a need to recognise, as

Desmond does, the levels on which white Western artists made appropriations from colonised groups. There is also, however, a need to move beyond a 'political correctness' which defines the 'right' anti-racist, anti-colonial stance because this position is still achieved through enforcing a single, overarching polarity between Western and 'non-Western', whereas what is needed is to dissolve binary polarities and to appreciate rather than fear differences.

There is nothing inherently wrong with making an imaginary division between self and Other, and indeed psychoanalysts argue that such a division is essential to well being. The relationship between self and Other is not fixed but should be shifting and dynamic. Sander Gilman has suggested that stereotypes arise when self-integration is threatened:

> The fear we have of our own collapse does not remain internalised. Rather, we project this fear onto the world in order to localise it and, indeed, to domesticate it. For once we locate it, the fear of our own dissolution is removed. Then it is not we that totter on the brink of collapse, but rather the Other.
>
> (Gilman 1988: 1)

One of the ways in which concerns about the alienating effects of modernity were dealt with in the inter-war years was through an ambivalent response to the 'primitive' as Other that was simultaneously one of disgust and fascination. Because dance uses the body as its primary means of expression, early modern dancers using 'primitive' dance material literally embodied this ambivalence when their encounters with the Other led to loss of self as their bodies became the alien bodies of these Others. The three examples I am considering in this chapter all involve the performance of movement material that induced disassociational auto-hypnotic changes in the dancer's consciousness – what are sometimes called dances of possession. This is the encounter to which Graham was referring when she wrote that 'You get to the point where your body is something else and it takes on a world of cultures from the past' (1991: 13). What is at issue therefore is how the stagings which Dunham, Graham and Wigman created out of ritual practices articulated the difference between modern and 'primitive': did their performances define difference in terms of a rigid separation or was the imaginary division fluid and dynamic?

In order to answer this question, this chapter proceeds as follows. First it places intellectual ideas about ritual within their historical context by locating them within the discourses of modernism, psychoanalysis and anthropology. It then examines the connections between Dunham's *Shango* and her anthropological studies, focusing on the functionalist, theoretical framework that she developed for conceptualising the dances of Haiti. The distinctions Dunham defines between different categories of sacred dance are then used as a basis for discussing *Monotony: Whirl Dance* and *Primitive Mysteries* and the religious ceremonies on which each drew. It concludes by contrasting and comparing the different ways in which Dunham, Graham and Wigman each understood the relationship between their position as a member of modern Western society and the social groups whose rituals they appropriated.

Modernism, psychoanalysis and anthropology

Three discourses about 'primitive' ritual govern the ways in which *Monotony: Whirl Dance*, *Primitive Mysteries* and *Shango* defined the difference between modern and primitive: modernism, psychoanalysis and anthropology. Susan Hiller, as we have already seen, characterises modernist uses of ethnographic material as the erasure of a people's self-representation into a Western artistic style (Hiller 1991: 2). This use of ethnographic material, however, was central to the development of modernism both in the visual arts and in choreography. In the first twenty years of the century Cubist and Fauvist artists in Paris, the artists of Die Brücke group in Dresden, the Blaue Reiter group in Munich, and the Dadaists in Zurich all used 'primitive' art as an inspiration for their own break with nineteenth-century artistic conventions and their radical reconfiguration of the means of visual expression. Ideologies of primitive ritual were equally important in the development of modernist choreography. Nijinsky's *Le Sacre du printemps* (1913) is the seminal work within this tradition. Both Lynn Garafola (1989) and Millicent Hodson (1985; 1986; 1996) have argued from different premises that Nijinsky's use of ritualistic movement in *Le Sacre* marked a decisive break with nineteenth-century theatrical practice – from ideologies of ballet as a mimetic and narrative medium towards a modernist conception of theatre dance as abstracted, formal and expressive movement. In *Le Sacre* Nijinsky's dancers performed movements that had an expressive effect independent of the fact that they were dancing the role of a Slavic tribe.

Since Nijinsky's original version of *Le Sacre* there have been a number of other versions, including ones choreographed by Leonid Massine (1920 and 1930), Mary Wigman (1957), Pina Bausch (1975) and Martha Graham herself (1984).[3] The fact that Martha Graham danced the role of the Chosen One in Massine's 1930 revival of his version of *Le Sacre* in Philadelphia and New York has been cited as a key moment in Graham's artistic development and an inspiration for her own *Primitive Mysteries* (1931) (Hodson 1985: 38; Jowitt 1988: 182). Leroy Leatherman commented on the connection in his review of the 1944 revival of *Primitive Mysteries* (quoted in Sears 1982: 25). There are similarities between the two pieces in their use of abstracted, ritualistic movement and gesture. Furthermore, some choreographic motifs which Graham first used in *Primitive Mysteries* she undoubtedly encountered in *Le Sacre*: circle dances, processionals, leaps. This is undoubtedly a key lesson that Graham herself learned from her involvement with the production. One may assume that Massine's 1930 production of *Le Sacre*, like his 1920 production, diluted the radicalism of Nijinsky's original version; but it must nevertheless have conveyed some sense of the expressive power of ritual movement independent of any mimetic signification. One could even go further and say that ideologies of ritual dance were an essential factor in the development of American modern dance. When Doris Humphrey famously stated that modern dance works from the inside out, she might almost have been describing the effects of performing auto-hypnotic ritual movement. Humphrey herself did not dance in Massine's 1930 revival of *Le Sacre* but most of her dancers did. She herself choreographed and danced in Rouben Mamoulian's production of Schöenberg's *Glückliche Hand* which was performed with *Le Sacre* making up a double bill. It seems very probable therefore that Humphrey's *The Shakers* (1931) which, like *Primitive Mysteries* explores movement derived from religious ritual, was itself partly inspired by the modernist notion of ritual as non-mimetic, expressive movement.[4]

A basic awareness of psychology was a factor in Dunham, Graham and Wigman's understanding of 'primitive' dance. Psychoanalytic theory, by equating children and the mentally ill with 'primitive' people, reinforced a basic European spatial and temporal model of the world. Western people are not only at the top of the hierarchy but also occupy the position of the modern present while 'primitive' peoples are consigned to the pre-modern past. Graham herself evidently thought in these temporal terms when she wrote: 'You get to the point where your body is something else and it takes on a world of cultures *from the past*' (1991: 13, my emphasis). Psychoanalytic ideas determined the ways in which all three choreographers understood the religious rituals they appropriated in their work and offered them a model for conceptualising how audiences responded to their work.

It is generally acknowledged that Graham started reading the works of Jung in the late 1930s, possibly at the time Joan Erdmann, then a dancer in her company, married Joseph Campbell (who wrote Jungian interpretations of myth and literature). During the 1940s Graham underwent Jungian analysis, partly provoked by difficulties in her relationship with Erick Hawkins (Graham 1991: 178). Graham will undoubtedly have had a more general awareness of psychology and psychoanalysis much earlier than this. Her father was an alienist – a pre-Freudian psychologist. In the 1920s she settled in Greenwich Village in New York. Ann Douglas has documented the widespread interest in Freudian and Jungian psychoanalysis among artists and writers in Greenwich Village during this period: it contributed, Douglas claims, to the development of the ethos of the period which she calls a 'terrible honesty'. Douglas sees Freud as a key figure for a whole generation of New Yorkers to whom she says he unwittingly issued a call to take up the task of ruthlessly interrogating past and present lies (Douglas 1996: 31). She cites as a further instance T. S. Eliot, who wrote in 1933 that 'anyone who does not wish to deceive himself by systematic lies' must acknowledge 'the agony and horror of modern life' (ibid.). Douglas is surely correct when she cites Graham's work as an example of 'terrible honesty' (ibid.: 51). Indeed the phrase seems particularly appropriate to the radical process of stripping away sentimentality and lyricism to which Graham subjected her choreography, starting in the late 1920s. As Bessie Schöenberg, who danced in the premiere of *Primitive Mysteries*, observed to Deborah Jowitt:

> I found that everything [Graham] was doing was extremely posi-
> tive. It was all discovery. She came, after all, from a school of
> pseudoism into trying to find honesty. And there was really nothing
> very negative to say about any of it. It was very deep and very real –
> this was what was so extraordinary about studying with her during
> the 1930s.
>
> (Jowitt 1981: 40)

It is in this way that *Primitive Mysteries*, which marks the high point and culmination of Graham's rejection of the pseudoism of Denishawn,[5] can be seen as part of a wider movement among artists and intellectuals in New York to which a general awareness of Freud's work made a significant contribution.

Wigman spent the years 1914–19 in Zürich and Ascona. The psychoanalyst Carl Jung was living at the time in Zürich and had contacts with the vegetarian anarchist colony at Ascona in which Laban and Wigman were involved. Indeed Otto Gross, who Martin Green (1986) cites as one of the founders of the colony, was a renegade pupil of Jung's. Living in Dresden in the 1920s Wigman had a relationship with Herbert Binswangwer who was a practising psychoanalyst (see Müller 1986: 159). Both Green and Susan Manning cite Wigman's contact with psychoanalysis as a significant factor in her intellectual and artistic development. In so far as there is any similarity between Wigman's abstracted 'absolute dance', of which *Monotony: Whirl Dance* is an example, and Graham's 'terrible honesty', both can be seen as the result of a stripping away of inessentials that was informed in part at least by a general awareness of psychoanalysis.

Underlying Dunham's functionalist analysis of folk and religious dance is her awareness of the importance of subconscious motivations conveyed through dance. As Joyce Aschenbrenner has observed: 'Dunham's functionalism reflects the Malinowskian imperatives of fulfillment of biological and psychological needs rather than the *status quo*-oriented structural-functionalism of Radcliffe-Brown' (Aschenbrenner 1980: 86). Important for Dunham's exposure to psychoanalytic ideas was her acquaintance with the German psychologist Erich Fromm. She initially met Fromm not through her university but at a dinner given by the Rosenwald Foundation at which they were both guests. This foundation gave money to African American artists and writers, and it was with two fellowships from it that Dunham was able to go to the Caribbean. Fromm had come to Chicago to attempt to interest the Rosenwald Foundation in supporting the resettlement of German Jewish academics in the United States. The foundation was unable to do this, and Fromm wrote to it in support of Dunham's work.[6] In *Island Possessed* Dunham states that by the time she arrived in Haiti she was already interested in using Fromm's ideas to help understand what she found there (1994b: 42, 67). What a basic awareness of psychology and psychoanalysis also gave Dunham was a means with which to understand her own responses to what she experienced in vaudun ceremonies and hence a means through which to conceptualise how audiences responded to her choreographic work. Dunham became aware of the need to draw not only on psychology and anthropology but also on the teachings of the cult in order to try to understand the experiences she had while dancing in vaudun ceremonies.

This leads me on to the third discourse that defined the difference between modern and primitive: anthropology. Early nineteenth-century, 'scientific' ideas of racial difference conceived of the white races as more advanced than the backward non-white races. By the end of the century, Social Darwinian ideas contributed to the view that the expanding Western colonial domination of non-Western peoples was an example of the survival of the fittest. Early twentieth-century anthropologists in Britain and the United States, including Robert Redfield, Katherine Dunham's professor at the University of Chicago, saw the process of contact between 'primitive' and 'peasant' peoples and modern urban culture as one of acculturation, as the 'weaker' culture became assimilated into the stronger tradition of modern Western society. Melville Herskovits, however, with whom Dunham also studied, controversially proposed the idea that people of African descent in America and the Caribbean were not a 'weaker' social group but possessed a distinctive and non-assimilable culture through the retention of Africanisms (Herskovits 1958).

John O. Perpener has argued that, where an understanding of race was concerned, there was a significant difference between the sociological positivism of the so-called Chicago School of Sociology at the University of Chicago, where Katherine Dunham was an undergraduate, and the view of racial difference put forward by Herskovits, who supervised Dunham's field work in the Caribbean. Dunham recalls that one of the main reasons why her professors were keen for her to do field research in the Caribbean was because they were interested in acculturation.[7] This was the theory of interaction between societies or groups and of consequent social changes. Perpener points out that Robert E. Park, founder of the Chicago School, developed a theory which proposed that acculturation was a process that occurs in four stages. Initial competition between minority and majority ethnic groups leads to conflict, but conflict brings about a process of social self-consciousness which forms a basis for social and political development that makes possible the third stage: accommodation. The final stage, according to Park, is assimilation as differences between the minority and majority groups are eroded. The problem with this theory was that the white majority resisted accommodation with groups like African Americans and Asians whose inborn 'racial traits' remained a visible source of racial discrimination. Park tried to move away from a biologically determinist model of racial difference by contending that different groups had characteristics which could contribute positively to the advancement of group interaction and assimilation. 'For example, Jews were characteristically intellectual; Anglo-Saxons were restless explorers and adventurers; and Negroes found their most characteristic forms of expression in the arts' (Perpener 1994: 25).

As Perpener points out, there are two significant problems with this theory. First is the question of whether these supposed group characteristics are themselves biologically determined or socially and historically constructed. For example, where dance is concerned, the notion that racial characteristics are biologically determined gave rise to the idea that all black dancers are innately talented performers and their skills are therefore not the result of conscious development and achievement. Second is the positivist assumption of the inevitability and desirability of complete assimilation of minority groups into the majority. Herskovits not only presented a strong argument against biological essentialism but also provided a basis for recognising the value and distinctness of the African American cultural heritage.

When Dunham was a student, acculturation was still seen in evolutionary terms – generally with a positivist inflection. The assimilation of modern ideas and technologies was seen as a contributory factor in the decline of traditional practices and rituals. Robert Redfield, Dunham's professor at the University of Chicago and a student of Park's, proposed a positivist view of ritual in his 1930 book *Tepoztlan: A Mexican Village*:

> In the simpler societies the rites of passage are an inseparable mixture of practical, magical, and religious elements. The disposition to do something which accompanies the crisis results in behaviour which is in part practical and in part merely expressive. . . . But in modern Western societies the expressive and the practical elements diverge into two quite different contexts. From the former the magical elements tend to fall away; what is done is more rationally comprehended and is year by year modified in accordance with the development of technique. The expressive elements are institutionalised and in part fall under the direction of the church. The technique of the obstetrician is remote from the religious ritual of baptism; the practical problem of disposing of a dead body is attacked by a practical specialist, while the expression

of the feelings of the bereaved is assisted by conventionalised ritual which is religious rather than magical.

(Redfield 1968b: 133–4)

In Tepoztlan, the Mexican village which Redfield studied, the richer towns-people who were more accustomed to city ways were known as 'los correctos', amongst whom Redfield observed: 'a tendency to relegate the non-practical usages to the rank of superstitions, and to omit them entirely. The tendency grows, and grows slowly; the society is not breaking down; it is merely changing' (ibid.). For Redfield, ritual serves no rational function. What is modernist in this view is the almost unquestioned assumption that acceptance of rational, scientific practices leads to general improvements in the quality of life. Redfield's positivism is, however, accompanied by the almost nervous assertion that society is not breaking down as a result of the changes.

If Redfield saw no rational function served by what to him constituted superstition and ritual, Herskovits argued that a greater knowledge and understanding of the retention of Africanisms among people of African descent in the New World would lead to a better understanding of the social issues faced by African Americans in the United States. In this context, Herskovits' judgement in 1947 of Katherine Dunham's work is instructive. After describing the aims of her field work in 1936, he goes on to discuss her subsequent choreography:

> The popular successes achieved by her reproductions of the dances she studied add weight to the testimony of numerous dancers and laymen as to the familiarity of her dances to them in the light of their own experience with Negro dancing in this country, or of these dance patterns as diffused to the whites. Such reactions, despite their impressionistic nature, are not without significance in terms of the search for African survivals, pointing to the rich returns to be gained from systematic scientific analysis of African dance styles and the effect of acculturation on New World Negro dancing.
>
> (Herskovits 1958: 270)

Herskovits' disappointment at Dunham's defection from the field of system-atic scientific analysis is thinly veiled. Dunham herself recalled in *Island Possessed* that Redfield said 'What's wrong with being a dancer' when she announced her decision to concentrate on running her company. Herskovits' reaction was completely different. Dunham says she

> stammered and stuttered into the phone on an icy day a few weeks after my return from Haiti, spoke to Herskovits in his office on the

campus of Northwestern and told him my decision, then repeated
my message at the end of a long silence.

(Dunham 1994b: 67)

Dunham also reveals that Herskovits had written to her while she was in
Haiti to discourage her from becoming too deeply involved with the vaudun
cult in which she had been initiated. Herskovits had been 'categorically
against' Dunham's plan at the time to undergo the 'canzo' or trial by fire
(1994b: 227). He himself had commented that:

> Much nonsense has been written about the need for the student of
> the customs of a people to become a 'participant observer' of those
> customs, by doing what, in common parlance, is termed 'going
> native'. . . . The ethnographer . . . especially if he be a white man,
> has what is called a high degree of social visibility, and any attempt
> to live according to the canons of native life would forthwith expose
> him to the thrusts of a deadly weapon in the hands of the Negro,
> the weapon most destructive of that mutual respect that is the basis
> of all free and friendly intercourse between two human beings,
> whatever their race – ridicule.

(Herskovits 1964: 323)

Herskovits believed that the anthropologist in the field will form 'warm
friendships among the native folk after he comes to know them well, so that
as a friend it will not be denied to him to share with them their inner values'
(ibid.). Herskovits' professed aim here is free and friendly discourse between
two human beings regardless of race, yet he is far from disregarding race.
When he mentions social visibility and implies the dangers of 'going native'
he is stressing the polarities that create difference and with it the distanced
detachment which in his view is what the anthropologist needs to create a
cogent, rational account.

Dunham, through not being content to rely on 'warm friendships' as a
source of information, adopted the role of participant observer which had
been used by sociologists studying urban life at the University of Chicago.
As a participant observer Dunham drew on her knowledge of psychology to
help her understand her subjective response to the experience of dancing in
vaudun rituals. As I have already argued, psychoanalytic ideas therefore
enabled Dunham to become involved in the vaudun cults she investigated,
and her involvement led her to question whether the kind of systematic
scientific analysis Herskovits advocated was the only way to do research. To
put this another way, by questioning scientific notions of detachment and
objectivity, Dunham came to see the boundary between the modern Western
subjectivity and notions of the 'primitive' Other in fluid and dynamic terms
and not as a rigid boundary.

Shango

Shango was initially choreographed as the Act 1 Finale of the 1945 musical comedy *Carib Song* and was subsequently performed as a stand-alone piece within mixed programmes of dance.[8] Shango is a West African god, who survived as part of the group of gods in the Shango cult in Trinidad, the Rada-Dahomey cult in Haiti and the Santos cult in Cuba. Dunham's *Shango* drew on elements from all three. The piece starts with a burst of jazz music and a few performers revelling and cavorting on stage, drinking rum and dancing. Then the mood changes, more dancers come on stage singing a hymn and carrying benches and the altar for the ceremony. Drummers take up position to one side of the altar – this is a simple table with a print of a Christian saint on it. When the congregation has sat down, a white cock is ritualistically sacrificed and taken round the participants seated on the benches, who each become affected by it in different ways. At the end of the last bench a young boy who took part in the sacrifice shows signs of becoming possessed and is held down and looked after by attendants. He crawls across the floor like a snake (Shango in Haiti is a snake deity) with writhing movements in his spine and torso until he reaches the altar onto which he climbs. Facing him centre stage is a priest and together they stretch out their arms in symmetrical gestures before the boy faints and is caught by the priest who carries him over his shoulder off stage. A few other members of the congregation now come forward and dance one by one different dances of possession by other gods in front of the altar before the boy comes back sitting astride a huge drum carried on its side above the heads of five men. At the same time many of the women in the congregation perform a fast, driving, unison dance with a rhythmic stepping pattern and a characteristically African forwards-backwards jerking of the shoulders. The action on stage has built up to an almost orgasmic peak of intensity that does not diminish as the lights fade and the curtain is lowered. In *Shango* Dunham clearly gives an almost educational example of the intoxicating power of Afro-Caribbean religious rituals, showing the forms that create cult solidarity and induce hypnosis, and showing what dances of possession look like – all condensed into a short, intense piece of theatre. As Charles Moore, a past member of Dunham's company, recalls: 'When I danced in Katherine Dunham's *Shango* I wasn't Charles Moore anymore, I was possessed'.[9]

In her 1941 essay 'Form and function in primitive dance' (1978b) Dunham presented the theoretical framework she developed for evaluating the functions of the dances of Haiti which can be used as a key to show what Dunham understood she was showing in *Shango*. In this, she distinguishes between 'seasonal dances', 'dances at occasional small gatherings' and 'sacred dances'.

Dunham demonstrates the inter-relationship between the dance forms she found and their social function. The 'danse grouillière' which consists of 'a

Figure 8 An acolyte holds a bowl of chicken's blood over the boy possessed by a snake in *Shango*, photo by Roger Wood

Source: © New York Public Library Dance Collection

Seasonal

play – recreation
externalisation of inhibitions
externalisation of energy

social cohesion
greater social integration
sexual stimulus and release

Occasional small-gathering dances

sexual selection
sexual attraction
development of artistic values through
  exhibition of skill

development of the artist
social cohesion
gratification of exhibitionist
  tendencies through audience-
  performance relationship

Sacred

cult dances

ritual preparation for reception
  of 'loa'

secret ritual functions to
  induce and break hypnosis

establishment of cult solidarity
  by motivation and direction
  of religious ecstasy through
  dance

'loa' dances

represent or symbolise 'loa'

establish contact between
  individual and deity

funeral dances

externalisation of grief

escape from emotional
  conflict

Figure 9 Function of the dances of Haiti

Katherine Dunham 'Form and function in primitive dance', *Educational Dance*, October 1941

grinding movement of the forward thrust hips' and is 'directly associated with sexual activities' (Dunham 1978b: 193) occurs in many contexts including festivals like Mardi Gras but also at funerals where it brings about a release of tension and hence externalisation of grief. This sexual character of funeral dances, Dunham observes, is 'in keeping with African philosophy which closely associates procreation with death, perhaps as a compensatory effort' (ibid.). Another function that Dunham finds in some Haitian dance forms is the generation of a sense of communality: in the large 'danse collé' (literally meaning stuck or glued together): 'the closeness and compactness of the mass engenders social cohesion, while at the same time the gregarious-recreation impulses and desire to externalise and share experiences draws people together in mass form' (ibid.).

Dunham found much the same types of functions in sacred dances. She divides sacred dances into three categories. First, cult dances: these prepare individuals for possession, enact secret rituals and induce or break hypnosis, or establish cult solidarity by motivation and direction of religious ecstasy through dance. Second, 'loa' dances: these 'represent or symbolise "loa"' and 'establish contact between individual and deity' (including possession by a deity). Last, she cites funeral dances whose function is the 'externalisation of grief [and] escape from emotional conflict' (1978b: 192). Cults used dances to engender a sense of communal identity among cult membership and also used dances to build up or release tension in order to motivate participants towards religious ecstasy. One key difference between social and sacred dances in Dunham's framework is that it is only in the sacred dances that participants become possessed by spirits known in Haitian vaudun as 'loa'. Possession is achieved through ritual dance movements whose performance leads to a dissociative change in the consciousness of the dancer – a sort of hypnosis. Dunham gives as an example the 'yonvalou'. This is a dance she learnt in the rituals of the Rada-Dahomey cult within which she became initiated:

> The movement of the 'yonvalou' is fluid, involving spine, base of head, chest and solar plexus. The effect is complete relaxation . . . a constant circular flow which has acted as a mental narcotic, and figu-ratively speaking, physical purgative. The dance, is decidedly soothing, rather than exciting, and one is left in a state of complete acceptance. It is in this state most often that contact with 'loa' occurs.
>
> (ibid.: 195)

In *Shango* the boy dances the 'yonvalou' at the beginning of his possession. Dunham gives another example of this type of dance, the 'zepaules'. This stresses shoulder action:

> But here the ecstasy is of a slightly different quality than in the 'yonvalou'. It seems that the regular forward-backward jerking of the shoulders, a contraction and expansion of the chest, insures regular breathing, and this regular breathing brings about hypno-tism or auto-intoxication, states bordering on ecstasy.
>
> (ibid.)

The group of women at the end of *Shango* are dancing the 'zepaules'. Dunham also contrasts the relatively peaceful Rada-Dahomey cult, in which she became initiated and on whose ceremonies *Shango* is partly based, with the Petro cult which she says is known for its violence and as a cult of blood.[10] Whereas in her view the Rada-Dahomey ceremonies aim to relax tensions, the Petro bush priests use dance to generate psychological tension that builds up to a violent explosion. Dunham observes that there are fewer 'possessions' by gods at a Petro ceremony: 'the form of the dance apparently leads to uncontrolled motor activity, hysteria, rather than ecstasy or hypnotism . . . and cult solidarity [is] assured by the producing of similar effects in all of the worshipers' (ibid.: 194).

In *Shango* Dunham was showing a type of ceremony which, as she had already argued in her lectures and academic writing, is one through which dancers release their tensions in a way that is peaceful and beneficial. As Aschenbrenner observes, underlying Dunham's understanding of the function of ritual dances of possession is Malinowski's functionalist approach to anthropology: that anthropologists seek to explain social phenomena in terms of imperatives to fulfil biological and psychological needs. Whereas Charles Moore recalls that when he danced *Shango* he wasn't Charles Moore any more, he was possessed, not only did Dunham herself not dance in *Shango* but one of the most important experiences she herself derived through her participation in the Rada-Dahomey cult was her realisation of her inability to become possessed.

Dunham was initiated into the Rada-Dahomey cult. In this she was adopted by or 'married' to the snake deity Damballa. She writes in some detail about her initiation ceremony in her 1969 book *Island Possessed*. Before leaving Haiti in 1936 at the end of her field trip, she went through a further ceremony at the compound of a bush priest called Julien in which she promised to return and go through a further stage of initiation. After making these promises in the sanctuary, she then, with 'La place' (an acolyte), performed ritual dance steps of the yonvalou which were described earlier. This dance, Dunham says, is decidedly soothing, and should have left her in a state of complete acceptance. While performing it she should have become possessed by Damballa – in Haitian vernacular he should have 'mounted' her. A plate full of flour with an egg propped up on it – the snake deity's special food – was placed on the ground before the altar for her to break and eat. A sheet was spread above her head while this took place, but Dunham, however, 'succumbed to one of my old taboos, a revulsion towards eating raw eggs' (1994b: 234). Finding herself critically observed by the priest, Julien, she became frightened and for a while was unable to continue the ceremony. Then:

> Someone handed me a kerchief, I wiped my face and started to dance. I danced more than I have ever in my life, before or after. I danced out all my anger at unknown things and at myself for trying to know them, frustration at the rotten egg and weariness with strange mores. I found myself alone with one, with another, or just

myself while others clapped and sang and it dawned on me that it was with affection and encouragement.

(ibid.)

At last she caught Julien's eye and he nodded, telling her that all was well and the gods happy, and the ceremony finished. After making her promise in the sanctuary, the dance was a test in which the god showed his acceptance. During this Damballa should have entered into her, eaten the egg and danced his undulating, snake-like dance of possession. Dunham implies that this didn't happen, but that what she performed in its place was acceptable.

Writing about her experiences during vaudun ceremonies in 1936, Dunham says that she asked herself:

> Could Herskovits tell me, could Erich Fromm, could Téoline or Dégrassé tell me what part of me lived on the floor of the houngfor, felt awareness seeping from the earth and people and things around me, and what stood on one side taking notes?
>
> (1994b: 228)

Téoline and Dégrassé, who were not present at the ceremony with Julien, were the vaudun priestesses who oversaw Dunham's initiation into the cult, and 'houngfor' is the name for the vaudun temple. Dunham is implying here that she found it hard to sort out which part of her was drawing on her scientific, rational training as an anthropologist and which part of her was using what she had learned from the teachings of the cult itself in order to try to understand the experiences she had while dancing in vaudun ceremonies. So while on the one hand her experience in the ceremony made her aware of her difference from the Haitian villagers – she found herself weary 'with strange mores' and 'angry at unknown things' (ibid.) – on the other hand 'objective' anthropological methodologies and psychoanalysis offered her no comfort either. Joyce Aschenbrenner has observed about Dunham's book *Island Possessed*:

> It is a measure of Dunham's ethical sensitivity that she is constantly troubled by the fact that while she is able to gain a much higher quality of understanding through her open and sympathetic attitude towards the religions she has studied, she is not able to say unqualifiably that she is a believer. The people sense her sensitivity and her desire to believe – which is in itself a sign of respect for their beliefs – and they are not concerned that she has never experienced possession – as, indeed, many of them have not.
>
> (Aschenbrenner 1978: 189)

In speaking here of Dunham's sensitivity and respect for the beliefs of the people she was studying, Aschenbrenner is in effect saying that Dunham defined the boundary between herself and the Other as fluid and dynamic rather than rigid. In proceeding now to consider Wigman's *Monotony: Whirl Dance* and Graham's *Primitive Mysteries*, what is at issue is the extent to which Graham and Wigman, through dancing ritual material, came to define the boundary between self and Other in similar ways.

Monotony: Whirl Dance

Mary Wigman's *Monotony: Whirl Dance* was first performed as part of her 1928 dance suite *Celebration*. Just as *Primitive Mysteries* was an artistic response to the rituals of the Penitente Indians, *Monotony* was derived from the Sufi whirling ritual of the Mevlevi Dervishes. Wigman's early teacher and mentor Rudolf Laban was fascinated by Sufi whirling which he first saw as a child when living in Bosnia Herzogovina where his father was military governor (Laban 1975: 50–3). Wigman first started to choreograph ecstatic whirling dances in 1917 when she was still working with Laban, and she performed a whirling dance in his *Festival of the Sun* at Ascona (Manning 1993: 77–8). She went on making them until the mid-1940s, and also included spinning in the curriculum for her dance schools.

The Mevlevi Sufis are one of a number of Sufi brotherhoods, many of whom engage in ceremonies that use patterned movement practices through which they achieve disassociational states. Anthony Shay has argued that Western scholars are wrong to call the whirling ceremony of the Mevlevi Sufis dance.[11] Dance is not actually forbidden in the Koran but there is a strong prejudice against it that dates back to the times of Mohammed. Shay offers as one possible explanation for this prejudice the fact that singing and dancing girls were used in a satirical way by the enemies of Islam to discredit early Muslims (Shay 1995: 67). He points out that there is a long historical tradition within which Sufis have had to defend their dance-like practices against attack by orthodoxy and that, since 'the Sufis do not want their sacred practices to be thought of in terms of dance, it seems inappropriate for the uninitiated to do so' (ibid.: 69).

Theodore Barber (1986) has made a useful comparison between Wigman's *Monotony* and the actual Sufi ceremony. The Mevlevi Dervishes who perform this ceremony are all men and it is performed as a group, with one 'semazen-bashi' or dance leader outside the group who doesn't himself turn but arranges the participants and keeps them from getting out of order while spinning. In silence, all turn at the same comparatively slow pace, and at the end of ten or fifteen minutes the leader signals them to stop. The participants then bow in all directions around the hall before starting turning again. The spinning is controlled and no one should fall down. The participants, according to Barber, aim to become channels for spiritual energy, with one hand facing palm up to the sky, the other turned towards the ground.

Wigman's dance was a solo, performed by a woman – herself. She did not wear the distinctive high hat and long coat that is the traditional Mevlevi brotherhood costume and, while the Dervishes move in silence, her dance had a musical accompaniment of gong and percussion sounds. Again, unlike the Dervishes, Wigman spun around at varying speeds, using various gestures. At the end she accelerated to a virtuosic high speed, and at the climax when the music stopped, she halted, suspended for a moment before slowly falling to the ground as the curtain dropped. Of all the dances Wigman performed in the United States, Martha Hill particularly remembered her 'turning' dances:

> She came on stage and turned on the spot, faster, slower, with her body bending forward, rotating and spiralling, somehow similar to Martha's contraction and release. I saw her turn so fast that her hair was flowing across her face, and the dance would end in a gradual fall; immediately she rose and was perfectly on balance to take those beautiful bows. Wigman's turning dances were completely mesmerising.
>
> (Partsch-Bergsohn 1994: 66)

Here is part of Wigman's own account of the piece:

> Fixed to the same spot and spinning in the monotony of the whirling movement, one lost oneself gradually in it until the turns seemed to detach themselves from the body, and the world around it started to turn. Not turning oneself, but being turned, being the centre, being the quiet pole in the vortex of rotation!
>
> Arch and dome, no sky above me . . . a tender rocking, with the arms reaching out, painful and blissful again in a crescendo of self-destructive lust, surging and ebbing, flowing back higher and faster, ever faster. . . . Will it never end? Why does no one speak the redeeming word, stopping this madness? With a last desperate exertion, control over one's willpower is found again.
>
> A jerk pierces the body, compelling it to stand still at the moment of the fastest turn; now the body is stretching high, lifted on tiptoe, with the arms thrown up, grasping a non-existent support. A breathless pause, an eternity long, lasting only a few seconds. And then the sudden letting go, the fall of the relaxed body into the depth with only one sensation still alive: that of a complete incorporeal state. And in that state only one wish: never be forced to get up again, to be allowed to lie there just like this, through all eternity.
>
> (Wigman 1966: 39)

But as Hill pointed out, Wigman did, of course, get up and take her bows to the audience, and Wigman's reminiscence ends with 'Once more it had turned out well. Once more I had got away by the skin of my teeth' (ibid.). Barber (1986) argues that what Wigman felt may have been similar to the sorts of spiritual experiences that the Dervishes attributed to their ceremony. In Dunham's functionalist terms, the group of male Dervishes establish cult solidarity through performing hypnotic movement, and enact symbolic rituals when they stop and bow to all sides of the hall. Wigman used similar hypnotic movements to establish contact between herself and a great, transcendent power of unity within the cosmos.

Barber points out that, where the performer's posture was concerned, Wigman and the Mevlevi Dervishes inclined their head to one side in similar ways. The Mevlevi Dervish spins with his head inclined towards his right shoulder. Wigman turns with her upper torso and head leaning in opposite directions; this can be observed in a section in Allegra Fuller Snyder's documentary film about Wigman where, as an old woman, she demonstrates whirling to a class of students.[12] The position of the head determines the physiological effect of dancing. Both the Dervishes and Wigman lean the head to one side, which is likely to induce a hypnotic state. Keeping the head upright would lessen the performer's chances of becoming hypnotised.[13] Barber says that the Dervishes focus their concentration through repeating the name of God. Wigman in her dance, however, seems to be aiming to blur the distinction between consciousness and the unconscious, an outcome that was not that of the Mevlevi brotherhood. Another important distinction between Wigman's dance and the ceremonial practice of the Mevlevi Dervishes is the fact that she was a woman on her own and a dancer, while they were men in a group and did not see their practice as dance.

Primitive Mysteries

Martha Graham first came across the Penitente Indians of New Mexico in 1930 when driving back to the East Coast after performing in California. The Penitente sect had originally been converted to Roman Catholicism by Spanish missionaries in the seventeenth century, but by the time Graham encountered them, their harsh, masochistic rituals included retentions from pre-Christian practices. Graham wrote at the end of her life that the Penitente Indians were

> a sect which believes in purification from sin through penance. Even today, the sect practices its ancient rites, though they are banned by the Catholic Church. I saw a woman in a pueblo walk on her bare knees over cactus leaves, as the rites were performed.
>
> (Graham 1991: 176)

Graham did not, however, borrow from or directly represent anything from the dances and rituals she observed, but made an austerely formal, modernist piece in response to them.

Her interest in ritual dance at this time must also have been partly prompted by her experience dancing the role of 'The Chosen One' in Massine's 1930 revival of the ballet *Rite of Spring* in Philadelphia.[14] Louis Horst, who already knew of the Penitente Indians, took Graham to see them. They were already reasonably well known, however, particularly among artists and writers. While in New Mexico, Graham visited Mabel Dodge McLuhan, a wealthy New York hostess who in the 1910s held an artistic salon and who in 1917 moved to Santa Fe (see Graham 1991: 177). Among the European and American modernists who visited New Mexico during the 1920s and 1930s are Antonin Artaud, Rudolf Laban, D. H. Lawrence, and Georgia O'Keefe. Horst and Graham's interest in Native American culture was therefore far from unique. Bessie Schöenberg has suggested that it was Horst who was primarily interested in the native peoples, especially their music. Graham, she says, 'really did a mixture of the Indian and the Spanish-American . . . almost a montage of two cultures there in some ways. But she spoke more about the Indian. She *used* more of the Spanish American' (Jowitt 1981: 47, emphasis in the original).

Graham herself had been brought up in a Protestant family in New England which traced its ancestry back to the Mayflower (Graham 1991: 18). She nevertheless seemed to have felt a life-long affinity between her own puritan sensibility and the extreme asceticism of these Native Americans. After she died her ashes were scattered in the New Mexican desert. More than one person has also commented on the irony that *Primitive Mysteries* was inspired by the Catholic cult of the virgin, but that many of the original dancers were first generation Jewish immigrants from Eastern Europe. Ernestine Stodelle (1984: 72) says that Graham was attracted by the Catholic side of what she found in New Mexico. She points out that Graham had been brought up by a Catholic nurse, Lizzie Prendergast, who was still living with Graham's mother and Graham would have seen her when she visited them in Santa Barbara just before her trip to New Mexico. Schöenberg says that, while making *Primitive Mysteries*, Graham was particularly interested in the qualities of one of her dancers, Mary Rivoire. Rivoire was a Catholic and Schöenberg says Graham 'would turn to Mary in rehearsal and say, "This is right?" ' (Jowitt 1981: 48). Schöenberg also says that Graham brought back 'Santos' from New Mexico – simple carved wooden saints made by Spanish-American Catholics – and that these were an inspiration for some of the stark, simple gestures dancers take up in many of the tableaux.

Primitive Mysteries has three parts, titled 'Hymn to the Virgin', 'Crucifixus', and 'Hosanna'. A chorus of twelve dancers (all of whom were women) wore plain dark blue woollen dresses with tight bodices[15] while

Graham, who was set apart from them in some special but unidentified role which I shall call the Virgin, was dressed in a long loose brilliant white calico dress. Before and after each section the dancers process on or off stage in silent formations.

In the first part, when they have all processed on stage the chorus divide into three groups, four dancers squatting in a line across the rear of the stage

Figure 10 'Hymn to the Virgin' from *Primitive Mysteries*, photo by Edward Moeller

Source: © New York Public Library Dance Collection

and two groups of four mid stage on either side. The Virgin moves from one to the other of these two groups and poses in front of them while they make up angular patterns with their hands and arms or form little circle dances around her; this and subsequent circle dances are all reminiscent of *Le Sacre* (or at least to Millicent Hodson and Kenneth Archer's reconstruction of it).[16] Stodelle likens this alternation between soloist and chorus to a concerto, and it is reminiscent of a similar alternation in Graham's earlier *Heretic*. The chorus seem to worship the soloist as if she were the Virgin. Some accounts suggest she blesses them, but the dancer Yuriko who learnt the role from Graham for the 1964 revival recalled: 'Martha told me when I danced the role I wasn't blessing them. "Oh, no, Yuriko," she said, "they are blessing you"' (Sears 1982: 26). Eight of the dancers kneel down to form two lines through which the Virgin processes and accepts blessings and then all twelve dancers form a circle around her which moves in an increasingly complicated, halting sequence – a few steps clockwise and back again – before the music unexpectedly stops. The dancers then reform in a stark rectangular formation with which the piece began, and process in silence off stage.

Yuriko said she interpreted her role in the second section as the Virgin Mary watching her son suffering on the cross. The Virgin stands with head bowed while two women stand facing front either side of her, place their outside hand on their hip and raise their inside arm on the side above the Virgin's head; their hand points up so that their arms frame her with a gothic arch. Stodelle says they are pointing to the invisible figure of Christ suffering on the cross behind the Virgin's back (Stodelle 1984: 76). At the moment of Jesus' death the Virgin stretches her arms out vertically to make the sign of the cross. Marcia Siegel suggests that at this moment she might be Christ himself suffering or dying.[17] This moment seems to be the high point of the ritual as a whole. As the Virgin takes up the cross stance, the remaining ten members of the chorus, who have formed a close group in front and to one side, each bends slightly forwards and raises one hand to their forehead with its fingers pointing stiffly forwards. Stodelle says this is a crown of thorns and Schöenberg says this motif came from a 'Santos'. One by one the dancers break out of the group into slow dragging leaps with their hands held behind their backs. They circle around the Virgin and their dance gradually but painfully builds up speed. Again, as in the first section, the music stops, the dancers reform and process off stage in silence.

The mood of the final section – 'Hosanna' – is more celebratory, with a moderate, tripping melody played on a flute to which the chorus of dancers skip lightly though still in a slightly constrained way. The Virgin, however, still seems to be involved in grieving for Jesus' death in the 'Crucifixus' and an assistant enacts with her the descent from the cross and the pietà. This too ends up with a circle of dancers while the Virgin sits on the ground and her assistant kneels behind her in the middle. This time both make a cross with their arms. As Yuriko observes about this stance:

There was inner joy, a light that comes from within, coming out of the contraction itself. It goes down the thighs, and you even have it in the hands. They aren't free, but cupped with a tension on the inside of the palm, like holding a candle. It is weight, depth of feeling. These are not just positions.

(Sears 1982)

In Dunham's functionalist terms the dance performed creates a sense of group solidarity; but whereas ritual movement in the Haitian Rada-Dahomey cult functioned through releasing tension, in *Primitive Mysteries* tension was built up during the piece somewhat in the way Dunham says it was built up in Haitian Petro ceremonies. This can be seen in the silent processions at the beginning and end of each section. Each is different but all have halting rhythms and a weightiness to them. Dancers take one step and then pause, then step again with the same foot. Shurr says 'On the entrances and exits we walked on a contraction, and we felt each other. Our arms almost touched' (ibid.). Pearl Lang remembered that:

The uniqueness of that walk, and the awesomeness of it, is that it's done in complete silence. The dancers listen to each other. She has to watch them and they have to watch her in order to keep this together. It's very difficult. And that's part of the mystery . . .

(ibid.: 27)

Although all the dancers move on the same beat, in some of the processions some groups have to cover more ground than others and thus take longer steps so as to change the linear procession in which they leave the wings into a rectangular formation by the time they reach the middle of the stage. Accounts speak of the processions being rehearsed for six months or more before Graham was satisfied with them. Graham wouldn't allow the dancers to count to keep in time, but insisted that they 'keep together on the beat by breathing together, and [that they] must take their signals from the smallest indications of breath and reflex, until they moved as one organism with a collective mind' (De Mille 1992: 178).

Following Dunham's schema of sacred dances, the processions, together with many other ritualised gestures in the piece, had the function of establishing cult solidarity by motivation and direction of religious ecstasy through movement; this was generated not through hypnosis but by the production of similar effects in all of the participants. Like the Petro priest in Dunham's example, Graham built up tension in her dancers, both within the rehearsal period and through the choreographed movements themselves. Dorothy Bird recalled that at the end of the silent processions: 'When Louis [Horst's] music began we all but cracked open with relief, because the silence had been so agonising' (quoted in De Mille 1992: 178). When taking up the cross stance Yuriko spoke of tension in the palm of the hand. Tension was also a factor in the leaps at the climax of the middle, 'Crucifixus' section. The result of holding the hands behind the back during the leaps was that only limited release of tension was allowed. Dunham says the result of building up tension in this way was that few participants became possessed but there were hysterical outbursts.

The dancers who worked with Graham were almost a cult group in their dedication to her work. Gertrude Shurr observed:

> In those days you had to believe thoroughly in the person you were working with. Otherwise you shouldn't have been with that person. You absolutely had to believe. That's what I was doing. We believed in it [*Primitive Mysteries*], and it was wonderful.
>
> (Sears 1982: 26)

Evidence suggests however that Graham also terrified her dancers. The myth of the first performance of *Primitive Mysteries* is a case in point. Rehearsing on stage in the early hours of the morning before its premiere Graham screamed at the dancers for making a mistake and walked out on them saying they were ruining her piece and she was withdrawing it altogether. Horst kept everyone on stage, Graham eventually reappeared and finished the rehearsal. Thirty-three years later Graham terrorised another cast of *Primitive Mysteries*. Jean Nuchtern, who danced with Yuriko in the 1964 revival of the piece, later wrote:

> I remember feeling afraid and isolated during rehearsals – afraid because I couldn't do the movement and isolated because I didn't want to reveal how scared I was. . . . I remember when Martha came to rehearsals I wanted to disappear. I wanted her only to look at me if she'd think I was a great dancer. . . . I remember Martha punching a dancer in the arm because she felt the dancer wasn't working hard enough. I remember the company manager trying to calm Martha but being unable to comfort her . . . I remember us dancers scattering like pigeons whenever Martha approached.
>
> (Nuchtern 1977: 28–9)

Graham clearly dominated her dancers during the rehearsal period and did the same on stage. This was another lesson she evidently learnt from *Le Sacre*. Dorothy Bird has spoken of her first class with Graham at the Cornish School in Seattle. Graham told the students:

> I have something very exciting that I want to share with you. I have just come from dancing the role of The Chosen One in *Le Sacre* on the great stage of the Metropolitan Opera in New York. I discovered

something as I stood still for a long period of time in the work with the dancers all around me. I learned how to command the stage while standing absolutely still. And I'm going to teach you how to do that.

(Bird, quoted in Horosko 1991: 47–8)

Bessie Schöenberg, who had been in the audience at the Met, commented on precisely this quality:

What fascinated me was that Massine had moved her out almost onto the apron and the orchestra was going tutti, during the section before the Danse Sacrale. And the chorus on-stage, the dancers, were going tutti, all full force. And this small figure was standing there absolutely quietly. And you couldn't take your eyes off her. Even before she danced. She was magnetic.

(Jowitt 1981: 54)

The Virgin does very little dancing in *Primitive Mysteries* and is often still while the others dance, yet she always remains the centre of attention. While the others have occasional moments when their tension bursts into a temporary release, like the leaps at the climax of the middle, 'Crucifixus' section, it is only the Virgin who seems, at the two moments when she makes the sign of the cross, to experience any connection between individual and a deity.

Conclusion

What *Shango, Monotony: Whirl Dance* and *Primitive Mysteries* therefore have in common is their use of movement material that has the potential to lead to disassociational states of consciousness. In each case this movement material itself was derived from a religious ceremony performed by a group whose culture was radically different from that of the choreographer. Not all of the pieces, however, acknowledged this, as each referred to the religious ceremony in different ways and with different consequences.

Shango is a much more direct representation of the religious ceremony on which it is based than *Primitive Mysteries* or *Monotony: Whirl Dance*, but it is nevertheless theatricalised and conventionalised. This is most obvious in terms of time and space: the ceremonies described by Herskovits and Herskovits (1947), Herskovits (1964) and Dunham (1994b) generally went on all night whereas the action in *Shango* is compressed into less than ten minutes. Herskovits' (1964) photographs of a vaudun ceremony show a crowded space with no particular focus, rather like photographs of dancers at a crowded disco; in contrast there is lots of space for the dancing and action in *Shango* which is clearly arranged frontally before the altar and behind a proscenium arch. Costume also has been generalised. In *Shango* all wear uniform white dresses or trousers, whereas Herskovits' photographs show the men wearing suits and shoes; the male dancers in *Shango* are bare breasted and bare foot. During the Shango ceremony Herskovits and Herskovits (1947) describes the attendants tying a ribbon in a particular god's colour on a participant who has become possessed by that god; this does not happen in *Shango*.

Monotony: Whirl Dance does not directly refer to the Sufi ceremony at all. Although Wigman's students seem to have known that the whirling exercises that Wigman taught them were derived from the Sufi whirling ceremonies, there is no mention of the Sufis in the passage Wigman herself wrote about the piece or in any of the reviews and reminiscences of the piece that I have read. Not mentioning the Sufi aspects of the piece has the effect of making the piece more generalised and abstracted, and of drawing attention to Wigman's act of dancing in a disassociational state, blurring the distinction between consciousness and the unconscious.

Primitive Mysteries like *Monotony: Whirl Dance* is a generalised and abstracted version of Penitente Indian and Spanish American ceremonial practices. But whereas *Monotony: Whirl Dance* plays down its relation to the Sufis, Graham seems to have emphasised the inspirational role of Penitente Indian ceremonies in *Primitive Mysteries*: she herself spoke of its Native American connections and these are frequently mentioned in reviews. Precisely what the connection was, however, is less clear. Gertrude Shurr, who was with Graham and Horst in New Mexico during the summer of 1930, recalls their watching a dance in which villagers took an icon of the Virgin Mary out of a church and walked her through the village square (Sears 1982: 25). In *Primitive Mysteries* she says: 'Martha was the Virgin. She has many ideas now, but the very first idea was that she was the appointed figure, and we were the people doing this miracle play' (ibid.). Whereas *Shango* aimed to show what a group of related Caribbean religious ceremonies looked like, *Primitive Mysteries* in many ways asserts its modern Western origins. The chorus of dancers wear long, tight fitting sheath dresses that do not look particularly 'Indian', but are made of the same type of woollen jersey tubes which Graham used to costume most of her 'long woollen' pieces. Marcia Siegel says the Virgin's dress 'might be a plain version of a party dress for a Southern belle, in white organdie with flowing panels and sleeves, a dress that is almost demurely feminine yet conceals the shape of the body' (1979: 52). Therefore this costume too did not look 'Indian' but distinctly Western.

In *Primitive Mysteries* Graham distances herself from Native American ritual practices, just as Wigman distances herself from Sufi practices, in order to emphasise the specificity of the movement she herself has made for the piece: both *Primitive Mysteries* and *Monotony: Whirl Dance* are modernist pieces. But unlike Wigman's piece, in *Primitive Mysteries* the existence of a Native American (if not a Catholic) referent is given emphasis. By explicitly naming the source of her inspiration, Graham was suggesting that she had a particular affinity with this particular group: that she as a modern American was primitive in ways that these native peoples were primitive. Dunham, as an African

American, had an affinity (that Graham and Wigman lacked) with the Caribbean communities whose dances she used through shared African descent. What is at issue here, however, is not the act of appropriation which all three choreographers made but the underlying ethics of the act – the sensitivity and respect each showed for those whose rituals were appropriated.

In so far as all three dance pieces involved possession, all three point to the possibility of defining the imaginary boundary between self and Other as not just fluid and dynamic but actually as permeable. The problem is that this positive outcome is undermined by some of the ways in which these dance pieces mediated notions of the primitive. Distinguishing between those who speak *as* 'natives' and those who speak *about* them, Trinh T. Minh-ha has made an observation that is useful for understanding what is at stake here. Trinh observes: 'Terming "us" the natives focuses on *our* innate qualities and our belonging to a particular place by birth; terming "them" the natives on *their* being born inferior and "non-European"' (Trinh 1989: 52, emphasis in the original). Wigman speaks *as* a 'native' and focuses on innate qualities that she shares with fellow Europeans; furthermore, because she does not speak *about* the 'natives' she does not consign anyone as 'inferior' and 'non-European' through her piece. Dunham speaks both *as* and *about* the 'natives' but does so with a sensitivity and respect that does not consign them to an inferior position. Graham speaks *as* a 'native' in *Primitive Mysteries* when she focuses on innately American qualities that she believes she shares with Amerindians. Through her seriousness she expresses a great respect for what she imagines to be Penitente mores, although she undoubtedly misrepresented these by mediating them in assimilationist terms. Graham does not speak *about* the 'natives' in the exoticised stylistic terms through which Shawn, St Denis and many others represented Amerindian dance.[18]

Speaking *as* a 'native' allows Graham to escape from objectification as a woman and with it from demands to conform to stereotypical notions of how femininity should be represented in dance. She also escapes objectification as Other through appealing to universals of which 'we' (Americans) 'are all a part' (Armitage 1966: 105). In *Primitive Mysteries* Graham may be articulating her own fantasies (as Susan Hiller puts it) about the meanings of Penitente Indian practices, but she is including rather than excluding these Native Americans as part of modern America. She doesn't take the easy way out and simply objectify Penitente Indians as Other, but blurs the boundaries between modern American and Amerindian through performing movement that leads to 'possession'. Rather than deny that there are contradictions within the binary polarity between modern and 'primitive', Graham honestly and uncompromisingly articulates these. What makes *Primitive Mysteries* stand out among the other American modern dance pieces of the period is the terrible honesty, to use Ann Douglas' phrase, with which it articulates a conflictual fear and fascination with the Other that itself articulates in sublimated form a deep ambivalence about modernity itself.

9

CONCLUSION

Reeling through a microfilm of Katherine Dunham's scrapbooks of press cuttings at the New York Public Library Dance Collection, a headline caught my eye: 'German Dances Foretold War; Jitterbugs a Sign of US Stability'. This headed a short feature in the *Detroit Free Press*, 11 February 1945, written by Katherine Lynch. Dunham had given her an interview when she and her company had performed in Detroit the previous week. The feature begins: 'If the State Department authorities really wanted to know ten years ago what Germany's intentions were towards the world, there was an easy way to find out. They should have asked a serious student of the dance' (Dunham Scrapbooks Vol. 4, page un-numbered). It goes on to cite Dunham's training as an anthropologist in support of her opinion of the difference between the 'national mental health' of America and Germany. Dunham told Lynch that:

> All of ten years ago in Germany and Italy they began doing modern equivalents of Aztec and Mayan war dances. These are mass dances, regimented dances. The fascists sponsored them and taught them. They're callisthenics dances done to percussion and wind instruments, designed to build tension rather than to relieve it.
>
> (ibid.)

Dunham then compares these mass dances with the jitterbug which she suggests is imported from Jamaica. She observes that, although this dance is also done in large groups, 'the individual jitterbug improvises with the greatest freedom as he goes along. The same is true of Cuban festival dances, and of all dances danced for individual pleasure' (ibid.). Dunham's theories about dance and social tension have already been discussed in the previous chapter in the context of 'primitive' society. What is fascinating about this newspaper cutting is that Dunham extends her ideas to include the social impact of modernity:

Our industrial civilisation builds up tension: it confines people to patterns. The jitterbug relieves the tension in violent dance very free and unconfined. This freedom in the dance is an indication of freedom in our society. The fact that it is an adopted dance shows a change in our mode of thinking; a community of thought with other peoples; a turning away from isolationism. In Germany, the dance does not relieve tension. It builds it up to stimulate the mass idea of war and regimentation.

(ibid.)

Colour and 'race' are not directly mentioned here but they are implicit: the jitterbug has been adopted by Americans (both black and white) from Jamaicans and is of African origin. When Dunham speaks of a community of thought shared between Americans and Jamaicans, and of a turning away from isolationism, she is interpreting social and political shifts optimistically. Dunham goes on to mention Mary Wigman 'who at one time was one of the world's foremost exponents of free, flowing, individual expression in the dance' but is 'no longer permitted to dance in the way which made her famous or to teach it' (ibid.). While the whole issue of Wigman's degree of complicity with the Nazi regime is still today a matter of some disagreement, and Dunham is incorrect in supposing Wigman had been forced to stop performing and teaching, it is nevertheless interesting that Dunham should be thinking about Wigman at all, especially during war time.

What is fascinating about this interview is the fact that here in 1945 is Dunham talking about what Kracauer in 1927 had called the mass ornament, and trying to answer one of the major questions that has preoccupied so many people since then: how could the German people have accepted or perhaps even actively supported the National Socialist regime and (though at the time Dunham gave the interview their full horrors were yet to be revealed) its horrendous anti-Semitic policies? Her questioning of what role the performance of mass choreography might have played in this brings her concerns close to those being developed around this time by Erich Fromm and Siegfried Kracauer. As I have already pointed out, Dunham had known Fromm since the mid-1930s. Although she herself did not know Kracauer, Fromm had known him in Frankfurt during the 1920s and renewed an acquaintance with him in New York when Kracauer escaped there from France in 1941. Fromm helped Kracauer to develop the psychological categories for Kracauer's 1947 book *From Caligari to Hitler: A Psychological History of German Cinema*.

In his 1941 book *Escape from Freedom*, Fromm argues that human beings only developed a sense of individuality and subjectivity in modern times. Before this they had been more willing to accept authority, but along with the development of a greater awareness of individual identity went a more mature sense of individual responsibility. Hitler and the Nazis succeeded,

Fromm argued, because of people's immaturity and their longing to revert to being ruled in an authoritarian way. This is very similar to the view of the mass ornament that Kracauer proposed in *From Caligari to Hitler*. It was on his arrival in the United States that Kracauer began to write this book, and in it he identified signs in Weimar cinema of a German disposition towards accepting authoritarianism which in his view contributed to their acceptance of fascism.

> *Triumph of the Will*, the official Nazi film of the Nuremberg Party Convention in 1934, proves that in shaping their mass-ornaments the Nazi decorators drew inspiration from *Nibelungen* [directed by Fritz Lang 1924]. Siegfried's theatrical trumpeters, showy steps and authoritarian human patterns reappear, extremely magnified, in the modern Nuremberg pageant.
>
> (Kracauer 1947: 95)

I pointed out in Chapters 4 and 5 that Kracauer's ideas about the mass ornament went through a series of changes between 1927 and 1947 in response to changing political circumstances. The events of the Second World War mark a turning point, a historical moment when artists and intellectuals finally gave up many of the hopes, beliefs and ideas that I have traced in this book, if they had not already abandoned them. Theodor Adorno had already dismissed the avant-garde. In an often quoted section from a letter he wrote to Walter Benjamin in 1936 after reading the manuscript of the latter's 'The work of art in the age of mechanical reproduction', Adorno is critical of Benjamin's avant-garde blurring of modernism and mass culture. Both of these, Adorno argues: 'bear the scars of capitalism, both contain elements of change. Both are torn halves of freedom to which, however, they do not add up' (Harrison and Wood 1992: 522). At the end of the 1930s as we have seen, Clement Greenberg formulated his view that modernism was a guarantee of freedom only where it purified itself of any associations with kitsch – mass culture.

Greenberg and Adorno were both in fact formulating their ideas about modernism and kitsch at around the same time; both were responding in different ways to the rise of totalitarianism in Europe. The positions they marked out in the late 1930s and 1940s have affected the way the dance of the period considered in this book was subsequently conceptualised. In Greenbergian modernism, the notion of an avant-garde became lost in a move to the idea of an apolitical, ahistorical, modernist formalism. For art to be progressive, Greenberg argued, it had to be free of any social or political co-ordinates. Thus the avant-garde stance of artists like Valeska Gert and Jean Börlin was marginalised because it could not be recognised without acknowledgement of the social and political agenda of the avant-garde. Furthermore, when the 'purist' formalism inherent in Greenbergian modernism was adopted by dance historians, the formalism of dancers like Graham and Wigman ceased to be considered modernist because of its so-called 'primitivism'. Posterity's view of the work of most early modern dancers in Germany has been indirectly affected by Adorno and Kracauer's writings because their rational, intellectual suspicion of the somatic body contributed to the development of ideologies of the supposed fascism of 'body culture'.

Writing in America in 1949, Margaret Lloyd observed: 'There are no reds in modern dance today' (1974: 173). It could equally have been said in Germany around the same time that there were no more nationalistic German modern dancers. It is the connections between art, the body, politics and notions of national identity that were lost in the nervous shifts away from a nationally focused, modern dance in the aftermath of the Second World War. Up until then in the United States, modern dancers who spanned a range of political positions from liberalism to communism were largely united around an isolationist but assimilationist nationalism. In Germany philosophical and cosmological ideas had informed a modern dance that created an exclusive, anti-assimilationist notion of German national identity. Graham's shift from her publicly stated, liberal view of America in *American Document* to the private, largely obscure, psychoanalytic concerns of her 'Greek' pieces, like *Dark Meadow* and *Night Journey*, constitutes an internal migration at the time of the national move to the right during the so-called McCarthy era. Katherine Dunham made a de facto migration to Europe around the same time. Returning to the United States in the 1960s, she was surprised to discover that civil rights had not only not progressed while she had been away but had actually regressed. In terms of European artists, the greatest casualty were modern dancers in Germany who became in effect part of an underground movement which did not re-emerge until the late 1960s and early 1970s in the work of Pina Bausch and the Tanztheatre movement: too late for Dore Hoyer who committed suicide in 1967.

What was forgotten or unacknowledged in the view of modernism that developed during and after the Second World War are what Zygmunt Bauman calls the deconstructive aspects of critical modern consciousness. A revisionist view of early modern dance and ballet recovers the ways in which the modern dancing body had been a site at which extra-linguistic meanings about the social and psychological experience of modernity were contested. The alien dancing bodies of modern dancers exemplified what modernity could do for you and what it did to you. As the dancer took modernity inside him or herself s/he embodied it through dancing to jungle music and the song of the machine like Baker and the Tiller Girls, or to its new accent, sharp, staccato, zigzag as identified by Graham. Alien bodies dynamically interacted with and within the new spaces of modernity in a positive and exciting way in Graham's *Celebration* or Humphrey's *New Dance*, or in a way that was determined by its disturbing, agoraphobic or neurasthenic nature, like the Apache in *Skating Rink* or the woman driven to prostitution in *The Green Table*; they could be kaput like Gert's prostitute or blasé and worn out like the rain soaked dancers on the street in *Stormy Weather*. Those modernist dances that expressed positivist dreams of what modernity could do for society contained within them, in repressed and sublimated form, acknowledgements of the disturbing nature of modernity. What was disturbing re-emerged in the form of silences and exclusions, and through projection onto the simultaneously fascinating and repellent, alien bodies of Others. Those avant-garde dances like *Relâche* and Gert's *Canaille* that turned their focus critically and deconstructively on modernity itself did so by attempting to break down barriers between art and life through rejecting conventions and traditions which up until then had been considered essential to theatre dance. Avant-garde artists attempted to break down the divisions between high and mass culture, and between performance and ceremony.

In Dunham's functionalist terms, tight, rigidly defined boundaries build up tensions that can be released through vigorous dancing (which breaks down the rigidity of boundaries) or contained and channelled in dangerous and authoritarian ways. When she saw Wigman as a libertarian rather than an authoritarian (because she was the leading exponent of free dance) Dunham was recognising a possible relationship between dance and an embodied ethics. In identifying jitterbugging as a sign of community of thought with other peoples and a turning away from isolationism, Dunham was making connections between the dancing body and the social and psychological construction of national identities. To acknowledge a community of thought with other peoples is to recognise sameness across difference. It was the ways in which alien modern dancing bodies allowed such a recognition to be made that was nervously forgotten and was subsequently discarded in the post-war period.

For Julia Kristeva the recognition of sameness across difference is an ethical imperative and necessitates admitting that what is disturbing about strangers is a projection of a sense of uncanny strangeness that is inscribed within oneself (Kristeva 1991: 169–92). In calling this book *Alien Bodies,* my intention has been to examine ways in which the alien dancing bodies of modernity embodied this uncanny strangeness that is inscribed within. To dance is to take into and find within one's own body possibilities of moving that express otherness – like Graham and her company in *Primitive Mysteries* or the unidentified man dancing with Baker in her Parisian night club. I have argued that to dance in this way is to reject ideologies of national and 'racial' identity (and superiority), and thus to blur boundaries that have been defined as tight and rigid. During the period covered in this book, these alien dancing bodies have issued a challenge to make public things that are private and interior by mixing this intimate personal space of the performer's body and the broader public space on stage. The deconstructive tendencies of critical modern dance have treated the border between the two as fluid and dynamic. On an individual level, to have a rigid definition of the difference between self and Other is unhealthy, just as, at the other extreme, having no sense of difference leads to psychosis. Therefore, to define the difference between self and Other in fluid and dynamic ways, is not just essential to well-being but is also ethical. This is the distinction Dunham was making between the jitterbug and the mass ornament. It would be an exaggeration to claim that, within their social and political contexts, some of the dance artists whose work has been discussed in this book successfully challenged the rigidities of the boundaries that reinforced normative definitions of 'racial' and national identities; yet the ideal of opening up new ways of relating to one another that were healthier and more just was evidently one that a few of them at least would have recognised. The critical, deconstructive work of the more radical dance modernists constituted the type of critical ontology to which Michel Foucault was referring when he postulated: 'a critique of ourselves [that] is at one and the same time the historical analysis of the limits that are imposed upon us and an experiment with the possibility of going beyond them' (Rabinow 1986: 50). The alien dancing bodies of the 1920s and 1930s were themselves experiments with the possibilities of going beyond the limiting ways in which bodies were conditioned to conform to 'modern forms of gendered, racial and national identity.

NOTES

1 INTRODUCTION

1 This is the same group that Malcolm X would later join.

2 Duncan Grant lived most of his life with Vanessa Bell, Virginia Woolf's sister. As well as *You'd be Surprised* he also designed the decor for Rupert Doone's *The Enchanted Grove* (1932) and a production of *Swan Lake*.

3 *Ringside* is less well known than Humphrey's two pieces. Choreographed by Charles Weidman and with music by Winthrop Sargeant, it was first performed at the Civic Repertory Theatre, New York, on 28 October 1928. It apparently showed a boxing match. A photograph in the collection of the New York Public Library from 1931 shows Charles Weidman as the referee and José Limón and William Matons as boxers. Information from New York Public Library Dance Collection Catalogue.

4 Siegel says that by the late 1930s Humphrey was known and trusted by both Weidman and Limón as a choreographic advisor (1993: 188); writing about *Sing Out, Sweet Land* (1944) she comments, 'given Charles' increasing undependability, she probably doctored his work as well as directing her own' (ibid.: 224); and in 1948 she writes that she had to 'bail Charles out of trouble again' on another show (ibid.: 253).

5 She made this comment during a questions and answers session at a conference in Leeds, 8 June 1996.

6 Too often not even the totality of the United States is included, but only dancers active in New York: consider the marginalisation for example of Lester Horton and other modern dancers like him who were active in California.

7 The Ballets Suédois and the Ballets Russes, who were both based in France, toured in the United States and danced in New York. Jooss won the international ballet competition in Paris and he and his company subsequently appeared in New York. Balanchine moved from Paris to New York during the period, while Josephine Baker moved in the opposite direction. Valeska Gert performed in both cities and was liked by neither. As far as I know none of the American modern dancers performed in Paris in the 1930s, but Wigman, who spoke both French and English, performed in both New York and Paris.

8 'All communities larger than primordial villages of face-to-face contact (and perhaps even these) are imagined' (Anderson 1991: 6).

2 CHOREOGRAPHING THE DISTURBING NEW
SPACES OF MODERNITY

1 Grand Concours Internationales de la Danse founded by Les Archives Internationales de la Danse. See Markand and Markand 1985: 45–9.

2 Jill Lloyd has pointed out that this French modern subject came to Germany through connections between the fauve painter Kees Van Dongen and Die Brücke member Max Pechstein. Similarly cabaret and variety themselves initially developed in Paris and then spread to Berlin and other German cities. See Lloyd 1991: 85–101

3 There was actually more than one Queen of the Night, as Laban explains in this chapter of his autobiography.

4 Kenneth Archer and Millicent Hodson found a review of *Jeux* in the London press in which the writer mentioned recognising steps from these popular dances. Personal communication.

5 Garafola and Baer both presume that *Les Biches* was a Cocteau ballet, although Aschengren denies this.

6 Both John Berger and Lincoln Kirstein describe a riot. Berger 1965: 84–90; Kirstein 1970: 210–11. Richard Buckle, however, states that 'the uproar that greeted *Parade* has been greatly exaggerated' (Buckle 1979: 331).

7 *The Sleeping Princess* was the name Diaghilev gave to the ballet now of course known in English as *The Sleeping Beauty*. The comédie-ballet *Les Fâcheux*, by Molière, was originally performed for Louis XIV at Vaux in 1661.

8 I am very grateful to Millicent Hodson and Kenneth Archer for inviting me to Zurich to observe the final stages of their work with Zurich Ballet and generously sharing their research with me, and to Zurich Ballet for giving me access backstage to watch rehearsals. My travel to Zurich was funded by a grant from De Montfort University.

9 At first the Poet does not notice that the Young Woman has fallen but is exultant about his victory over the Apache Man. When he does notice he makes a cry which Millicent Hodson wanted the dancer playing the Poet to make cartoon-like, and in her drawing the mouth crying forms a square. Whether or not one thinks the Young Woman dies depends on how one interprets this cry. Personal communication, Millicent Hodson.

10 They deduced this from closely studying black and white photographs of dancers in the original production. The men's 'jackets' were actually made in two parts – a 'shirt' of relatively soft material and an armless 'jacket' of stiffened cloth, both in the same colour, so that from any distance they appear to be one item. Kenneth Archer found by using a magnifying glass on the photographs that a gap can be seen where the softer material of the sleeve appears from underneath the stiffer cloth of a separate 'coat' that covers the torso. Personal communication.

11 The 1932 version of Jooss' ballet was called *Grosstadt von Heute* (*The Big City*). In 1935, shortly after the Ballets Jooss had taken up residence at Dartington Hall, they premiered *Grosstadt*. I take the latter to be a revised version of the former as it has the same composer and designer though I am unaware of how much alteration took place at that time.

12 First, *Skating Rink* was performed in Germany in 1922 and it is not impossible that Jooss may have seen it then or heard of it from someone who had. Second, Jooss would undoubtedly have met de Maré, as the latter organised the competition that *The Green Table* (*Die Grühne Tisch*) won. The competition was held in

memory of Börlin and that year de Maré published a book about Börlin's ballets. It is not therefore impossible that Jooss may have heard of *Skating Rink*.

13 The full evening's programme consisted of *Pavane* (1929), *A Ball in Old Vienna*, *The Big City* and *The Green Table*, all created in 1932. See Kersley and Kersley 1986.

14 However, Marcia Siegel, writing about the 1975 version of *The Big City* described the wealthy night club scene as follows: 'The scene fades back to the night club; the dancers look even more kinky than before, jerking their torsos around in a frenzy of dissipation' (Siegel 1976: 146).

15 For example many paintings by Otto Dix and George Grosz, films like *Joyless Street* and *Pandora's Box* by Pabst, novels by Döblin, Heinrich Mann and operas like Brecht and Weill's *Happy End*.

16 Petro (1989) argues this in her discussion of prostitution in the 'street films' made in Weimar Germany. I have found this study extremely useful in formulating my argument about dance and modernity in this chapter.

3 'SAVAGE' DANCER: TOUT PARIS GOES TO SEE JOSEPHINE BAKER

1 For a contemporary review of *Paris qui Remue* see MacCormack 1930. For a discussion of Balanchine and Baker and other African American dancers see Gottschild 1996: 59–79 and Banes 1994: 53–69.

2 The honourable exception is Christy Adair (1992: 165–7).

3 Her previous autobiographies were 'ghosted' by Marcel Sauvage (Sauvage 1927 and 1931).

4 Baker would have thought of herself as a Negro not as an African American. While I recognise that the term Negro is implicitly derogatory, to speak of her as African American would be anachronistic. The title of the show that made her a star was after all *La Revue Nègre*.

5 Baker's original comments are in Sauvage 1927: 89.

6 I take this to mean it didn't help her to be seen as a person first and black second.

7 During Baker's first shopping trip in Paris when she was taken to the legendary couturier Paul Poiret, Baker was stripped naked while a bolt of silvery silk was fetched. Poiret, she later wrote, 'poured the gleaming torrent over me, rolled me up in it, draped it around my body, pulled it tight, ordered me to walk, then loosened it around my legs. I felt like a sea goddess emerging from the foam . . .' (Baker and Bouillon 1978: 52). Could de Maré have shown her a reproduction of Botticelli's painting of Venus emerging from the foam when explaining Levinson's review to her? And could Angela Carter have read Baker's autobiography before she wrote her own story *Black Venus* (1985) about Baudelaire and Jeanne Duval which mentions Baker and has the image of Duval as the Black Venus coming eastwards across the Atlantic on a wave of foam? For a fascinating discussion of Carter's story see Heather Johnson (1995) 'Black Venus returns: the inverted body of colonialism', University of Hull Body Matters Conference, July 1995.

8 I am not discussing Baker's impact in Berlin in this chapter. There is a general discussion of this in the biographies of Baker. For further reading see the last chapter of Louise Brooks' 1982 autobiography and Towers (1990). For a general discussion of German attitudes towards Africans and African Americans in the 1920s see Grimm and Hermand (eds) 1986, in particular Lester 1986 in that collection.

9 I am grateful to Thea Barnes for pointing this out to me.

10 There appear to have been variations on this famous costume. Some photographs show Baker bare breasted with a girdle of bananas that hang downwards, while others show ones that are gilded and covered with little glittering jewels or studs. These bananas stick outwards and upwards and some of the photographs of these show Baker wearing a bra decorated with jewels. In the film she wears a white bra.

11 I am not aware of any evidence that Baker and Jackson ever met. However, along with Ethel Waters, there does seem to be a lot they had in common.

12 In a similar vein hooks has also written: 'One exciting dimension to cultural studies is the critique of essentialist notions of difference. Yet this critique should not become a means to dismiss differences or an excuse to ignore the authority of experience. It is often evoked in a manner which suggests that all the ways black people think of ourselves as "different" from whites are really essentialist, and therefore without concrete grounding. This way of thinking threatens the very foundations that make resistance to domination possible' (hooks 1990: 130). See also Trinh T. Minh-ha's *Woman, Native, Other* especially Chapter 3: 'Difference: "A special Third World women issue"' (1989: 79–118).

13 Sally Banes, in her essay 'The Charleston in Moscow' has shown that when the dancers and musicians in *The Chocolate Kiddies* (a touring version of *The Chocolate Dandies* that Baker herself had been in on Broadway) arrived in Moscow, the Muscovites, just like de Maré and his colleagues, found the show didn't fit their idea of what black dancing should be. Banes 1994: 161–8.

14 At this time Europeans were still more ready to pay serious attention to theatre dance than Americans, and Europeans were much more ready to pay serious attention to African American artists than white Americans for example Baker's recognition was repeated for Dunham in 1948.

15 Thea Barnes suggests that instead of 'wild abandon' I should write 'instinct for survival'.

16 The cruel irony here is that Baker did want to marry and have children, and subsequently found her inability to have children a personal tragedy. This is a sad example of the way that the star image, as it is commodified and interpreted by the star's audience, is by no means identical with the star's private needs and desires.

4 THE CHORUS LINE AND THE EFFICIENCY ENGINEERS

1 The mass ornament did have a military source. A former Tiller Girl from the early years told Doremy Vernon that they had received training in military drill from a Sergeant Major (Vernon 1988: 36). Busby Berkeley, whose extravagant production numbers for Ziegfeld on Broadway and later in Hollywood are among the best known examples of the mass ornament, trained at an East Coast Military Academy and gained experience arranging special parade ground drill routines as an officer with the American army in France during the First World War before starting his career in the theatre: see Thomas and Terry 1973.

2 They were of course a product of Lancashire business acumen and not American industrial efficiency. Furthermore Doremy Vernon (1988) states that Tiller troupes first appeared in New York during the First World War, and that they made a big impact there in the 1920s, dancing for Florenz Ziegfeld and Fred Stone, eventually inspiring American imitations like the Rockettes (Vernon 1988: 91–103). See also Parker and Parker 1975: 102–12.

3 Another reason for Kracauer's increasing pessimism in 1931 were his personal circumstances. In 1931 he was working as Berlin head of the features section of the *Frankfurter Zeitung*. The paper had been owned, since 1929, by the industrial conglomerate I G Faben who were influencing its editorial policy away from the uncompromisingly left-wing stance of which Kracauer's pieces were the prime examples.

4 Van der Rohe's early work was within the Expressionist tradition, just as Taut's later work was in the new International style.

5 It must be a possibility that Kracauer had seen Josephine Baker perform, as the Tiller Girls were often on the same bill as her.

5 TOTALITARIANISM AND THE MASS ORNAMENT

1 Horst Koegler quotes a contemporary review of the dance festival opening the 1936 Olympic Games in which Medau gave a rhythmic gymnastic demonstration. I am assuming that the mass spectacle under discussion here was also arranged by Medau (Koegler 1974: 47).

2 It was international in the sense that gymnastics was a field of international competition between countries, rather than being international in a cosmopolitan way, or based on a notion of community or 'common humanity' that transcends national allegiances. It was not just in Germany that gymnastics was a vehicle for the definition of a purified national body. I am grateful to Bodil Persson for pointing out to me that in the 1930s the Swedish people, under a Social Democratic government, also attached great significance to the practice of Swedish gymnastics.

3 I came across this photograph while looking through *The Times* for coverage of the Olympics.

4 Dziga Vertov (1896–1954) was a Russian director of avant-garde documentary films during the 1920s, including his film magazine *Kino-Pravda* (1926) and *Man with a Movie Camera* (1929).

5 Susan Manning has argued that modern dance in Germany does not fit 'the master-narratives of a transition from expressionism to the "new objectivity" in the mid-twenties, the persecution of the avant-garde after 1933, or the de-Nazification of the arts after 1945' (Manning 1993: 4). For further discussion see Koegler (1974; 1996); Müller and Servos (1982); Müller (1987); Preston-Dunlop (1989); Servos (1990); Manning (1993; 1995); Karina and Kant (1996); Huxley and Patterson (forthcoming). Green (1986) and Wollen (1995) are also interesting but weak on supporting factual information.

6 One possible explanation of the German people's submission to Nazi propaganda, as Taylor and van der Will have pointed out, is the idea that: 'Hitler merely represented the culmination of a process within German history stretching back to the times of Luther and the Obrigkeitstaat (a state demanding unquestioning obedience from its subjects) which made possible the fashioning of subservient religious minds and apolitical citizens' (Taylor and van der Will 1990b: 8).

7 On whether or not one can say Laban was not until then fascist, see Preston-Dunlop (1989), Karina and Kant (1996) and Koegler (1996).

8 Three works exemplify the differences between various approaches. George Mosse's *The Nationalization of the Masses* (1991) presents a solidly researched, meticulously supported interpretation of complex class interests in early twentieth-century Germany. Klaus Theweleit's two volume *Male Fantasies* (1987/9)

looks at the psychology of the political responses of conservative, middle-class German soldiers in order to develop an account of the appeal of fascism based on radical psychoanalytic ideas. Daniel Jonah Goldhagen's *Hitler's Willing Executioners: Ordinary Germans and the Holocaust* (1996) makes the controversial claim that it was not just the fanatical National Socialist party members and members of the SS that were involved in the atrocities of the Holocaust but also 'ordinary' Germans.

9 Sixty years on, it is probably not possible to establish whether or not all the women in the mass gymnastic display are members of Bünd Deutsches Mädel or any similar organisation, nor whether any who were members entirely accepted the National Socialist view of sport as a means of aiding women's destiny as mothers.

10 See also Hans-Ulrich Thamer's 'The orchestration of the national community: The Nuremberg Party Rallies of the NSDAP' (1996).

11 Lucy Fischer (1981), writing about Busby Berkeley's cinematic mass ornamental fetishism, takes the opposite point of view.

12 Sontag's essay ends, however, with a discussion of the use of Nazi regalia within sado-masochistic practices. In the light of her discussion of thematics within Riefenstahl's work, Sontag is curiously silent about questions of the politics and ethics of sado-masochistic practices. Sado-masochism is an area that some libertarian theorists (following Foucault) have subsequently argued presents a model of power relationships which challenges conventional assumptions about the ahistorical nature of ethics.

6 DANCING ACROSS THE ATLANTIC

1 'The Four Pioneers' is the title of a documentary film about the modern dance summer schools at Bennington College during the 1930s, and refers to Holm, Graham, Humphrey and Weidman – thus, as Christina Schlundt (1989) has pointed out, excluding Tamiris. It is nevertheless true that Holm distanced herself from Wigman and Nazi Germany and that this must have contributed to the fact that the German roots of her work have subsequently been ignored.

2 'How Meyerhold trained his actors' by John Martin in Law and Gordon 1996: 228–33 reprinted from *Theatre Guild Magazine*, November 1930: 26–30.

3 Kreutzberg and Georgi were on the same bill as Graham at the opening of the Radio City Music Hall and Graham reportedly used to sit in the wings and watch them. In 1928 Louis Horst (who accompanied everybody) played for Kreutzberg at his first American dance recital at the Cosmopolitan Theater in New York with Tilly Loesch. See Partsch-Bergsohn 1994: 58.

4 Among other things, Dunham was in the early 1930s a protégé of Ruth Page's. Page and Kreutzberg toured together in 1931. He made a significant impact in the United States as a teacher as well as a performer. Margaret H'Doubler asked Kreutzberg to teach at the University of Wisconsin in 1931. Kreutzberg returned to New York in 1947 to teach and perform. Margaret Lloyd says 'his delighted audiences were ready to pick up where he left off' (1974: 22). However, a *Dance Observer* reviewer of his concert on 9 November 1947 was less impressed. In the light of 'what has been happening in the past ten years' in dance in the US, 'we have come to expect far more basic, organically developed and psychologically penetrating work than this from modern dance' ('Old worlds for new: The return of Harald Kreutzberg, Ziegfield Theater No. 9 1947' *Dance Observer* December 1947: 113). Clearly dance had developed in the US in ways that it had not been able to develop in Germany. In the late 1920s

and 1930s when Kreutzberg and Wigman first appeared in the US, it was their work which was more developed.

5 Among the many artists who were involved with the Beggars Bar were Judith Malina and Julien Beck who went on in the 1950s to found the Living Theatre.

6 I am grateful to Stacy Prickett for pointing out to me that Sokolow, the New Dance Group, and other members of the workers' dance movement were much more international in their outlook even before the advent of the Popular Front. This, she suggests, was

> due to their immigrant backgrounds and growing up in the Lower East Side neighborhoods, the union related families, and being part of the international Jewish community which meant that there was a lot of interaction and awareness of the world outside US boundaries prior to the Popular Front. Even Jane Dudley, who was immersed in the left-wing contingent despite her more privileged background, embraced an international rather than American outlook. I'm thinking of early dances such as *Van der Lubbe's Head* and a turn towards not just the Soviet Union but towards some of America's first generation's parental homelands, and a sense of belonging to the world in addition to America. This may be specific to the New York area groups, but I never got a sense of isolationism from the left wingers which was apparent in government policy. The union papers and *Daily Worker* were filled with international news. The dancers with whom I spoke gave the impression that they were very aware, hence the level of criticism of Graham and Humphrey (among others).

(Personal communication April 1997)

7 See Prickett 1989, 1990, 1994a; Graff 1994; Franko 1995.

8 Open University broadcast *A315 Modern Art and Modernism* programme no. 26 MOMA, 27 August 1988.

9 It is worth pointing out that no love was lost between the followers of Trotsky and members of the Communist Party. Jane Dudley commented 'The Trots were always out to do the party down' (private communication 1994).

10 The dancer and choreographer Anna Sokolow made a surprisingly similar statement: 'Art should recognise all our needs. I don't believe in Ivory towers. The artist should belong to his society, yet without feeling that he has to conform to it. He must feel that there is a place for him in society, a place for what he is. He must see life fully, and then say what he feels about it. Then, although he belongs to his society, he can change it, presenting it with fresh feelings, fresh ideas' (Sokolow in Morrison Brown 1980: 108).

11 Dudley wrote an article in 1934 called 'The mass dance' describing how the sorts of mass choreographic techniques pioneered by Laban and Dalcroze could be used for left-wing 'revolutionary' purposes (reprinted in Franko 1995: 119–22).

12 My argument here follows the proposals Henning Eichberg makes in his essay on Nazi Thingspiel (Eichberg 1977: 133–50).

13 I am not claiming that Matons was in any way typical of American modern dance or even of the choreography of other members of the workers' dance movement. I am pointing out that certain signifying practices which communicated political messages were in themselves value free. I am also trying to put the charges about political involvement that are frequently made against German dancers into a broader context.

14 Susan Manning discussed this in a paper ' "Danced Spirituals": The performance of race in American modern dance' (part of her ongoing research) presented at a research seminar at Roehampton Institute, London, 13 March 1997. See also Schlundt 1989: 107.

7 AMERICAN MODERNS

1 According to Isa Partsch-Bergsohn the first German modern dancer to appear in New York was Eugen von Grona in 1925. Two years later his *Spirit of Labour* 'attempted to mirror the functioning of a machine in robot-like motions made by the dancers and supported by realistic sound effects' (1994: 57). There was of course a tradition of machine ballets in Soviet Russia, of which the Ballet Russe's *Pas d'Acier* was an isolated European example. There are however no other obvious examples. John Martin makes a similar comment about European machine dances (1968: 72) to which I refer to later in this chapter. Oliver M. Sayler, in his book *Revolt in the Arts* (1930) to which Graham had contributed, had asked the question: what is the function of the arts in the machine age?

2 In writing this section and in applying this theoretical argument later in the chapter I am indebted to Richard Dyer's essay 'Entertainment and utopia' (1981).

3 I saw the Graham Company's reconstruction of *Celebration* as part of their programme 'Radical Graham' at the 1996 Edinburgh Festival.

4 Dudley presumably chose that poem because of its relevance to audiences from the Needlework Union.

5 Ralph Taylor 'Martha Graham, Guild Theatre, November 4th 1934' on page 88; Henry Gilfond 'Workers Dance League, Civic Repertory Theatre, November 25th 1934' on page 89. Dudley had not yet become a member of the Graham company.

6 'I feel that the old technique was foreign in every way to the world we live in and must be discarded. . . . The ballet group had been based on the social scene of which it was a part. The leading dancer was either King or Queen, the next important dancers served as all the ranks of nobility, and the corps de ballet was just as unimportant as the "rest of the people" were at that time' (Humphrey in Kriegsman 1981: 284).

7 Balanchine arrived in New York in October 1933. Details about the dates of the premiere of *Serenade* are sometimes slightly confusing. *Serenade* was scheduled to be shown by his students on 9 June 1934 at the country estate of Felix M. Warburg: although this date is often cited in the literature on *Serenade* it apparently rained on the day and the piece was actually performed on 10 June. It was shown by the student company of the American Ballet School at the Avery Memorial Theatre, Hartford, Connecticut on 9 December 1934 and received its New York premiere during the American Ballet Company's first season at the Adelphi Theatre on 1 March 1935. *Serenade* may therefore have undergone revision between June 1934 and March 1935.

   New Dance was premiered on 3 August 1935 at Bennington College during the summer school, with a preview on 1 August at the University of Vermont, Burlington. The 'Variations and Conclusion' had not yet been choreographed and were not shown until the New York premiere on 27 October 1935. Clearly therefore the two pieces were made and first shown at very much the same time.

8 'The leading role in *Serenade* was first danced by a group of soloists rather than by one principal dancer. In a number of productions, however, I arranged it for one dancer. But when the New York City Ballet was to make its first appearance

in London, at the Royal Opera House, Covent Garden, in the summer of 1950, it seemed appropriate to introduce the company by introducing its principal dancers and the leading role was again divided and danced by our leading soloists' (Balanchine 1968: 365).

9 'For the peoples that the ethnologist studies today, there is no term free from criticism. Even the neutral "preliterate" will not quite do, for there are some peoples who have for a long time some use of reading and writing and yet show none of the consequences of literacy which we find in civilised societies' (Redfield 1968a: 13).

10 *With My Red Fires* is divided into two parts. The following is from the original programme:

Part 1 – Ritual

For the Divine appearance is Brotherhood, but I am Love,
Elevate into the Region of Brotherhood With My Red Fires.

Part 2 – Drama

the Great Selfhood . . .
Having a white Dot call'd a Center, from which branches out
A Circle in continual gyrations: this became a Heart
From which sprang numerous branches varying their motions,
Producing many Heads, three or seven or ten, and hands and feet
Innumerable at will of the unfortunate contemplator
Who becomes his food: such is the way of the Devouring Power.

(Kriegsman 1981: 139)

Given that Humphrey chose the verses after completing the piece, one can infer that she was struck by parallels between the movement imagery in the poetry and in the piece, as well as the references to brotherhood, selfishness, and devouring power.

11 Lena Horne had taken over Katherine Dunham's role as Sweet Georgia Brown in *Cabin in the Sky* when the original Broadway musical was made into a film by MGM. On one level Dunham seems to be almost a dancing double for Horne in the *Stormy Weather* dream ballet.

12 Telephone conversation with Katherine Dunham, 21 October 1996.

13 Dunham performed traditional ballet solos and aesthetic interpretations in her concert at the Rex Theatre in Port au Prince, Haiti in 1936 which were much appreciated by the local Creole elite (Dunham 1994b :152–4).

14 John E. Perpener III in his PhD thesis cites many examples of John Martin's reviews of African American dance concerts during the 1930s and 1940s in which Martin constantly judges the work he writes about in relation to what should be defined as his imaginary notion of African American energy and otherness. See Perpener 1992.

15 See Cappetti 1993. Cappetti identifies Simmel's 'stranger' as a precursor for Park's 'marginal man' (1993: 63).

8 PRIMITIVISM, MODERNISM AND RITUAL IN THE WORK OF MARY WIGMAN, KATHERINE DUNHAM AND MARTHA GRAHAM

1 Vaudun is the creole name for the religious practices that English and Americans call voodoo. Following Herskovits and Dunham I am using the term vaudun out of respect for members of vaudun cults.

2 At the time she was making *The Dark Meadow* (1946) Graham copied into her notebooks quotes from Wolfgang Paalen's book *Totem Art* about American Indian art and mythological beliefs (Graham 1973: 205). Paalen, a painter who was interested in Jungian psychoanalysis, was associated with the Surrealists and with the New York School.

3 For an interesting discussion of German productions of *Le Sacre du printemps* see Manning (1991a) 'German rites', *Dance Chronicle* 14 (2–3).

4 Marcia Siegel devotes a whole chapter of her excellent *Shapes of Change: Images of American Dance* to ritual, in which she discusses *Primitive Mysteries* and *The Shakers* (Siegel 1979: 50–67).

5 Graham herself wrote at the end of her life: 'It was at this period that I was doing what the critics called my long woollen dances of revolt, and looking back on them, they were revolting. But I was really casting off Denishawn and its veils of exoticism' (1991: 123).

6 Telephone conversation with Katherine Dunham, 21 October 1996.

7 Telephone conversation with Katherine Dunham, 21 October 1996.

8 The following discussion is based on viewing two versions of the dance on video: one performed by the Charles Moore Dance Company filmed at the Brooklyn Academy of Music during the Dance Black America Festival, 21–4 April 1983; and the other performed by dancers and ex-dancers from the Katherine Dunham Dance Company at the Katherine Dunham Gala at Carnegie Hall, New York, on 15 January 1979. In addition, in Richard Buckle's 1949 book *Katherine Dunham: Her Dancers, Singers and Musicians* there are fifteen photographs of the Katherine Dunham Dance Company in *Shango* taken in London in 1948.

9 From the videotape of the Dance Black America festival.

10 Herskovits suggests that the name Rada-Dahomey is derived from the ancient principality of Allada in Dahomey, West Africa and the gods worshipped are of African origin (1964: 149), whereas the gods worshipped in the Petro cults may be of New World origin. The name Petro, he goes on to suggest, might derive from the so-called Dom Pedro worship or from the name of one of its supposed founders, a Spanish Negro from Petit-Gôave (ibid.: 150). Herskovits discounts the suggestion that the Petro priests use only malignant magic.

11 Anthony Shay presented a paper on this at the 1996 CORD Conference at the University of North Carolina Greensboro. I am grateful to him for giving me a copy of his longer version of this paper in *Iranian Studies* (see Shay 1995).

12 *When the fire dances between the two poles: Mary Wigman, 1886–1973*, director Allegra Fuller Snyder, video recording 1982.

13 Barber compares Wigman's dance with other versions of the Mevlevi Sufi ceremony performed during the 1920s including one by the followers of Gurdjieff. The Gurdjieff dancers spin with the head vertically aligned with the spine. This also can be seen in Peter Brook's 1978 film of Gurdjieff's 1960 autobiography *Meetings with Remarkable Men* for which Olga de Hartmann reconstructed several of the original movement exercises.

14 She also saw Mary Wigman dance at the Chanin Theatre in New York in December 1930, just a few weeks before the premier of *Primitive Mysteries*.

15 According to Jean Nuchtern, Graham added white frills to the hems of these skirts in the 1964 production because she said the dancers were a softer generation (Nuchtern 1977: 28).

16 My analysis of *Primitive Mysteries* is based on watching the film of the 1964 production of the piece, together with Barbara Morgan's famous photographs from 1941 (Morgan 1980). I have also been helped by reading Marcia Siegel's discussion of the piece (1979: 50–8), reminiscences compiled by David Sears (1982) and other published reminiscences by dancers who performed in the piece. Erick Hawkins, who was with Graham when she revived *Primitive Mysteries* in the mid-1940s, called the spatial patterns of the piece mandalas (Hawkins 1992: 5).

17 Although it is outside the immediate scope of this chapter I think Siegel's suggestion that Graham represented a female Christ figure is worth further consideration. I disagree with Susan Manning's (1991b) proposition that the fact that all the dancers in *Primitive Mysteries* are women did not give any gender-specific meanings to the piece. Siegel suggests the opposite when she argues that the fact that all the dancers were women, 'fully capable of conducting a religious observance, [and] that they do not need male priests or teachers to channel their worship or intercede for them with God, is one of the boldest of *Primitive Mysteries*' many achievements' (1979: 58). In this context see Theresa Berger's fascinating account of the tradition of female devotional imagery in the European Christian tradition in her essay 'A female Christ child in the manger and a woman on the cross, or: the historicity of the Jesus event and the inculturation of the gospel' (Berger 1996).

18 For an interesting account of Lester Horton's early experiences dancing in popular amateur pageants on Native American themes and of his own early 'Indian' dances, see Warren 1977: 14–38.

BIBLIOGRAPHY

Acocella, J. (1987) 'Book review: Frank W. D. Ries, The Dance Theatre of Jean Cocteau' *Dance Research Journal* 19 (1) Summer: 44–5.

Acocella, J. and Garafola, L. (eds) (1991) *André Levinson on Dance: Writings from Paris in the Twenties* Hanover and London: Wesleyan University Press.

Adair, C. (1992) *Women and Dance: Sylphs and Sirens* London: Macmillan.

Adorno, T. W. (1991) 'The curious realist: on Siegfried Kracauer' *New German Critique* Fall: 159–78.

Altman, R. (ed.) (1981) *Genre: The Musical: A Reader* London: Routledge and Kegan Paul: BFI.

Anderson, B. (1991) *Imagined Communities* (2nd edn) London: Verso.

Anderson, J. (1975) 'New York Newsletter' *Dancing Times* April: 363.

Archer, K. and Hodson, M. (1994) 'Ballets lost and found: restoring the twentieth-century repertoire' in J. Adshead-Landsdale and J. Layson (eds) *Dance History* (2nd edn) London: Routledge, 98–116.

—— (1995) 'Skating Rink: cubism on wheels' *Dance Now* 4 (4): 14–18.

Arendt, H. (1958) *The Origins of Totalitarianism* (2nd edn) London: Allen and Unwin.

Armitage, M. (ed.) (1966) [1937] *Martha Graham* New York: Dance Horizons.

Armitage, M. and Stewart, V. (1970) [1935] *The Modern Dance* New York: Dance Horizons.

Aschenbrenner, J. (1978) 'Anthropology as a lifeway: Katherine Dunham' in V. Clark and B. Wilkerson (eds) *Kaiso! Katherine Dunham: An Anthology of Writings* Berkeley, CA: Institute for the Study of Social Change, University of California, 186–91.

—— (1980) 'Katherine Dunham: Reflections on the Social and Political Context of Afro-American Dance' *Dance Research Annual: CORD*: 12.

Baer, N. Van N. (1978) *Bronislav Nijinska: a Dancer's Legacy* San Francisco, CA: The Fine Arts Museums of San Francisco.

Baker, J.-C. and Chase, C. (1993) *Josephine: The Hungry Heart* New York: Random House.

Baker, J and Bouillon, J. (1978) *Josephine* London: W. H. Allen.

Balanchine, G. (1968) *New Complete Stories of the Great Ballets* New York: Doubleday.

Banes, S. (1980) *Terpsichore in Sneakers: Post-modern Dance* (1st edn) New York: Houghton Mifflin.

—— (1987) *Terpsichore in Sneakers: Post-modern Dance* (2nd edn) New York: Houghton Mifflin.

—— (1989) letter (Terpsichore in Combat Boots) *TDR* T-121 Spring: 13–15.

—— (1993) 'Balanchine and Black Dance' *Choreography and Dance* 3 (3): 57–99.

—— (1994) *Writing Dancing in the Age of Postmodernism* Hanover, NE: Wesleyan University Press.

Barber, T. X. (1986) 'Four interpretations of Mevlevi Dervish Dance 1920–1929' *Dance Chronicle* 9 (3): 328–55.

Barzel, A. and Turbyfill, M. (1983) 'The untold story of the Dunham/Turbyfill alliance' *Dance Magazine* January: 91–8.

Bauman, Z. (1991) *Modernity and Ambivalence* Cambridge: Polity.

Benjamin, W. (1970) *Illuminations* (trans. Harry Zorn) London: Fontana.

Berger, J. (1965) *Success and Failure of Picasso* Harmondsworth: Penguin.

Berger, T. (1996) 'A female Christ child in the manger and a woman on the cross, or: the historicity of the Jesus event and the inculturation of the gospel' *Feminist Theology* (11): 32–45.

Berghaus, G. (1988) '*Girlkultur* – feminism, Americanism, and popular entertainment in Weimar Germany' *Journal of Design History* 1 (3 & 4): 193–219.

Bordo, S. (1993) *Unbearable Weight: Feminism, Western Culture and the Body* Berkeley: University of California Press.

Brender, R. (1986) 'Reinventing Africa in their own image: the Ballets Suédois' "Ballet nègre" La Création du Monde' *Dance Chronicle* 9 (1): 119–47.

Brooks, L. (1982) *Lulu in Hollywood* New York: Knopf.

Buchloh, B. (1981) 'Figures of authority, ciphers of aggression' *October* 16 Spring: 39–68.

Buck-Morss, S. (1989) *The Dialectics of Seeing: Walter Benjamin and the Arcades Project* Cambridge, MA: MIT Press.

Buckle, R. (1949) *Katherine Dunham, her Dancers, Singers, Musicians* London: Ballet Publications Ltd.

—— (1979) *Diaghilev* London: Weidenfeld and Nicolson.

Burt, R. (1995a) *The Male Dancer: Bodies, Spectacle, Sexualities* London: Routledge.

—— (1995b) 'Humphrey, modernism and postmodernism' *Dance Theatre Journal* 12 (2): 10–13.

Cappetti, C. (1993) *Writing Chicago: Modernism, Ethnography and the Novel* New York: Columbia University Press.

Carter, A. (1985) *Black Venus* London: Chatto and Windus.

Chadwick, W. (1995) 'Fetishizing fashion/fetishizing culture: Man Ray's "Noire et Blanche" ' *The Oxford Art Journal* 18 (2): 3–17.

Clark, V. and Wilkerson, M. (1978) *Kaiso! Katherine Dunham: an Anthology of Writings* Berkeley, CA: Institute for the Study of Social Change: CCEW Women's Centre, University of California.

Clifford, J. (1988) *The Predicaments of Culture: Twentieth-Century Ethnography, Literature and Art* Cambridge, MA: Harvard University Press.

—— (1989) 'Negrophilia' in D. Holier (ed.) *A New History of French Literature* Cambridge, MA: Harvard University Press.

Cockcroft, E. (1985) 'Abstract Expressionism, weapon of the Cold War' in F. Frascina (ed.) *Pollock and After: The Critical Debate* London: Harper and Row, 125–34.

Cocteau, J. (1926) *Call to Order* London: Faber and Gwyer.

Cohen, M. (1981) 'Primitivism, modernism and dance theory' G. Fancher and G. Myers (eds) *Philosophical Essays on Dance* New York: Dance Horizons, 138–56.

Cohen, S. J. (1972) *Doris Humphrey – An Artist First* Middletown, CT: Wesleyan University Press.

—— (1974) *Dance is a Theatre Art* Pennington, NJ: Dance Horizons, Princeton Book Company.

Copeland, R. (1996) 'The search for origins' *Dance Theatre Journal* 13 (1): 8–14.

Coton, A.V. (1946) *The New Ballet: Kurt Jooss and His Work* London: Dennis Dobson.

Daly, A. (1987) 'The Balanchine woman: of hummingbirds and channel swimmers' *TDR* 31 (1) (T113) Spring: 8–21.

de Francia, P. (1983) *Fernand Léger* New Haven and London: Yale University Press.

de Grazia, V. (1989) 'The arts of purchase: how American publicity subverted the European poster' in B. M. Kruger and P. Mariani (eds) *Remaking History* Seattle, WA: Bay Press, 220–57.

De Mille, A. (1992) *Martha: The Life and Work of Martha Graham* London: Hutchinson.

De Valois, N. (1957) *Come Dance With Me: A Memoir 1898–1956* London: Hamish Hamilton.

Desmond, J. (1991) 'Dancing out the difference: cultural imperialism and Ruth St Denis's "Radha" of 1906' *Signs* 17 (1): 28–49.

Douglas, A. (1996) *Terrible Honesty: Mongrel Manhattan in the 1920s* London and Basingstoke: Picador.

Douglas, M. (1966) *Purity and Danger* London: Ark.

Douglas, P. (1995) [1935] 'Modern dance forms' in M. Franko *Dancing Modernism/ Performing Politics* Bloomington and Indianapolis, IN: Indiana University Press, 137–42.

Downing, T. (1992) *Olympia* London: BFI Publishing.

Dunham, K. (1978a) 'Statement' in V. Clark and B. Wilkerson (eds) *Kaiso! Katherine Dunham: an Anthology of Writings* Berkeley, CA: Institute for the Study of Social Change, University of California, 199.

—— (1978b) 'Form and function in primitive dance' (first published in *Educational Dance* October 1941) in V. Clark, and B. Wilkerson (eds) *Kaiso! Katherine Dunham: an Anthology of Writings* Berkeley, CA: Institute for the Study of Social Change, University of California, 192–6.

—— (1978c) 'The Negro dance' in V. Clark and B. Wilkerson (eds) (1978) *Kaiso! Katherine Dunham: An Anthology of Writings* Berkeley, CA: Institute for the Study of Social Change, University of California, 66–74.

—— (1994a) *A Touch of Innocence* Chicago, IL: University of Chicago Press.

—— (1994b) *Island Possessed* Chicago, IL: University of Chicago Press.

Dunleavy, R., Reynolds, N., Russell, R., Simon, V. and Taras, J. (1983) 'Staging Balanchine's ballets: a symposium' *Ballet Review* 11 (3) Fall: 81–96.

Dyer, R. (1979) *Stars* London: BFI.

—— (1981) 'Entertainment and Utopia' in R. Altman (ed.) *Genre: The Musical* London: Routledge and Kegan Paul, 175–89.

—— (1987) *Heavenly Bodies: Film Stars and Society* London: BFI/Macmillan.

Eichberg, H. (1977) 'The Nazi *Thingspeil*: theatre for the masses in fascism and proletarian culture' *New German Critique* 11 Spring: 133–50.

Ellison, R. (1972) [1964] *Shadow and Act* New York: Random House.

Emery, L. F. (1988) *Black Dance from 1619 to Today* Princeton, NJ: Dance Horizons.

Fabre, G. and O'Meally, R. (eds) (1995) *History and Memory in African-American Culture* New York and Oxford: Oxford University Press.

Fabre, M. (1995) 'International beacons of African American memory: Alexandre Dumas père, Henry O. Tammer, and Josephine Baker as examples of recognition' in G. Fabre and R. O'Meally (eds) *History and Memory in African-American Culture* New York and Oxford: Oxford University Press, 122–9.

Fischer, L. (1981) 'The image of woman as image: the optical politics of *Dames*' in R. Altman (ed.) *Genre: The Musical* London: Routledge and Kegan Paul, 70–84.

Forster, E. M. (1927) *Aspects of the Novel* London: E. Arnold.

Foucault, M. (1977) *Discipline and Punish: The Birth of the Prison* Harmondsworth: Allen Lane.

—— (1980) *Power/Knowledge* Brighton: Harvester Press.

Franko, M. (1995) *Dancing Modernism/Performing Politics* Bloomington and Indianapolis, IN: Indiana University Press.

Freeman, J. (1995) 'Fernand Léger and the Ballets Suédois. The convergence of avant-garde ambitions and collaborative ideals' in Exhibition Catalogue *The Swedish Ballet 1920–1925* New York: Museum at the Fashion Institute of Technology, 86–107.

Freud, S. (1951) 'The "Uncanny" ' in *The Standard Edition of the Complete Psychological Writings of Sigmund Freud* Vol. XVII London: Hogarth Press, 218–52.

Fromm, E. (1941) *Escape from Freedom* New York and Toronto: Rinehart and Co., Inc.

Fry, R. (1928) *Vision and Design* (4th edn) London: Chatto and Windus.

Gadberry, G. (1980) 'The Thingspeil and Das Frankenberger Wurfenspiel' *TDR* 24 (1) March: 103–14.

Garafola, L. (1989) *Diaghilev's Ballets Russes* Oxford: Oxford University Press.

Gert, V. (1990) [1930] 'Dancing' in V. Preston-Dunlop and S. Lahusen (eds) *Schriftanz: A View of German Dance in the Weimar Republic* London: Dance Books, 13–16.

Gilman, S. (1985) *Difference and Pathology* Ithaca, NJ: Cornell University Press.

—— (1988) *Disease and Representation: Images of Illness from Madness to AIDS* Ithaca and London: Cornell University Press.

Gilroy, P. (1989) *Small Acts* London: Serpent's Tail.

—— (1996) ' " . . . to be real": the dissident forms of black expressive culture' in Catherine Ugwu (ed.) *Let's Get it On: The Politics of Black Performance* London: ICA; Seattle, WA: Bay Press, 12–33.

Goldhagen, D. J. (1996) *Hitler's Willing Executioners: Ordinary Germans and the Holocaust* New York: Little Brown.

Gordon, M. (1974) 'Meyerhold's Biomechanics' *The Drama Review* 18 (3) T-63 September: 73–88.

Gottschild, B. D. (1996) *Digging the Africanist Presence in American Performance Dance and Other Contexts* Westport, CT: Greenwood Press.

Graff, E. (1994) 'Dancing red: art and politics' *Studies in Dance History* 5 (1): 1–13.

Graham, M. (1973) *The Notebooks of Martha Graham* New York: Harcourt Brace.

—— (1991) *Blood Memory: An Autobiography* London: Sceptre Books.

Green, M. (1986) *Mountain of Truth: The Counterculture Begins, Ascona 1900–1920* Hanover, NH: University Press of New England.

Greenberg, C. (1961) *Art and Culture: Critical Essays* Boston, MA: Beacon Press.

—— (1983) 'Modernist painting' (1965) in F. Frascina and C. Harrison (eds) *Modern Art and Modernism: A Critical Anthology* London: Harper and Row: 5–10.

Grimm, R. and Hermand, J. (eds) (1986) *Blacks and German Culture* Madison, WI: University of Wisconsin Press.

Guillaume, P. and Munro T. (1926) *Primitive Negro Sculpture* New York: Harcourt, Brace and Co.

Håger, B. (1990) *Ballet Suédois* London: Thames and Hudson.

Hammergren, L. (1995) 'The re-turn of the flâneuse' in S. Foster (ed.) *Corporealities* London: Routledge, 53–69.

Hammond, B. and O'Connor, P. (1988) *Josephine Baker* London: Jonathan Cape.

Haney, L. (1981) *Naked at the feast: A biography of Josephine Baker* London: Robson Books.

Hansen, M. (1992) 'Mass culture as hieroglyphic writing: Adorno, Derrida, Kracauer' *New German Critique* 56 Summer: 43–75.

Hargreaves, J. (ed.) (1982) *Sport, Culture and Ideology* London: Routledge and Kegan Paul.

Harrison, C. and Wood, P. (eds) (1992) *Art in Theory: An Anthology of Changing Ideas* Oxford and Cambridge, MA: Blackwell.

Haskell, A. L. (1930) 'Further studies in ballet: negro dancing' *The Dancing Times* January: 455–6.

Haskell, M. (1974) *From Reverence to Rape* Harmondsworth: Penguin.

Hawkins, E. (1992) *The Body is a Clear Place and Other Statements on Dance* Princeton, NJ: Dance Horizon Books.

Hellman, E. (1990a) 'Shock of the "Bleu" ' *Ballet Review* 18 (1) Spring: 37–9.

—— (1990b) 'A conversation with Frank W. D. Reis' *Ballet Review* 18 (1) Spring: 40–8.

Hellman, R. and Hoshino, M. (1995) 'Theme and variation' *Ballet Review* 21 (3) Fall: 45–51.

Helpern, A. (1991) 'The technique of Martha Graham' *Studies in Dance History* 2 (2).

Herskovits, M. (1958) [1941] *The Myth of the Negro Past* Boston, MA: Beacon Press.

—— (1964) [1937] *Life in a Haitian Valley* New York: Octagon Books Inc.

Herskovits, M. and Herskovits, F. (1947) *Trinidad Village* New York: Alfred A. Knopf.

Hill, C. V. (1996) 'Jazz modernism' in G. Morris (ed.) *Moving Words: Re-Writing Dance* London: Routledge, 227–42.

Hiller, S. (ed.) (1991) *The Myth of Primitivism: Perspectives on Art* London and New York: Routledge.

Hinton, D. (1978) *The Films of Leni Riefenstahl* Metuchen, NJ and London: The Scarecrow Press.

Hoberman, J. (1993) *42nd Street* London: BFI Publishing.

Hodgson, J. and Preston-Dunlop, V. (1990) *Rudolf Laban: An Introduction to his Work* Exeter: Northcote House.

Hodson, M. (1985) 'Ritual design in the new dance: Nijinsky's Le Sacre du Printemps' *Dance Research* 3 (2): 35–45.

—— (1986) 'Ritual design in the new dance: Nijinsky's choreographic method' *Dance Research* 4 (1): 63–77.

—— (1996) *Nijinsky's Crime Against Grace* New York: Pendragon Press.

Hofmeister, E. B. (1993) 'Balanchine and Humphrey: Comparing *Serenade* and *Passacaglia' Choreography and Dance* 3 (3): 13–30.

hooks, b. (1990) *Yearning: Race, Gender and Cultural Politics* Boston, MA.: South End Press.

—— (1992) *Black Looks: Race and Representation* Boston, MA: South End Press.

Horosko, M. (1991) *Martha Graham: The Evolution of Her Dance Theory and Training 1926–1991* Chicago, IL: Capella Books.

Huxley, M. (1982) 'The Green Table – a dance of death: Kurt Jooss in an interview with Michael Huxley' *Ballett International* August/September: 8–10.

Huxley, M. and Patterson, M. (forthcoming) 'German theatre and dance' in W. van der Will (ed.) *The Cambridge Companion to Modern German Culture* Cambridge: Cambridge University Press.

Huyssen, A. (1986) *After the Great Divide: Modernism, Mass Culture and Postmodernism* London: Macmillan.

Jackson, M. (1983) 'Movin' on up' in E. Southern (ed.) *Readings in Black American Music* New York: W.W. Norton and Co., 291–7.

Jelavich, P. (1993) *Berlin Cabaret* Cambridge, MA: Harvard University Press.

Jeschke, C. (1995) 'Book review of Susan Manning's *Ecstasy and the Demon: Nationalism in the Dances of Mary Wigman' Dance Research Journal* 27 (2) Fall : 34–6.

Johnson, H. (1995) 'Black Venus returns: the inverted body of colonialism' *Body Matters Conference* University of Hull, 6–8 July.

Jowitt, D. (1981) 'A Conversation with Betty Schöenberg' *Ballet review* 9 (1): 31–63.

—— (1988) *Time and the Dancing Image* Berkeley and Los Angeles, CA: University of California Press.

Kakutani, M. (1981) 'An interview with Lena Horne' *New York Times* 3 May 1981, section D: 1, 24.

Karina, L. and Kant, M. (1996) *Tanz unterm Hakenkreutz. Eine Dokumentation* Berlin: Henschel Verlag.

Keersmaeker, A. T. de (1981) 'Valeska Gert' *TDR* 25 (3) Fall: 55–67.

Kersley, J. and Kersley, L. (1986) ' "Modern" – ancient and modern' *Dance and Dancers* April: 17–19.

Kirstein, L. (1970) *Movement and Metaphor* New York: Praeger.

Koegler, H. (1974) 'In the shadow of the Swastika: dance in Germany 1927–1936' *Dance Perspectives* 57 Spring

—— (1996) 'Book review: Tanz Unterm Hakenkreuz' *Ballett International/Tanz Aktual* July: 56–7.

Koonz, C. (1987) *Mothers in the Fatherland: Women, the Family and Nazi Politics* London: Jonathan Cape.

Kracauer, S. (1947) *From Caligari to Hitler: A Psychological History of German Cinema* London: Dennis Dobson.

—— (1960) *Theory of Film* New York and Oxford: Oxford University Press.

—— (1994) 'Girls and crisis' in A. Kaes, M. Jay and E. Dimendberg (eds) *The Weimar Republic Sourcebook* Berkeley, CA: University of California Press, 565–6.

—— (1995) *The Mass Ornament* (ed., trans. and with an introduction by Thomas Y. Levin) Cambridge, MA: Harvard University Press.

Kriegsman, S. A. (1981) *Modern Dance in America: The Bennington Years* Boston, MA: G. K. Hall.

Kristeva, J. (1986) 'Women's time' in T. Moi (ed.) *The Julia Kristeva Reader* Oxford: Basil Blackwell, 186–213.

—— (1991) *Strangers to Ourselves*, New York: Columbia University Press.

Laban, R. (1975) *A Life for Dance* (trans. Lisa Ullmann) London: Macdonald and Evans.

Lavin, M. (1993) *Cut With a Kitchen Knife: The Weimar Photomontages of Hannah Höch* New Haven and London: Yale University Press.

Law, A. and Gordon, M. (1996) *Meyerhold, Eisenstein and Biomechanics Actor Training in Revolutionary Russia* Jefferson, NC and London: McFarland and Co.

Layson, J. (1983) 'Methods in the historical study of dance' in J. Adshead and J. Layson (eds) *Dance History: An Introduction* London: Dance Books, 15–26.

Le Corbusier (1996) 'A contemporary city' in R. LeGates and F. Stout (eds) *The City Reader* London: Routledge, 368–79.

Léger, F. (1968) [1924] 'Vive Relâche' in H. Rischbieter (ed.) *Art and the Stage in the Twentieth Century* Greenwich, CT: New York Graphic Society,169.

—— (1973) *The Function of Painting* London: Thames and Hudson.

Lester, R. (1986) 'Blacks in Germany and German Blacks: a little known aspect of Black history' in R. Grimm and J. Hermand (eds) *Blacks and German Culture* Madison, WI: University of Wisconsin Press.

Levinson, A. (1929) *La Danse d'Aujourd'hui* Paris: Editions Duchartre et Van Buggenhoudt.

Lipton, E. (1982) 'The launderess in late nineteenth-century French culture' in F. Frascina and C. Harrison (eds) *Modern Art and Modernism: A Critical Anthology* Milton Keynes: Open University Press, 275–83.

Lloyd, J. (1991) *German Expressionism: Primitivism and Modernity* New Haven and London: Yale University Press.

Lloyd, M. (1974) [1941] *The Borzoi Book of Modern Dance* New York: Dance Horizons.

Loos, A. (1985) [1908]'Ornament and crime' in *The Architecture of Adolf Loos* London: Arts Council of Great Britain, 100–3.

Love, P. (1934) 'Martha Graham. Guild Theatre February 18 and 25, 1934' *The Dance Observer* 1 (2) March: 17.

Lowenthal, L. (1991) 'As I remember Friedel' *New German Critique* Fall: 5–18.

MacCormack, G. (1930) ' "Paris qui remue": brilliant dancing at the "Casino de Paris" ' *The Dancing Times* November: 164.

McDonagh, D. (1973) *Martha Graham* New York: Praeger Publishers.

Maier, C. S. (1970) 'Between Taylorism and technocracy: European ideologies and the vision of industrial productivity in the 1920s' *Journal of Contemporary History* 5 (2): 27–61.

Manning, S. (1988) 'Modernist dogma and post-modern rhetoric' *TDR* T-120 Winter: 32–9.

—— (1991a) 'German Rites: a history of Le sacre du printemps on the German stage' *Dance Chronicle* 14 (2–3): 129–58.

—— (1991b) 'The mythologization of the female: Mary Wigman and Martha Graham, a comparison' *Ballett International* 14 (9) September: 11–13.

—— (1993) *Ecstasy and the Demon: Feminism and Nationalism in the Dances of Mary Wigman* Berkeley, CA: University of California Press.

—— (1995) 'Modern dance in the Third Reich: six positions and a coda' in S. Foster (ed.) *Choreographing History* Bloomington and Indianapolis, IN: Indiana University Press, 165–76.

—— (1996) 'American document and American minstrelsy' in G. Morris (ed.) *Moving Words: Re-Writing Dance* London: Routledge, 183–202.

Markand, A. and Markand, H. (1985) *Jooss: Dokumentation von Anna und Hermann Markand* Köln: Ballett-Bühnen-Verlag.

Martin, J. J. (1965a) [1933] *The Modern Dance* New York: Dance Horizons.

—— (1965b) [1939] *Introduction to the Dance* New York: Dance Horizons.

—— (1968) [1936] *America Dancing* New York: Dance Horizons.

—— (1978) 'The dance: a Negro art. Katherine Dunham's notable contribution – programs of the week and after' in V. Clark and M. Wilkerson (eds) *Kaiso! Katherine Dunham: an Anthology of Writings* Berkeley, CA: University of California, 63–5 (reprinted from the *New York Times* 25 February 1940).

Mason, F. (1991) *I Remember Balanchine: Recollections of the Ballet Master by Those Who Knew Him* New York: Doubleday.

Morgan, B. (1980) *Martha Graham: Sixteen Dances in Photographs* Dobbs Ferry, New York: Morgan and Morgan.

Morris, G. (ed.) *Moving Words: Re-Writing Dance* London: Routledge.

Morrison Brown, J. (ed.) (1980) *The Vision of Modern Dance* London: Dance Books.

Mosse, G. (1991) *The Nationalization of the Masses. Political Symbolism and Mass Movements in Germany from the Napoleonic Wars through the Third Reich* Ithaca, NJ: Cornell University Press.

Müller, H. (1986) *Mary Wigman: Leben und Werk der grossen Tanzerin* Berlin: Quadriga.

—— (1987) 'Wigman and National Socialism' *Ballet Review* 15(1) Spring: 65–73.

Müller, H. and Servos, N. (1982) 'From Isadora Duncan to Leni Riefenstahl' *Ballett International* 5(4) April: 14–23.

Nijinska, B. (1981) *Early Memoirs* London: Faber and Faber.

Nijinsky, R. (ed.) (1937) *The Diary of Vaslav Nijinsky* London: Jonathan Cape.

Nuchtern, J. (1977) 'Primal memories of *Primitive Mysteries*' *The Soho Weekly* 26 May: 28–9.

Orme, F. L. (1978) 'Negro in the dance as Katherine Dunham sees him' in V. Clark and M. Wilkerson (eds), 59–62 (reprinted from *American Dancer* March 1938).

Orton, F. and Pollock, G. (1985) 'Avant-gardes and partisans reviewed' in F. Frascina (ed.) (1985) *Pollock and After: The Critical Debate* London: Harper and Row, 167–83.

Parker, D. and Parker, J. (1975) *The Natural History of the Chorus Girl* Indianapolis and New York: Bobbs-Merrill.

Partsch-Bergsohn, I. (1994) *Modern Dance in Germany and the United States* Chur, Switzerland: Harwood Academic Publishers.

Patterson, M. (1981) *The Revolution in German Theatre* London: Routledge and Kegan Paul.

Perpener, J. O. III (1992) *The Seminal Years of Black Concert Dance* (unpublished PhD thesis) New York: New York University.

—— (1994) 'African American dance and sociological positivism' *Studies in Dance History* 5 (1): 23–30.

Peters, F.-M. (1987) *Valeska Gert: Tänzerin, Schauspielerin, Kabarettistin* Berlin: Edition Hentrich.

Petro, P. (1989) *Joyless Street: Women and Melodramatic Representation in Weimar Germany* Princeton, NJ: Princeton University Press.

Phelan, P. (1993) *Unmarked: The Politics of Performance* London and New York: Routledge.

Pollack, B. and Woodford, C. H. (1993) *Dance is a Moment: A Portrait of José Limón in Words and Pictures* Pennington, NJ: Dance Horizons, Princeton Book Co.

Preston Dunlop, V. (1989) 'Laban and the Nazis' Towards an understanding of Rudolf Laban and the Third Reich' *Dance Theatre Journal* 6 (2): 4–7.

Preston-Dunlop, V. and Hodson, J. (1990) *Rudolf Laban: An Introduction to his Work and Influence* Plymouth: Northcote House.

Preston-Dunlop, V. and Lahusen, S. (eds) (1990) *Schriftanz: A View of German Dance in the Weimar Republic* London: Dance Books.

Prickett, S. (1989) 'From workers' dance to new dance' *Dance Research* 7 (1) 47–54.

—— (1990) 'Dance and the workers' struggle' *Dance Research* 8 (1) 47–61.

—— (1994a) ' "The people": issues of identity within the revolutionary dance' *Studies in Dance History* 5 (1): 14–22.

—— (1994b) 'Reviewing in the left: the dance criticism of Edna Ocko' *Studies in Dance History* 5 (1): 65–104.

Rabinow, P. (ed.) (1986) *The Foucault Reader* Harmondsworth: Penguin.

Redfield, R. (1968a) *The Primitive World and Its Transformations* Harmondsworth: Penguin.

—— (1968b) *Tepoztlan, A Mexican Village: A Study of Folk Life* Chicago, IL: The University of Chicago Press.

Richardson, A. (1990) 'The Nazification of women in art' in B. Taylor and W. van der Will (eds) *The Nazification of Art: Art, Design, Music, Architecture and Film in the Third Reich* Winchester: The Winchester Press, 53–79.

Rischbeiter, H. (ed.) (1968) *Art and the Stage in the Twentieth Century* Greenwich, CT: New York Graphic Society.

Rorty, R. (1989) *Contingency, Irony and Solidarity* Cambridge: Cambridge University Press.

Rose, P. (1990) *Jazz Cleopatra* London: Vintage.

Roth, M. (1981) 'Some Warner musicals and the spirit of the New Deal' in R. Altman (ed.) *Genre: The Musical* London: Routledge and Kegan Paul, 41–56.

Roussel, R. (1966) *Impressions of Africa* Berkeley, CA: University of California Press.

Rowbotham, S. and Weeks, J. (1977) *Socialism and the New Life: The Personal and Sexual Politics of Edward Carpenter and Havelock Ellis* London: Pluto.

Sauvage, M. (1927) *Les memoires de Josephine Baker: recueillis et adaptes par Marcel Sauvage* Paris: Editions Kra.

—— (1931) *Voyages et Aventures de Josephine Baker* Paris: Editions Marcel Sheur.

Sayler, O. (ed.) (1930) *Revolt in the arts: a survey of the creation, distribution and appreciation of art in America* New York: Brentano's.

Schama, S. (1991) *Dead Certainties (Unwarranted Speculations)* London: Granta Books.

Schlundt, C. (1989) 'Tamiris: A chronicle of her dance career 1927–55' *Studies in Dance History* 1 (1): 65–156.

Scholz, D. (1989) 'The Triptych Metropolis by Otto Dix' in B. Reinhardt (ed.) *Otto Dix* Stuttgart: Galerie der Stadt, 73–82.

Sears, D. (1982) 'Graham masterworks in revival' *Ballet review* 10 (2): 25–34.

Servos, N. (1990) 'Pathos or propaganda? On the mass choreography of fascism. Some conclusions for dance' *Ballett International* 13 (1) January: 62–6.

Shay, A. (1995) 'Dance and non-dance: patterned movement in Iran and Islam' *Iranian Studies* 28 (1–2): 61–78.

Siegel, M. B. (1976) 'Time Collapsule' in *Watching the Dance Go By* Boston, MA: Houghton Mifflin, 144–6.

—— (1979) *Shapes of Change: Images of American Dance* New York: Avon Books.

—— (1993) *Days on Earth* New Haven, CT: Yale University Press.

Silver, K. (1984) 'Jean Cocteau and the Image d'Epinal: an essay on realism and naiveté' in *Jean Cocteau and the French Scene* New York: Abbeville, 81–105.

Simmel, G. (1971) 'The metropolis and mental life' in Donald E. Levine (ed.) *On Individuality and Social Forms: Selected Writings* Chicago, IL: Chicago University Press, 324–39.

Sokolova, L. (1960) *Dancing for Diaghilev* London: John Murray.

Sontag, S. (1983) 'Fascinating Fascism' in *Under the Sign of Saturn* London: Writers and Readers, 73–105.

Souritz, E. (1990) *Soviet Choregographers in the 1920s* ed. S. Banes and trans. L. Visson Durham, NC: Dukes University Press.

Southern, E. (ed.) (1983) *Readings in Black American Music* New York: W.W. Norton and Co.

Speer, A. (1970) *Inside the Third Reich* London: Weidenfeld and Nicolson.

Stearn, J. and Stearn, M. (1968) *Jazz Dance: The Story of American Vernacular Dance* New York: Schirmer Books.

Steegmuller, F. (1970) *Cocteau: A Biography* Boston, MA: Little Brown.

—— (1984) 'Jean Cocteau 1889–1963: A brief biography' in *Jean Cocteau and the French Scene* New York: Abbeville, 15–38.

Stodelle, E. (1984) *Deep Song: The Dance Story of Martha Graham* New York: Schirmer Books.

Stratyner, B. (1994) ' "Significant historical events . . . thrilling dance sequences": Communist Party pageants in New York, 1937' *Studies in Dance History* 5 (1): 31–49.

Stuart, A. (1994) 'Looking at Josephine Baker' *Women: A Cultural Review* 5 (2): 137–43.

Taylor, B. and van der Will, W. (eds) (1990a) *The Nazification of Art: Art, Design, Music, Architecture and Film in the Third Reich* Winchester: The Winchester Press.

—— (1990b) 'Aesthetics and National Socialism' in B. Taylor and W. van der Will *The Nazification of Art: Art, Design, Music, Architecture and Film in the Third Reich* Winchester: The Winchester Press, 1–13.

Thamer, H.-U. (1996) 'The orchestration of the national community: The Nuremberg Party Rallies of the NSDAP' in G. Berghaus (ed.) *Fascism and Theatre: Comparative Studies on the Aesthetics and Politics of Performance in Europe, 1925–45* Providence and Oxford: Berghahn Books, 173–90.

Theweleit, K. (1987) *Male Fantasies I: Women, Floods, Bodies, History* Cambridge: Polity Press.

—— (1989) *Male Fantasies II* Cambridge: Polity Press.

Thomas, T. and Terry, J. (1973) *The Busby Berkeley Book* New York: A&W Visual Library.

Towers, B. S. (1990) 'Jungle music and the song of machines: Jazz and American dance in Weimar culture' in *Envisioning America* Cambridge, MA: Harvard University Press, 87–105.

Trinh, T. Minh-ha (1989) *Woman, Native, Other: Writing, Postcoloniality and Feminism* Bloomington, IN: Indiana University Press.

Trotsky, L. (1938) 'Art and politics' *Partisan Review* 5 (3) August–September: 3–10.

Tucholsky, K., Kustner, E., Lenz, S. and Hildesheimer, W. (1969) *Humour and Satire* Munich: Max Hueber Verlag.

van der Will, W. (1990) 'The body and the body politic as symptom and metaphor in the transition of German culture to National Socialism' in B. Taylor and W. van der Will *The Nazification of Art: Art, Design, Music, Architecture and Film in the Third Reich* Winchester: The Winchester Press, 14–52.

Vernon, D. (1988) *Tiller's Girls* London: Robson Books.

Vidler, A. (1991) 'Agoraphobia: spatial estrangement in Georg Simmel and Siegfried Kracauer' *New German Critique* Fall: 31–46.

Volta, O. (1991–2) 'Les "Fêtes Nègres" de Blaises Cendrars' *Continent Cendrars* 6–7: 36–45.

Warren, L. (1977) *Lester Horton, Modern Dance Pioneer* New York and Basel: Marcel Dekker.

Waters, E. (1983) 'His eye is on the sparrow' in E. Southern *Readings in Black American Music* New York: W. W. Norton and Co.

West, C. (1992) 'Nihilism in Black America' in G. Dent (ed.) *Black Popular Culture* Seattle, WA: Bay Press.

Wigman, M. (1966) *The Language of Dance* Middletown, CT: Wesleyan University Press.

Willett, J. (1978) *The New Sobriety 1917–1933: Art and Politics in the Weimar Period* London: Thames and Hudson.

Williams, R. (1989) *The Politics of Modernism* London: Verso.

Witte, K. (1975) 'Introduction to Siegfried Kracauer's "The Mass Ornament" ' *New German Critique* 5 Spring: 59–66.

Wolff, J. (1990) *Feminine Sentences* London: Polity.

Wolff, J. and Seed, J. (eds) (1987) *The Culture of Capital* Manchester: Manchester University Press.

Wollen, P. (1993) *Raiding the Icebox* London: Verso.

INDEX